Contents

Editors' Preface

In the winter term of 1974–1975, Max Delbrück gave a course of twenty lectures (listed as Biology 129) at the California Institute of Technology (Caltech) on what he called "evolutionary epistemology." He spoke only from notes and reference cards, without a prepared text. Delbrück repeated that course two years later. The second version of his lectures was recorded on tape, and the tapes were transcribed by one of his students, Judith Greengard. Delbrück entitled this transcript *Mind from Matter?* and added the charts, illustrations, and reading references that he had distributed to his students. He intended to publish the lectures eventually as a book-length essay, as indicated by a letter he sent to a San Francisco publishing house on 17 March 1977. Delbrück then wrote

> I have done some mild editing [of the transcript] just to correct gross errors and misunderstandings . . . . Some of the early lecture transcripts were quite condensed by the student editor and I would intend to expand them considerably. The lecture on Gödel's proof needs considerable revision . . . I think a reasonable estimate for producing a definitive manuscript may be something between a year and a year and a half from now.

The onset of Delbrück's fatal illness prevented him from carrying out that project. However, in the summer of 1977, he condensed the Greengard transcript to a single lecture, for delivery at the XIIIth Nobel Conference at Gustavus Adolphus College, St. Peter, Minnesota. According to Delbrück, he "seized this occasion to try to condense twenty lectures into one, in order to find out whether or not I had something worthwhile to say." This highly abbreviated version of *Mind from Matter?* was published in the proceedings of this conference (*The Nature of Life*, ed. W. H. Heidecamp [Baltimore: University Park Press, 1978] 141–169) and in *American Scholar* 47 (1978): 339–353. By the time of Delbrück's death on 10 March 1981, no further progress had been made in the project of publishing *Mind from Matter?* as a book length essay.

In consultation with Delbrück's widow, Mary, a group of his friends, colleagues, and students decided to edit and prepare the manuscript for posthumous publication, addressed to a general readership technically less qualified than Delbrück's Caltech student constituency. This turned out to be a very difficult task. First, the topics covered by Delbrück are so wide ranging that no one person could have been expected to possess the breadth of professional expertise necessary for a critical editing of the whole essay. Second, the transcript reflects the extemporaneous nature of Delbrück's lectures, which—though perfectly evoking the memory of his uniquely effective colloquial and humorous style—did not seem suited to the printed page. Indeed, Delbrück's own condensation of the transcript for the *American Scholar* essay embodies extensive revisions for that very reason.

Therefore, as Delbrück himself had realized, to convert the lecture transcript into a book, it was necessary to make many editorial changes. These changes include not only stylistic and organizational revisions, corrections of errors, and updating of references, but also additions to and emendations of the text that seemed needed to make it comprehensible to a general reader. The principle guiding any of these revisions was to ask "would Max himself have made this change or addition had *he* edited the transcript?" In line with this principle, portions of the *American Scholar* essay were substituted whenever possible for the corresponding passages of the transcript. Otherwise we have retained as much as possible of the wording of the transcript. We firmly believe that none of Delbrück's ideas have been distorted by our editing. Unfortunately, Delbrück's treatment of Gödel's proof could not be given the "considerable revision" he thought it needed, since to provide a more rigorous and yet generally comprehensible presentation of that proof would have been, as Delbrück hinted in his lecture, a formidable undertaking. Instead, we have left more-or-less intact Delbrück's nonrigorous, highly abbreviated outline of Gödel's general argument.

For helpful comments on chapters 9 and 10, we thank Doris and Norbert Bischof, and on chapter 13, E. Engeler and B. L. Van der Waerden, all of the University of Zurich; for helpful comments on chapters 1 through 8 we thank Florence Presti. We also acknowledge the assistance of Margery Hoogs.

Gunther S. Stent, *University of California, Berkeley*

Ernst Peter Fischer, *University of Konstanz*

Solomon W. Golomb, *University of Southern California*

David E. Presti, *University of Oregon*

Hansjakob Seiler, *University of Cologne*

MIND FROM MATTER?

An Essay on Evolutionary Epistemology

Introduction
and Overview
by Gunther S. Stent

In the summer of 1932, one year after Max Delbrück had spent six months as a postdoctoral fellow in Niels Bohr's laboratory, he returned to Copenhagen to hear Bohr deliver a lecture entitled "Light and Life." In that lecture, Bohr outlined the philosophical implications for the life sciences of the fundamental changes that the quantum theory had brought to the conception of natural law. One of the most profound of these changes is that the quantum theory forces us to renounce the possibility of a complete causal account of phenomena and to be content with probabilistic rather than deterministic laws. This revised view of the foundations of natural law, which extends to the very idea of the nature of scientific explanation, Bohr thought not only to be essential for the full appreciation of the new situation brought to physics by the quantum theory, but also to have created an entirely new background for the problems of biology in their relation to physics. That new background is provided by the insight that we face a fundamental limitation in defining the objective existence of phenomena independently of the subjective means we employ for their observation. Five years later in Bologna, Bohr presented a lecture entitled "Biology and Atomic Physics," in which he likened this aspect of his philosophy to the world view taught by Buddha and Lao Tzu, who long before him had addressed the epistemological problems arising from our being both observers and actors in the great drama of existence. In his lecture Bohr conjectured that we might have to discover some still missing fundamental traits in the analysis of natural phenomena before we can reach an understanding of life in physical terms. Fascinated by

1

this conjecture, the young Delbrück's principal scientific interest turned from physics to biology.

Most contemporary philosophers of science are quite familiar with Bohr's philosophical stance, and they are fully aware of the role it has played in the development of modern physics. Indeed, a generation ago many of them wrestled with its epistemological implications for their doctoral theses. But few, if any, have taken Bohr's stance seriously as a general world view, with implications that transcend physical science and inform our ideas in nearly all domains of human interest. In Delbrück, Bohr eventually found his most influential philosophical disciple outside the domain of physics. Through Delbrück, Bohr's epistemology became the intellectual infrastructure of molecular biology, the reason, perhaps, for its hegemony over twentieth century life sciences. It provided for molecular biologists the philosophical guidance for navigating between the Scylla of crude biochemical reductionism, inspired by nineteenth century physics, and the Charybdis of obscurantist vitalism, inspired by nineteenth century romanticism.

Although this approach to nature found lifelong reflection in Delbrück's personality and scientific attitudes, by the time he was in his sixties he had published only one explicit statement of his philosophical views, the 1949 essay "A Physicist Looks at Biology." Most of the pioneer molecular biologists of Delbrück's circle then laying the groundwork for the eventual rise of their still unnamed discipline found that essay hard to read. They couldn't see what philosophical point Delbrück was trying to make, and they considered his fascination with paradoxes as one of those foibles to which even the greatest minds are not immune. Finally, on receiving the Nobel Prize for Physiology or Medicine in 1969, Delbrück presented the philosophical essay, "A Physicist's Renewed Look at Biology: Twenty Years Later," as his acceptance speech in Stockholm. Here Delbrück previewed the topics that, five years later and nearing retirement, he would treat in his Caltech *Mind from Matter?* lectures and that he epitomized as an "investigation into human cognitive capabilities, as expressed in various sciences."

The sciences within Delbrück's purview ranged from cosmology through evolutionary biology, neurobiology, anthropology, psychology, mathematics, and physics, all the way to linguistics, and his motivation for presenting the lectures was to summarize his lifelong exploration of the implications of Bohr's philosophy for the possible sources of human knowledge. In particular he sought to examine whether there remain some areas of study for whose elucidation the complementarity concept could provide some decisive help. These lectures should not be regarded

A colloquium at Bohr's Copenhagen Institute of Theoretical Physics in 1936. In front row (from left): Niels Bohr, Paul Dirac, Werner Heisenberg, Paul Ehrenfest, Max Delbrück, and Lise Meitner. (Courtesy of Herman Kalckar)

as authoritative treatments of the enormously diverse topics covered— no denizen of the sublunar sphere could provide such a summary in twenty lectures—rather they should be read as the philosophically moti- vated explorations of one of the sharpest and most versatile scientific intellects of our postmodern age.

Delbrück's avowed objective is to formulate and, if not answer, at least examine three principal questions:

1. How is it possible that mind came into being in an initially lifeless, and hence mindless, universe?

2. If, by way of answer to the first question, we envisage that mind arose from mindless matter by a Darwinian evolutionary process of natu- ral selection favoring caveman's reproductive success, then how did this process give rise to a mind capable of elaborating the most profound insights into mathematics, the structure of matter, and the nature of life itself, which were scarcely needed in the cave?

3. Indeed, how can the capacity for understanding and knowing the truth arise from dead matter?

Delbrück begins *Mind from Matter?* by tracing the evolutionary origins of matter in general, of living matter in particular, and of man and his brain most especially. For this purpose, he professes to take the stance of naive realism, that is, the epistemological viewpoint of the man in the street, who believes that there exists a real world of things external to him and independent of his experience of it, and that, moreover, this real world actually is as he sees, hears, feels, and smells it. Delbrück eventually abandons naive realism, but he evidently starts from it because of its immediate and intuitive acceptability. In any case, naive realism seems as good as any other philosophical stance from which to give an account of our evolutionary history.

Neither the transcript of Delbrück's lectures nor his published writings contain an explicit statement of what his understanding of the term *mind* is or how he thinks the mind is related to the brain. It is clear that Delbrück holds that mental processes, such as feelings, thoughts, and consciousness, arise in the human brain and that the evolutionary origins of the mind are to be understood in terms of the development of the brain. Moreover, during the first part of his essay, while he is still adopting the epistemological stance of naive realism, Delbrück seems to take it for granted that mental phenomena are merely direct products (or epiphenomena) of human brain function. But as he abandons naive realism in later parts of his essay, Delbrück also abandons the notion of the mind as an epiphenomenon of the brain. It transpires that he regards human consciousness as a unitary phenomenon, which we must necessarily consider from two different aspects. One aspect is provided by extrospection, from outside, which reveals the brain as a network of a myriad of nerve cells. The other aspect is provided by introspection, from inside (directly in ourselves and indirectly, by empathy, in others), which reveals the mind as a complex of thoughts and feelings.

Matter came into existence with the "big bang" that gave rise to a gas of cosmic protons, electrons, and neutrons. Delbrück reviews the astrophysical evidence that such an event actually did happen about ten billion years ago, followed eventually by condensation of the primeval gas into local pockets of matter, such as galaxies, stars, and planetary systems, producing the elements along the way. In this history, our own planet Earth was formed about 4.5 billion years ago, with the oldest terrestrial rocks dating to about 3.8 billion years ago. The physical mechanisms underlying these processes are still imperfectly understood. Moreover, cosmic history was only partly predetermined, in the sense that it might have had quite a different outcome. This intrinsic historical indeterminacy has its roots in astrophysical processes that enormously amplify tiny random fluctuations. Living matter entered the terrestrial scene about 3 billion years ago, not long after the formation of the oldest

see p. 279

rocks. Very little is known about the processes responsible for the origin of life, except that some more-or-less plausible proposals trace it to a putative organochemical "primal soup" formed spontaneously under the conditions of the primitive Earth.

Although he was one of the main spiritual fathers of molecular biology, Delbrück is not very interested in the molecular origins of life. Satisfied that, one way or another, living matter did arise, he is more interested in the subsequent evolution of what he refers to as "real life." He traces organic evolution from bacteria to man and explains how biochemistry, genetics, and molecular biology have recently advanced our understanding of that process. The outcome of the history of life was even less predetermined than that of cosmic history, since in organic evolution tiny random fluctuations are amplified to an even greater extent than in astrophysical evolution. (Delbrück had a long-standing interest in the role of amplified microscopic fluctuations as a shaping force of macroscopic phenomena. He published a theoretical paper on that subject in 1940, which also underlies his and Salvador Luria's 1943 proof of the spontaneous origin of bacterial mutants.) Presaging the importance of perception in his later considerations, Delbrück points out that perception, which he explicates as the "reception and interpretation of signals from the environment," must be of high evolutionary antiquity, being a common attribute of all contemporary forms of life.

As for man and his brain, his ancestors diverged from the apes about 5 million years ago; the species *Homo erectus* appeared about 1.5 million years ago; and the species *Homo sapiens* several hundred thousand years ago. Only as recently as 40,000 years ago did one race of *H. sapiens*, namely our own kind, *H. sapiens sapiens*, manage to exterminate the other races of its species, such as *H. sapiens neanderthalensis*.

Among the important factors that shaped human evolution, Delbrück cites the initial transition from tropical forest to grassland habitat and its associated development of erect stature; the devising of the first crude stone tools and their subsequent refinement; the invasion of northern climes with their harsher conditions, which brought about the rise of social organization, use of fire, division of labor between the sexes, and linguistic capacity and communication; and, finally, the rise of culture, as reflected in the burying of the dead and the domestication of plants and animals (which Delbrück deems "a fantastic biological experiment").

This evolutionary progress from ape to man-in-the-street could not have occurred, of course, without the concomitant development of the human brain. By the standards of the animal kingdom, the weight of the human brain is very high. But Delbrück cautions that there is no simple connection between this well-known fact and our equally well-known high intelligence, since, as animals go, we are large animals, and large animals have large brains. Moreover, because the brain is a very complex organ, with many different types of cells and cellular assemblies carrying out different functions, the significance of inter- or intraspecies differences in brain size cannot be given a simple interpretation. Delbrück points out that if any correlation can be made, brain size has more to do with corporeal muscle mass than with cerebral intelligence or linguistic ability. So it is better, Delbrück says, to focus on the evolution of specific parts of the human brain circuitry than on its increase in total weight. For that purpose Delbrück considers vision, which, in however many neurobiological mysteries it may still be shrouded, is presently the best understood of all cerebral functions.

The evolution of vision in the primate line from lower mammals to man is characterized by three closely connected developments:

1. The transition from a primarily olfactory and tactile to a primarily visual mode of life.

2. The displacement of the eyes from a lateral position in the head, which provides panoramic, two-dimensional vision, to a frontal position, which provides focal, three-dimensional vision.

3. The differentiation of cone-photoreceptors in the retina that makes color vision possible.

These developments were, in turn, connected with a parallel growth and elaboration of those areas of the brain in which the visual sensory input is processed. Delbrück speculates that these improvements in processing visual input, coupled with an anatomical change in the structure of the upper lip, also provided for the use of facial expressions, such as smiling, frowning and baring of teeth, as means of social communication.

Delbrück now starts to undermine naive realism and to adumbrate an eventual conceptual link between brain and mind. The visual regions of the brain have so evolved that they process the sensory input by filtering out all information deemed to be irrelevant for the animal's interest. Thus relevant information content of the visual surround is abstracted from the input in a maximally meaningful form. Delbrück provides three examples.

1. The first example is the constancy with which we perceive the color of objects in a multicolored scene, regardless of the color of the light with

which that scene is illuminated. Thus a red apple is perceived as red, whether it is viewed in the bluish light of day, in the reddish light of dusk, or in the yellowish light of an incandescent lamp at night. We do not sense the actual wavelength of the light that forms the apple's image on our retina.

2. The second example is the constancy with which we perceive the position of objects in a stationary scene while we are voluntarily moving our head or eyes. Thus when we turn our head toward the table on which an apple is lying, we sense, despite the relative motion made by the apple's image on our retina, that it is our head and not the apple that has moved.

3. The third example is the constancy with which we perceive the size of objects as they approach us or recede from us. Thus when an apple is thrown at us, we sense that its diameter remains the same despite the constantly increasing size of the image on our retina as the apple flies toward us.

All three examples demonstrate that what we perceive are not raw sensory data but intrinsic (i.e., viewer-independent) qualities of objects abstracted from the raw data. Delbrück takes pains to emphasize that this abstraction process is *preconscious* and hence cannot be introspected, a point that "is often overlooked when [naive realist] physicists discuss the nature of reality, since they tend to equate sensation in the sensory organs with what is presented to the consciousness. The consciousness has no access to raw data; it obtains only a highly processed portion of the input." Such processing makes evolutionary sense, since the rate of visual input into our eyes is so enormous that without a preconscious filtering of raw data our minds would be overwhelmed by sensory overload.

Delbrück is now ready to ascend to a higher level of philosophical discourse, from the epistemology of naive realism to that of structuralist realism. He does not use this or any other particular term to designate the alternative to naive realism that he is about to develop. But he might as well have called it structuralist, since *structuralism* is the name generally given to the outlook shared by many of those whom he cites in support of his argument. The structuralist realist shares with the naive realist the fundamental belief in the existence of a real world external to him and independent of his experience of it. But understanding that what reaches his consciousness is a highly abstract structure of transformed raw sensory data, the structuralist realist recognizes that his internal reality is merely a construct whose true correspondence with the external reality of things is, in principle, unknowable. This insight dates back to Immanuel Kant, who revolutionized epistemology more than 200 years ago by pointing out that we construct first experience and then reality from sensation, by bringing to sensation such categories as time and space *a priori,* instead of inferring them from experience *a posteriori.* The modern neurobiological findings regarding the abstract nature of visual perception cited by Delbrück constitute an empirical validation of Kantian epistemology, in that they show that such categories as color, position and size of an object arise from the built in, or *a priori,* data-processing circuitry of our cerebral neuronal networks. But how can it be that if these categories are brought to reality *a priori* they happen to fit the external real world so well? Here Delbrück puts forward the answer provided forty years ago by Konrad Lorenz: what is *a priori* for the individual is *a posteriori* for his species. That is to say, the success of our built-in circuitry in perceiving reality is merely the product of natural selection having guided our evolutionary history: any early hominids who happened to perceive red apples as colorless, stationary apples as moving, or large apples as small, would have perished without issue.

Nevertheless, the findings of developmental neurobiology have shown, both at the neurophysiological and at the perceptive and cognitive level, that the designation of these categories as *a priori* does not mean that they are present already, full-blown, at birth. Instead, they arise post-natally, as the result of a dialectic interaction between the developing nervous system and the world. To illuminate the nature of that interaction Delbrück calls on Jean Piaget, one of the main figures in the landscape of structuralism. In the 1920s, Piaget opened what Delbrück calls "a goldmine for epistemological exploration, which was overlooked for millennia by philosophers," by initiating an empirical study of the development of cognitive functions in the infant and child. This study led to the recognition that the Kantian categories immanent in the mind are constructed gradually during childhood, in a succession of distinct developmental stages.

1. The first of these is the sensory-motor period (from birth to 2 years of age) during which the infantile mind constructs the categories of space, time, object, and causality. These categories arise *pari-passu* with the infant's development of hand-eye-ear-touch coordination and the capacity to follow and grasp moving objects. It should be noted, however, that in their initial form, these fundamental epistemological notions have not yet their adult (Kantian) character. As for space and time, they originally lack the

absolute and mutually independent quality they will later acquire and are instead conceived first as being relative and intertwined. As for causality, its origin is the child's posited link between what it wishes or intends and what actually happens; only subsequently does causality mature into the inferred link between events that are contiguous in time, although not necessarily in space. The hard-nosed scientific view of a deterministic world emerges on the eventual dissolution of the infantile connection between wishing and causality, and on the maturation of the belief that all connections linking events are physical rather than mental.

2. During the second, or preoperational period (2 to 5 years of age), the mind starts to reason from memory and by analogy, thanks to use of symbols, with objects being represented symbolically by words or other objects.

3. During the third, or concrete operational period (5 to 10 years of age), the mind gains the capacity to classify and order objects and also develops the concept of the conservation of their continuous properties, such as number, weight, and volume.

4. With the fourth and final, or formal, operational period (10 to 14 years of age), the mind begins propositional thinking, with assertions and statements which presuppose that what is actually the case in the real world is merely a subset of all that *could* be the case in a diversity of possible worlds.

At this point Delbrück presages a fundamental epistemological aspect of Bohr's position. The mind with its *a priori* categories, in its phylogenetic as well as ontogenetic origins, is evidently an adaptation towards coping with life in the real world of *middle dimensions*, that is, the world of our direct experience, give or take a few orders of magnitude. [This world has recently been designated the "mesocosm" by Gerhard Vollmer (1984), in an essay on evolutionary epistemology, whose viewpoint is remarkably similar to that presented here by Delbrück.] It is not surprising therefore that many of these categories fail, or have to be modified, when our quest for knowledge steps outside the middle dimensions (the mesocosm) and is directed to the very small and the very brief, as in atomic and elementary particle physics (i.e., to the microcosm), or the very large and the very long, as in cosmology or evolution (i.e., to the macrocosm). It is in these far reaches of our search for understanding of the world that we encounter deep paradoxes.

By way of further erosion of his initial naive realist stance, Delbrück considers the possibility that mathematics is a construct of the mind rather than a set of eternal truths independent of human experience. He explores that possibility, first by applying Piaget's studies of cognitive development to the foundations of mathematics. According to Piaget, the child acquires the spatial concepts of mathematics in exactly the reverse order in which they emerged in the history of that science: whereas metric (i.e., Euclidean) geometry was developed in the third century B.C., projective geometry in the nineteenth century, and topological geometry in the twentieth, children grasp the topological aspects of space first, its projective aspects second, and its metric aspects last. From the evolutionary point of view, projective, Euclidean, and topological geometries are conceptual adaptations to cope visually with a world in which, respectively, light propagates in straight lines, there are many solid objects, and these objects are structured rather than random. Delbrück then considers the theory of numbers, whose basic concept, the set, is grounded in topological notions. He outlines how the (intuitive) axioms of the theory of numbers arise from the spatial concepts of cognitive development, paying particular attention to the (still puzzling) nature of prime numbers. He surmises that a mouse, which has poor vision and depends primarily on tactile and olfactory clues for coping with its topologically restricted environment of the underground burrow, would have difficulty evolving the number concept and theories concerning the handling of numbers. But maybe lacking the concept of number, the mouse is better off, because, as we are about to learn, it has thereby been spared having to struggle with the logical difficulties that inhere in number theory. Delbrück points out one such difficulty: mathematicians have been unable to prove or disprove "Fermat's Last Theorem" (i.e., the conjecture that there are no positive integers which satisfy the relation

$$a^n + b^n = c^n$$

for any value of n greater than 2). Is it possible that there are mathematical propositions whose truth or falsity is not decidable? If the answer is "yes," then either mathematics is an open-ended construct of the mind, or, if numbers and their mathematical relations are constituents of the real world, the mind cannot adequately capture the definitions and axioms that reflect their "true" nature.

In any case, the basic concept of number theory, the set, is itself not free of paradox. For instance, there arise logical contradictions upon considering self-referential sets that are members of themselves, such as the set of all sets. Another paradox is presented by infinite sets, such as the set of integers, which have the bizarre property that they are equivalent to one of their own subsets, thus violating our intuitive understanding that in the real world the whole is greater than any of its parts. To compound the conceptual difficulty Georg Cantor showed in the 1870s that although the set of rational numbers is infinite, it is nevertheless "denumerable," and hence smaller than the "continuous" set of real numbers, of which the rational numbers form part. Cantor conjectured (without being able to prove) that there is no "medium-sized" infinite subset of numbers that is larger than the denumerable subset of rational numbers but smaller than the continuum of real numbers. Troubled by the paradoxes and unproven conjectures surrounding its very foundations, David Hilbert set out in the early years of this century to reduce mathematics to an axiomatic, formal system that would be both free of contradictions and complete, in the sense that the truth or falsity of any proposition could be derived logically from the axioms. By the 1930s, however, Kurt Gödel had shown that Hilbert's aim cannot be achieved: the formalization of mathematics does not produce a demonstrably consistent or complete system. Not only do there continue to exist propositions that are undecidable, but also there is not even a general way of deciding whether, with a given set of axioms, an as yet unproven proposition is or is not decidable. With his presentation of Gödel's proof, Delbrück renders one of Bohr's principal messages: the *a priori* conceptual equipment with which evolution has endowed us works very well only as long as we don't ask too much of it. Evidently, the category of number is wonderfully consistent and complete as long as it is applied to counting real apples, but it becomes paradoxical when it is extended to such things as infinite sets, which transcend our experience.

Next, Delbrück turns to the physical sciences, which have as their conceptual foundations not only the categories of object, number, space, and causality, but also the concept of the measurement of continuous quantities. That concept, in turn, depends on such subsidiary notions about the continuous quantities measured as their decomposability into additive units and their conservation by the objects that possess them. Delbrück traces the rise of astronomy, from the ancients—who, by projecting these notions into the heavens, provided a highly precise and detailed description of planetary motion in a conceptually orderly space, or *kosmos*—to Johann Kepler's recognition of the elliptical character of planetary orbits in the seventeenth century. Kepler's breakthrough permitted Isaac Newton to develop his unified celestial and terrestrial mechanics, based on the ideas of dimensionless mass points, or particles, subject to forces acting at a distance. Though these ideas were considered bizarre when Newton first put them forward, by the end of the eighteenth century they had become the cornerstone of physics. To account for how one object can interact with another at a distance, the notion of the "field" was developed in the nineteenth century, culminating in James Clerk Maxwell's unified field theory, which interprets light as a wavelike motion in an electromagnetic field. Concurrently, Newtonian physics was extended to the microscopic, or atomic and molecular domain, to provide a statistical–mechanical account of the phenomenon of heat. Thus, by the end of the nineteenth century physics had managed to provide a generally satisfactory account of the real world of matter, built on seemingly self-consistent notions that were, in turn, derived from our intuitive, *a priori* categories.

Meanwhile, however, some clouds had risen on the horizon of the sunny landscape of Newtonian physics. One of the most troubling of these concerned the nature of the medium, or "ether," in which Maxwell's electromagnetic waves are moving. That medium would have to possess two highly unusual features: it must be cohesive to carry waves, yet offer no friction to the motion of objects through it; and it does not permit the detection of motion relative to it. Early in the twentieth century, Albert Einstein resolved the dilemma posed by the paradoxical aspects of the ether by introducing fundamental changes in our intuitive categories of time and space, and in the concept of the measurement of continuous quantities. In developing his theory of relativistic physics, Einstein for-mulated the space–time framework of the real world as a continuum, in striking conflict with the preconscious dissection of our experience of that world into a three-dimensional visual space and a separate temporal dimension, as provided for us by our evolutionarily adapted nervous system.

Two intuitive notions in particular were violated by the formulations of relativity theory:

1. The absolute flow of time (since whether two events are or are not simultaneous here depends on the frame of reference of their observer)

2. The geometric relation between matter and space (since here the universe can be spatially unbounded yet contain a finite amount of matter)

These ideas, says Delbrück, appeared shocking to the first generation of scientists and the general public when they came to be confronted with the theory of relativity early in this century.

Another cloud on the horizon of turn-of-the-century physics arose from the finding that if light is really a continuous electromagnetic wave, then its observed interaction with matter does not conform to the predictions of statistical mechanics. To resolve this discrepancy, Max Planck introduced the notion of the quantum of energy: a minimum packet of energy that can be exchanged between an electromagnetic field and matter. Although Planck's formulation brought theory and observation into accord, it led to what Delbrück calls "an enormous calamity for physicists," namely to the paradoxical conception of light as a discontinuous wave. The sky of Newtonian physics darkened further when Niels Bohr extended the notion of the quantum of energy to the structure of the atom, by proposing that electrons circle the atomic nucleus in discrete orbits and jump from one orbit to the next by absorbing or emitting an energy quantum of light.

Thus Bohr's theory attributed counterintuitively discontinuous behavior not only to light but also to physical processes. For that reason the theory was vigorously opposed by most physicists, even though it evidently provided an understanding of the previously mysterious spectroscopic data, as well as of the structure of the periodic table of the chemical elements. By the 1920s these ominous developments had culminated in Erwin Schrödinger's and Werner Heisenberg's independent formulation of the quantum mechanics of the electron. Schrödinger's point of departure was the paradoxical speculation that electrons, though clearly material particles, resemble (nonmaterial) light in possessing wavelike properties. By contrast, Heisenberg's formulation depended on the assignment of mathematical properties to the position and momentum of the electron that are in conflict with our intuitive notions regarding the additivity and conservation of these continuous qualities as dynamic attributes of material objects. Heisenberg was able to justify his apparent violation of intuitive dynamic notions by demonstrating the existence of an uncertainty principle: position and momentum of a particle cannot, in principle, both be measured precisely in a single experiment, since any arrangement ✳ introduced to measure precisely one of these quantities causes loss of information regarding the other.

The epistemological implications of the development of the quantum theory became a major philosophical concern of Bohr's. In particular, Bohr envisaged that Heisenberg's uncertainty principle is only one example of a more general phenomenon designated as "complementarity." Delbrück paraphrases complementarity as a "conspiracy of nature" that prevents us from attaining a fully deterministic description of physical ✳ objects and thus places a limit on the empirical knowability of the real world. We cannot observe reality at its deepest level without disturbing it: every experimental arrangement we set up becomes part of the reality to be observed, and the conceptual cut between instrument and material object necessarily represents a subjective choice made by the observer. Because of this fundamental inseparability of object and subject Bohr came to the Buddhist-Taoist viewpoint that in the drama of existence we cannot do otherwise than play the dual role of actor and observer. With this insight, Delbrück abandons even the more sophisticated, structuralist version of realism. It is not merely some intrinsic limitation of our cognitive apparatus but the very nature of reality that prevents it from being fully knowable, since real objects do not move along deterministically governed trajectories, have no identity, and are not conserved.

But how is it possible that our mind can even conceive of complementarity, given our direct experience with the physical reality of the everyday world, where apples do indeed follow definite trajectories, have identities, and neither appear from nor disappear into nothingness? Delbrück's answer is that the world of complementarity is remarkably similar to the way an infant views reality, before it has fully consolidated the object category. Evidently the adult mind retains the ability to deal with the world on infantile terms. Since all of us did make the transition from the infant's world of evanescent apples to the adult's world of persistent apples, it is not incongruous that we are capable of returning to our ontogenetic cognitive antecedents.

Delbrück resorts to complementarity to develop an argument that is to show the inadequacy of all versions of realism. According to him, realism arises from an inadequate view of the relation between mind and matter. That view is represented by the "Cartesian cut," which splits existence between an internal world of thoughts, volitions, and emotions—the *res cogitans* or mind—and an external world of things—the *res extensa*, or physical reality.

The Cartesian cut, which has been the epistemological stance of science for the last 300 years, has provided the psychologists' principal research agenda, which is to bridge the cut and link mind and reality. But, as the latter-day neurobiological insights into the process of visual perception have shown, what the mind sees as an apple is literally worlds apart from the object that gives rise to the retinal image, and no conceptual link is as yet in sight. Could the reason why psychologists have not been able to tie the two worlds together be that the real apple and its percept should never have been dissected in this way in the first place? Could the very concept of a reality independent of our experience be an incoherent notion? To consider that question, Delbrück shows that even the laws of Newtonian (i.e., pre-quantum theory) physics directed to the everyday world do not describe the external world of things in an autonomous manner. Rather, the mathematical relations in terms of which these laws are expressed refer explicitly to situations actually or potentially experienced by an observer, and to nothing else. Thus physical laws are not propositions about an external world of things completely separate from the observer.

Is there then any sense in which physics can be said to be "objective"? Yes, insofar as its laws refer to classes of experiences that are reproducible for each observer and for different observers. But such reproducibility does not change the fact that physical laws concern personal experiences in however abstract a form, and hence pertain to the domain of the mind as much as any emotion or sensation. Admittedly, we do not explicitly refer to any observer when we say that the temperature of a body is 4°K or that a supernova exploded a billion years ago. But such a statement is meaningful only within the context of our total scientific discourse, reflecting our individual and collective experience and acts. Accordingly, Delbrück rejects the Cartesian cut; he claims that the antithesis of external and internal reality is an illusion, and that there is but one reality. The epistemological dust raised by the development of the quantum theory has merely reminded us of this fact, which had been lost in the abstractions of Newtonian physics.

But if the phenomena of mind are on a par with the phenomena of matter—if the Cartesian cut is but an illusion—is the mind then no more than a material machine, embodying complex cybernetic circuitry? Delbrück thinks that the general resistance to accepting that proposition and the widespread alternative belief that mind cannot be an ordinary phenomenon of matter are closely related to the fact that mental realities are predominantly communicated by language. After all, how could a machine have the gift of speech? Thus if we want to reify the mind, that is, outgrow the belief that mind transcends matter, then we have to be able to account for how a machine might possess the capacity to use language. Here it is important to be clear about the qualities that set human language apart from other forms of symbolic communication used by nonhuman species, such as honeybees. The most distinctive (and powerful) of these qualities is the syntactic character of human language, which makes possible the production of an unlimited number of meaningful sentences, built up from a large but finite set of symbols (words) logically connected by a finite set of rules (grammar). Accordingly, to have the gift of speech, each person must store in and be able to retrieve from memory the thousands of words and grammatical rules of his native language (and, in case of a polyglot, of several languages). How does the mind acquire that prodigous linguistic capacity? As all parents know, it is acquired in infancy. At an age when they are quite incapable of any comparable analytical task, all children are able to infer automatically the rules of any natural language, without explicit instruction and in a relatively short time, even though they are exposed only to fragmentary, and even faulty, samples of well-formed sentences. To account for how the infantile mind could possibly perform this cognitive feat, some linguists who form part of the structuralism movement (foremost among them Noam Chomsky) have postulated that all natural languages—however diverse their grammatical rules may appear on the surface—are actually transforms of a set of "deep" universals of which the infant has innate knowledge.

In any case, the deepest problem posed by language is not the capacity to memorize linguistic symbols and the rules that govern their manipulation. In fact, says Delbrück, at the present state of the art of the discipline styled artificial intelligence, or AI, it is already possible to design machines that can memorize symbols and the rules that govern their manipulation, as exemplified by chess-playing computer programs. No, the deepest question is how *meaning* is embodied in language, that is, the problem of semantics. That problem is deep because the intended meaning of a sentence usually cannot be decoded by a straightforward logical analysis of its strings of syntactically connected word–symbols. Instead, for semantic decoding it is necessary to take account of the *context* in which the sentence is produced.

Delbrück finds that even with regard to demystifying this deepest problem of language, the students of AI have made some progress; he cites the computer program devised by Terry Winograd, which has the capacity to perform quasi-semantic decoding of sentences that refer to a very narrowly circumscribed contextual world with a limited history and consisting of a limited number of solid objects on which a limited number of operations can be performed.

In the case of human language, the semantically relevant context is open-ended, however, encompassing all of human experience and history. For that reason it is not yet possible to design computer programs with quasi-human semantic competence, since such programs would have to have access to the sum total of conscious and subconscious memories stored in the human mind, that is, to have lived a human life. Moreover, in the mind these memories, or data about the contextual world, are precisely what is represented by language in the first place, and thus fathoming the nature of language amounts to uncovering the ways in which such representation is achieved. Thus the problem of semantics cannot be solved—as students of AI have attempted to do—

by invoking a strategy that calls on a stored contextual data base, since this strategy resembles that used by Baron Munchhausen, who as mentioned by Delbrück in his Summary lecture, pulled himself by his hair out of the mud.

From these shortcomings of the AI approach it does not, of course, follow that the mind *is* more than a material machine embodying complex cybernetic circuitry. What follows only is that the sense in which the mind could be said to be a computer is different from the sense in which the heart can be said to be a pump. The mind is not a *part* of the man-machine but an aspect of its entirety extending through space and time, just as, from the viewpoint of quantum mechanics, the motion of the electron is an aspect of its entirety that cannot be unambiguously dissected into the complementary properties of position and momentum.

Delbrück ends his lectures by wondering whether he has actually managed to answer the questions that he asked at the beginning. How *did* mind arise from matter? It seems to have arisen by organic evolution, probably thanks to natural selection. But in that case, how is it that the mind can transcend the tasks, such as managing stone tools and telling tales around the hearth, for which it was selected and handle number theory and quantum mechanics? How come so much more was delivered than was ordered? Delbrück does not answer that conundrum. But he thinks that, all the same, the problem of how mind can arise from no mind looks less puzzling than it used to. After all, he says, there is no inherent absurdity in organic evolution having turned up something much more refined than Terry Winograd's computer program. In any case, maybe we are greatly overestimating the knowledge of the world provided to us, individually and collectively, by the mind. Delbrück says, "The Stone Age people in England constructed Stonehenge 4000 to 5000 years ago . . . They probably thought very highly of themselves. Little did they know how much they didn't know." And what goes for them goes for us too.

REFERENCES

Bohr, N. 1933. Light and Life. *Nature* 131: 421–423, 457–459.

———. 1958. Biology and atomic physics. In *Atomic Physics and Human Knowledge*, 13–22. New York: John Wiley.

Cairns, J., G. S. Stent, J. D. Watson, eds. 1966. *Phage and the Origins of Molecular Biology.* Cold Spring Harbor, N.Y.: Cold Spring Harbor Laboratory of Quantitative Biology. A Festschrift in honor of Delbrück's 60th birthday, in which his collaborators and students present their personal accounts of his seminal role in the rise of molecular biology.

Delbrück, M. 1949. A physicist looks at biology. *Transactions of the Connecticut Academy of Science* 38: 173–190.

———. 1970. A physicist's renewed look at biology: twenty years later. *Science* 168: 1312–1315.

Vollmer, G. 1984. Mesocosm and objective knowledge. In *Concepts and Approaches in Evolutionary Epistemology*, ed. F. M. Wuketits, 69–121. Amsterdam: Reidel.

The world has been visibly recreated in the night.
Mornings of creation I call them.
In the midst of these works
of a creative energy recently active,
while the sun is rising with more than usual splendor,
I look back . . . for the era of this creation.
Not into the night, but to dawn
For which no man ever rose early enough.

Henry David Thoreau

One

Evolution of the Cosmos

In a diary entry for 1846, Søren Kierkegaard writes:

> . . . That a man should simply and profoundly say that he cannot understand how consciousness comes into existence—is perfectly natural. But that a man should glue his eye to a microscope and stare and stare and stare—and still not be able to see how it happens—is ridiculous, and it is particularly ridiculous when it is supposed to be serious . . . If the natural sciences had been developed in Socrates' day as they are now, all the sophists would have been scientists. One would have hung a microscope outside his shop in order to attract custom, and then would have had a sign painted saying: "Learn and see through a giant microscope how a man thinks (and on reading the advertisement Socrates would have said: 'That is how men who do not think behave')."

In this essay I propose, and propose seriously, to do that ridiculous thing, "look through the microscope," to try to understand how consciousness or, more generally, how mind came into existence. And with mind, how language, the notion of truth, logic, mathematics, and the sciences came into the world. Ridiculous or not, to look for the evolutionary origin of mind today is no longer an idle speculation. It has become an approachable, natural—indeed an unavoidable—question.

This essay, therefore, deals with truth and reality. Truth refers to knowledge; reality refers to the objects of knowledge. We will be dealing, then, with epistemology, the theory of knowledge. What do we know and how do we know it? Epistemology is a "metascience" in the sense that it presupposes science and reflects on the essence of science. (Another name for metascience is metaphysics. Although a derogatory connotation has been attached to the word *metaphysics* since the eighteenth century, it was originally used in a neutral sense, being named after the portion of Aristotle's writings that the first editor of Aristotle's manuscripts, 300 years after the author's death, placed after *(meta)* the natural sciences *(ta physika)*.) Our approach to epistemology will consist of an investigation into human cognitive capabilities, especially as expressed in various sciences. As we will see, each of these sciences has its own set of notions about truth and reality.

We begin our epistemological inquiry from the viewpoint of naive realism and consider our problem of truth and reality in the light of evolution. So we ask three naive questions:

1. How can we construct a theory of a universe without life, and therefore without mind, and then expect life and mind to evolve, somehow, from this lifeless and mindless beginning?

2. How can we conceive of the evolution of organisms with mind strictly as an adaptive response to selective pressures favoring specimens able to cope with life in the cave, and then expect that this mind is capable of elaborating the most profound insights into mathematics, cosmology, matter, and the general organization of life and mind itself?

3. Indeed, does it even make sense to posit that the capacity to know truth can arise from dead matter?

In light of these questions, the main topics addressed in the first half of this essay will be the origin of the universe and the origin of living matter in an initially nonliving universe, followed by the evolution of sentient forms of matter in an initially nonsentient universe, and culminating, at the endpoint of this astonishing twist of evolution, in an organ—the human brain—that is capable of introspection and language. In the second half, we will consider the ways in which modern scientific knowledge forces revisions of the naive view of reality with which we set out.

The currently accepted view of the creation of the universe is based upon the observation that the character of light reaching us from spiral nebulae is shifted from higher (blue) to lower (red) frequencies. This red shift is interpreted in terms of the Doppler effect, under which the frequency of a wave that reaches an observer from a given source decreases with the speed at which source and observer move away from each other. (We will consider the Doppler effect in more detail in chapter 15.) That

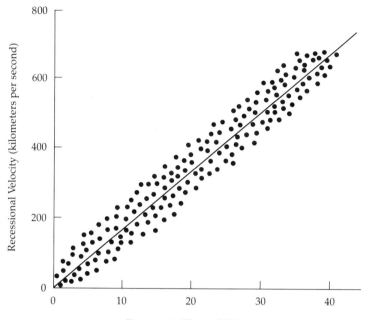

Distance (millions of light years)

The relationship between recessional velocity of galaxies (as determined from magnitude of red shift of the light received from them) and distance. Each point represents one galaxy. The proportionality factor between recessional velocity and distance—given by the slope of the line fitted to the points—is known as the Hubble constant and is currently considered to be about 17 kilometers per second per million light years. The reciprocal of the Hubble constant—approximately 18×10^9 years—gives the time taken by the galaxies to make their outbound journey since the big bang. This estimate assumes that the galactic recessional velocities have not changed, whereas it is currently believed that recessional velocities are declining due to the influence of mutual gravitational attraction. Thus the actual age of the universe is likely to be somewhat less than the reciprocal of the Hubble constant.

is to say, the red shift is due to movement of the nebulae (now known to be galaxies) away from us. In 1929 the astronomer Edwin Hubble showed that the velocity with which a distant celestial object moves away from us (as estimated from the red shift of its light) is correlated with its brightness: the fainter (and hence the more distant) an object is, the faster it seems to recede. The proportional increase of recession velocity with distance implies that the universe is expanding, as opposed to the alternative possibility of a universe of constant size, in which recession velocity would be *decreasing* with distance. Extrapolating backwards in time and supposing that the expanding universe originated from a very small volume as the result of an explosion, one can estimate when the expansion of the universe must have begun. One finds that this beginning, or creation of the universe by a "big bang," occurred roughly ten to twenty billion years ago.

Except for such local concentrations of matter as galaxies and clusters of galaxies, which correspond merely to minor inhomogeneities on the vast scale of cosmic dimensions, the universe appears to be homogeneous and isotropic: looking in any direction, one sees a uniform density of matter. This fact leads to a prediction—first made in the late 1940s by the physicist George Gamow and his colleagues—which can be stated in the following way: At the time of the big bang, the universe was at extremely high temperature and density, matter being in thermal equilibrium with radiation. In the expansion of the universe that began with the big bang, this (interconversion) equilibrium was lost when the density of radiation was reduced below a certain critical level. At that point, matter and radiation began to expand separately, without constant interconversion. The radiation extant at that time would be received now with an enormous red shift, corresponding to a source receding from us at a velocity befitting a celestial object at a distance of ten billion light years. The spectrum of frequencies present in that all-pervasive background radiation should appear to be that of radiation emitted by a blackbody at a temperature of only a few degrees kelvin (K). (Physicists define as a "blackbody" one that absorbs all incident radiation without reflecting any; the relation between temperature and frequency spectrum of radiation emitted by such a body will be considered in more detail in chapter 16.) This cosmic background radiation has indeed been detected in the frequency range of microwaves corresponding to emission from a blackbody at approximately 3°K. It is very highly isotropic, even more so than the cosmic distribution of matter, as embodied in the galaxies.

At first sight, the isotropy of the cosmic background radiation seems to imply the somewhat disturbing idea that our planet is at the center of the expanding universe. However, to avoid such cosmic geocentrism one can construct models according to which every point in the universe appears to be a center of expansion. One two-dimensional example of such models is provided by the surface of an expanding balloon, on which all points recede from all other points while retaining their relative positions. At each point on this surface an observer would see himself as being at the center of expansion. The expanding balloon surface illustrates the "cosmological principle," which states that all points in the universe are equivalent; in other words, the large-scale structure of the

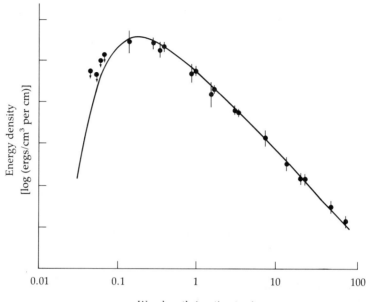

Wavelength (centimeters)

Spectrum of frequencies present in the cosmic microwave background radiation. Points represent experimental measurements of the spectrum. The curve is determined from the Planck blackbody radiation formula for a temperature of 3°K presented in chapter 16. The wavelength of the radiation shown on the abscissa is equal to the product of the reciprocal of its frequency times the speed of light.

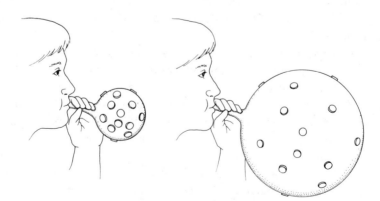

The inflation of a balloon covered with glued-on coins illustrates the isotropy of the expanding universe (the cosmological principle). As the balloon is inflated observers on each coin consider themselves to be at the center of the expansion.

universe appears to be isotropic to all observers, no matter where they are. Three-dimensional examples of such models are also available. The big bang creation theory and the cosmological principle are compatible with all observations and can be incorporated into the framework of Einstein's general theory of relativity to be considered in chapter 15.

The very early universe—say 1/100th of a second after the big bang— consisted of an undifferentiated soup of matter and radiation. Protons, neutrons, electrons, positrons, neutrinos, antineutrinos, and photons all existed in a state of thermal equilibrium, rapidly colliding and exchanging energy with each other. The temperature was probably in the vicinity of 100 billion °K. As expansion continued and temperature dropped, a point was reached (about 1 billion °K) at which protons and neutrons could associate to form stable atomic nuclei. This era of limited synthesis of atomic nuclei—lasting perhaps several minutes—resulted in the formation of a large amount of helium (about 25% of the mass of protons and neutrons was converted into helium) and of much smaller amounts of other light elements.

The next major event in the early evolution of the universe occurred when the temperature had dropped to a mere 3000°K. At that time, about 700,000 years after the big bang, free electrons combined with protons, helium nuclei and other atomic nuclei to form stable atoms. The disappearance of free electrons, and the attendant loss of their availability for interacting with photons, was the event that caused the end of the thermal equilibrium between matter and radiation. What we now observe as the 3°K cosmic background radiation is the red-shifted remnant of blackbody radiation from the era when matter and radiation were last in thermal equilibrium at 3000°K throughout the universe—some 10 billion years ago.

In the early universe, atomic matter probably formed an enormous gas of uniform density. As expansion continued, however, gravitational attraction caused local condensation in the primordial gas cloud. The huge masses formed by this condensation later underwent internal condensations that produced smaller masses. These smaller masses in turn formed galaxies, in which further condensation produced stellar clusters and, eventually, stars.

The evolution of the universe is only partly deterministic (i.e., accounted for by laws under which a given set of initial conditions leads to only one final state). It also has an indeterministic, or stochastic, component attributable to the gravitational forces to which a primordial gas cloud is subject and which enormously amplify infinitesimal fluctuations in the local density of matter. (Under an indeterministic law, a given set of initial conditions can lead to several final states.) A similarly indeterministic situation is encountered in meteorology, where infinitesimal fluctuations in initial atmospheric conditions can grow into large-scale phenomena within a few days, making any long-range predictions of the weather effectively impossible. An indeterminacy due to the amplification of small fluctuations also obtains in the processes of organic evolution. In this case, however, the indeterminacy is even greater, since fluctuations are amplified to an even greater measure in self-reproducing, living systems than in the mechanical systems of the evolving physical universe.

The future of the universe is as indeterminate as was its past. There may be enough matter in the universe to make gravitational attraction gradually slow the expansion set off by the big bang. In that case, the expansion would eventually halt and be followed by a contraction, or implosion. The result would be a "big crunch," perhaps followed by another "big bang" and a remake of the universe. However, the present best estimates indicate that there is insufficient matter in the universe for a big crunch, in which case the universe may continue to expand indefinitely.

A good deal of information about the evolution of stars is embodied in the Hertzsprung-Russell diagram, which consists of a plot of stellar luminosity against stellar surface temperature. On this diagram, most stars fall within a single band, known as the main sequence. To one side of the main sequence lies a class of stars designated as red giants; to the other side lies the class of white dwarfs. Stars begin their history as diffuse gas clouds, which condense in complex ways until they reach the main sequence. Computer modeling of stellar evolution predicts that clouds of different initial masses will arrive at different places on the main sequence. After burning for a long time on the main sequence, a star begins to deplete its nuclear fuel and expands, thereby evolving away from the main sequence to the red giant domain. Stars with high temperature and high luminosity use up their nuclear fuel faster and leave the main sequence more quickly than do slower burning stars such as our sun. After burning for a while as a red giant, the star may recollapse and finally die as a white dwarf, a neutron star, or a black hole.

Our sun, whose core is at a temperature of about 10 million °K, derives most of its radiant energy from a nuclear chain reaction, in which helium atoms are built from hydrogen through the fusion of four protons. Some of the sun's energy (less than 5%) is also derived from the carbon-nitrogen-oxygen (CNO) cycle, in which helium is formed from protons within carbon, nitrogen, and oxygen nuclei through a complex series of reactions. The CNO cycle is the dominant mode of energy production

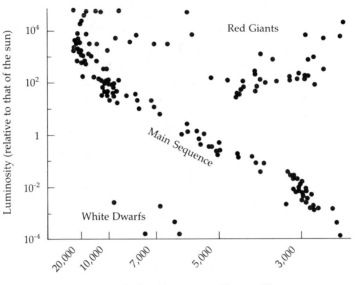

A Hertzsprung-Russell diagram of the nearest stars and those that appear brightest. Each point represents a star in our galaxy.

in stars more massive than the sun, which have higher interior temperatures. Nuclear fusion reactions leading to the formation of elements up to about the atomic number of iron (^{56}Fe) contribute to energy production in the dense, hot (up to 1 billion °K) cores of massive red giants. Formation of elements heavier than iron requires a net input of energy rather than leading to the production of energy. These heavy elements do not seem to arise within stellar furnaces; they are probably synthesized during the energetic explosion of stars known as supernovae. In view of the considerable abundance of heavy elements in our solar system, it appears that our sun is actually a second generation star, formed from the condensation of debris after an earlier star met explosive death as a supernova. Concomitantly with the formation of stars, their planetary systems came into existence. Our own solar system and with it the planet Earth, was formed about 4.5 billion years ago, by condensation of the same stellar debris from which our sun was formed.

When I was a student of astronomy in the 1920s, the knowledge of atomic physics was still quite primitive. Nevertheless, after solving the equations generated by his model of stellar structure (without the aid of computers), the English astrophysicist Arthur Stanley Eddington arrived at a core temperature of the sun of 10 million °K. At that time it was thought that 10 million °K was not hot enough to permit the nuclear reactions building helium from hydrogen to occur. Therefore, according to Eddington's calculations, all of the sun's energy would have to come from gravitational contraction of solar matter, and this would only last a few hundred thousand years. From geological records, it was known, however, that the earth was far older than this. Otto Stern, the great physicist, said "I went down on my knees and asked Eddington to raise the temperature of the sun, but he refused."

The current theory of the nuclear physics of the sun has one major flaw. According to present thinking, the fly in the ointment is the fate of the neutrinos which are produced by nuclear reactions in the solar interior. Because neutrinos interact very weakly with matter, they escape from the sun. Although the measurement of this solar neutrino efflux is difficult, it can be accomplished by using large detectors located deep underground to shield them from spurious signals generated by cosmic rays. It turns out that the neutrino efflux is three times lower than expected. This discrepancy between observation and theory remains unresolved.

Currently, the central region of the sun, in which hydrogen is converted into helium, is moving outward toward the solar surface as more and more hydrogen is consumed. When this helium core grows sufficiently large—in about 6 billion years—the sun will expand into a red giant and move away from its present position on the main sequence. At that time the earth's surface will be hot enough to melt lead, the oceans will boil, and life on earth will end.

REFERENCES

Fowler, W. A. 1967. *Nuclear Astrophysics.* Philadelphia: American Philosophical Society.

Gott, J. R., J. E. Gunn, D. N. Schramm, and B. M. Tinsley. 1974. An unbound universe? *Astrophysical Journal* 194: 543–553.

Hoyle, F. 1975. *Astronomy and Cosmology: A Modern Course.* San Francisco: W. H. Freeman.

Misner, C. W., K. S. Thorne, and J. A. Wheeler. 1973. *Gravitation.* San Francisco: W. H. Freeman.

Weinberg, S. 1977. *The First Three Minutes.* New York: Basic Books.

Wilson, R. W. 1979. The cosmic microwave background radiation. *Reviews of Modern Physics* 51: 433–445.

Two

Evolution of Life

We know enough about the history of the universe, the galaxies, the stars, the planets, and our own planet, to be certain that the earth started without life. It was only as the earth cooled that conditions began to approach those permitting the formation of life as we know it. The oldest terrestrial rocks are 3.8 billion years old and the earliest known forms of life date from at least 3 billion years ago, to the Precambrian geological age. In other words, life had appeared within about 700 million years of the earliest times that terrestrial conditions would have permitted it. On a geological time scale this can be considered "soon." How did life come to be present here? It is most unlikely that life flew in from outer space; there is none, and never was any, on the other planets of the solar system, and none would survive the exposure to the high intensity of cosmic rays in interstellar space during the journey from the far reaches of the universe. Thus there is a clear case for the transition on earth from no life to life. How this happened is a fundamental, perhaps *the* fundamental question of biology. The difficulty is not that we can't dream up schemes of how it might have happened. Many possible schemes can and have been proposed. The difficulty lies in the lack of data: there is *no* geological record of "prebiotic evolution." On the contrary, there is an immense conceptual gap between all present-day life and no life.

The generation of life ought to be almost a classroom experiment. All that is required is a body the size of the primitive earth, with its approximate temperature and composition. After 700 million years or so the body should be crawling with life. With more knowledge of the kind of processes involved, it should be possible to improve on nature and reduce the size of the body and the necessary waiting period.

The problem of spontaneous generation of life is a very old one for scientists. Until two or three centuries ago, it was universally assumed that life was being spontaneously generated all the time. Mice were thought to arise from dirty clothing, and maggots from meat exposed to the sun for a few days. A series of experiments then showed these notions to be false, culminating in Louis Pasteur's work, which finally placed the theory of spontaneous generation in disrepute. Since Pasteur's time, however, evidence has accumulated that indicates that at some time in the past, life did indeed emerge spontaneously from inanimate matter. Some scientists believe that new life may be emerging spontaneously even now, and that to demonstrate this it is only necessary to choose the correct experimental conditions. Otto Warburg, perhaps the most outstanding biochemist of our century, kept a sealed bottle on his shelf. When asked what the bottle was for, he shamefacedly admitted that he was attempting to demonstrate spontaneous generation. Similarly, the great microbiologist C. B. van Niel tells how, on visiting his old teacher M. W. Beijerinck in the late 1920s, he was asked if he were intending to do an experiment on the origin of life. When van Niel replied in the negative, he was admonished that unless he made a contribution to this field, he would never amount to anything. About this time, the Russian biochemist, Alexander Oparin, published a monograph in which he pointed out that if one is to do experiments on the origin of life, one must simulate the conditions of the primitive earth's "primal soup," that is, the mixture of spontaneously formed chemical molecules dissolved in the ancient oceans. Oparin proposed that conditions of the primal soup were highly reducing, with the atmosphere above it consisting of hydrogen, ammonia, and methane, in contrast to the present oxidizing atmosphere consisting of molecular nitrogen and oxygen. Before the appearance of life—that is, during the prebiotic phase of the earth's history—most terrestrial oxygen was tied up in the form of oxides in minerals and water. Molecular oxygen was not released into the atmosphere until about 2 billion years ago, with the advent of photosynthetic organisms that liberate oxygen from water.

After Oparin first made his proposal, more than two decades passed before someone finally decided to do an experiment to test it. This was Stanley Miller, who, at the suggestion of his teacher Harold Urey, made organic molecules in the early 1950s by passing ultraviolet light, or electric sparks through an atmosphere of hydrogen, ammonia, methane, and cyanide. Miller produced a large variety of such molecules, including several amino acids and sugars. This finding implied that the chemical composition of the "primal soup" could have been complex indeed. Since at the time of Miller's experiment very little was known about the structure of primitive life forms, it appeared plausible then that life could have evolved quite easily under these conditions. However, in light of more recent knowledge about the complexity of even the simplest organisms, the conceptual gap between nonliving and living matter has widened considerably, rather than narrowed.

For example, the intestinal bacterium *Escherichia coli*, a microorganism so tiny that it is barely visible under the microscope, is now known to contain a complex system of interacting protein and nucleic acid molecules that store a tremendous amount of highly specific biological information. The several thousand genes of *E. coli*, in which the structure of as many different protein molecules is encoded, appear to be the minimum number that even the most primitive autonomously living organism must possess. Viruses, albeit structurally less complex than bacteria and having fewer genes, do not qualify for the category of living organisms since they cannot translate their genetic information into proteins.

Biochemical systems extant today must represent a small subset of all the systems which presumably were tried out during the prebiotic phase. In recent years various theories have outlined the possible connections between molecular selection, natural selection, and irreversible thermodynamics in this prebiotic biochemical trial process. While all these theories seem quite plausible and very intelligent, in my opinion they tell us very little about the origin of life. I have made it my rule not to read this literature on prebiotic evolution until someone comes up with a recipe that says "do this and do that, and in three months, things will crawl in there." When someone is able to create life in a shorter time than was originally taken by nature, I will once more start reading that literature.

At this point we may consider real life. Real life used to be divided naturally into the plant and animal kingdoms since before the advent of the microscope there were no blurred distinctions between the two. Botany was studied in institutes at one end of town, and zoology in institutes at the other end. Recent discoveries have forced communication between the two disciplines. One of these discoveries is that plants and animals have a common biochemistry. Both are composed of the same basic chemical building blocks—namely lipids, carbohydrates, proteins and nucleic acids—which are synthesized from ingested raw materials via the same basic chemical reactions. Another discovery is that the principles of genetics are common to plants and animals: both encode their hereditary traits in nucleic acids and translate the encoded genetic information into the structure of proteins via the same mechanism, using the same genetic code. A third discovery is that certain single-celled organisms have both animal and plant characteristics. Ciliates swim like animals, while algae photosynthesize like plants. So the former seem to be animals and the latter plants. Flagellates, however, both swim and photosynthesize and hence cannot be placed in either kingdom. Current taxonomic practice, therefore, assigns ciliates, flagellates, and algae to their own separate kingdom, namely to that of the protists. Fungi, moreover, are plantlike, but they do not photosynthesize. So a fourth kingdom has been created especially for them.

Bacteria, the smallest organisms, are different from all other cellular forms of life and are the subjects of yet a fifth kingdom, namely that of the prokaryotes (meaning "having a primitive nucleus"). The other four kingdoms together constitute the superkingdom of eukaryotes (meaning "having a true nucleus"). Prokaryotes are undoubtedly the evolutionary ancestors of eukaryotes. Indeed, the prokaryotic–eukaryotic division is far less blurred and far more profound than the classical dichotomy of plant and animal kingdoms. Prokaryotes have only one chromosome; eukaryotes have several. Since prokaryotes have only one chromosome, division of that chromosome into a pair of daughter chromosomes is a relatively simple task that does not require a nuclear membrane to contain the process. Despite the absence of a nuclear membrane, however, the bacterial chromosome remains confined to a "nucleoid" domain of the cell. Division and orderly partition of the several daughter chromosomes of the eukaryotic cell is a much more complex process, termed *mitosis*, which proceeds at first within the confines of the nuclear membrane but later requires its breakdown.

Prokaryotes do not undergo cell fusion as part of their reproductive cycle. The reproductive cycle of eukaryotic organisms by contrast, includes an alternation between two phases: a haploid phase with a single set of chromosomes and a diploid phase with a double set of chromosomes. In the haploid phase two cells fuse to form a diploid cell. If the two fusing cells have arisen from separate organisms, genetic recombination is possible between different lines of descent. That diploid cell, or one of its descendants generated by a series of mitotic divisions, later undergoes *meiosis*, another even more complicated type of cell division, which reduces the double set of chromosomes to a single set and brings the cell back to the haploid phase of the cycle. The haploid–diploid cycle, the processes of mitosis and meiosis, and the "true" cell nucleus were all invented at the time when eukaryotes evolved from prokaryotes.

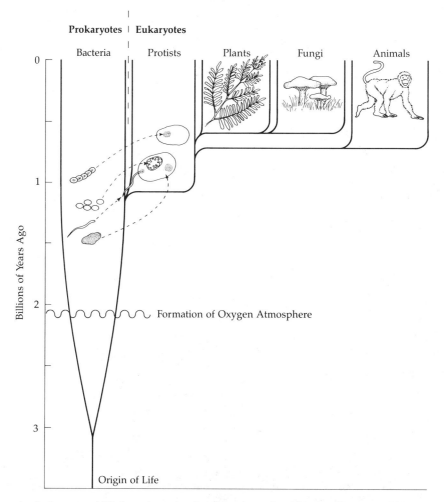

Prokaryotes | Eukaryotes

Bacteria   Protists   Plants   Fungi   Animals

Billions of Years Ago

0

1

2 — Formation of Oxygen Atmosphere

3

Origin of Life

A phylogeny of life based on the five-kingdom classification. Representative organisms are pictured within each of the kingdoms. Dotted arrows indicate probable symbiotic origins for components of eukaryotic cells: mitochondria from omnibacteria, chloroplasts from cyanobacteria, and cilia from spirochaete. [After Margulis and Schwartz, 1982]

Although bacteria do not undergo cell fusion in their reproductive cycle, they have developed other ways of achieving genetic recombination. In one such process, two bacteria mate and one of them, the donor, transfers a chromosome, or a chromosome fragment, to the other, recipient, cell. In another bacterial recombination process, extrachromosomal

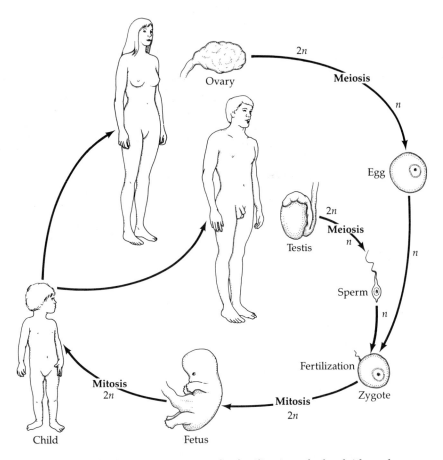

A human individual arises as a zygote, by fertilization of a haploid egg by a haploid sperm, each containing a single set of $n = 23$ chromosomes. The zygote containing a double set of $2n = 46$ chromosomes develops via a fetus into a multicellular man or woman by a series of mitoses. In the testis or ovary of the mature man or woman, haploid sperm or eggs are produced by meiosis.

genetic elements called plasmids, which can be inserted into and excised from chromosomes, are transferred from donor to recipient cell.

Eukaryotes derive their energy from respiration. In this process oxidizable foodstuff is ingested and oxidized by inspired oxygen in a series of chemical reactions called oxidative phosphorylation. In these reactions the energy liberated by oxidation of the food is used to generate adenosine triphosphate (ATP), which is the common carrier of chemical energy in the molecular transformations that take place in all living cells. To harness the energy provided by oxidation (i.e., by the loss of electrons),

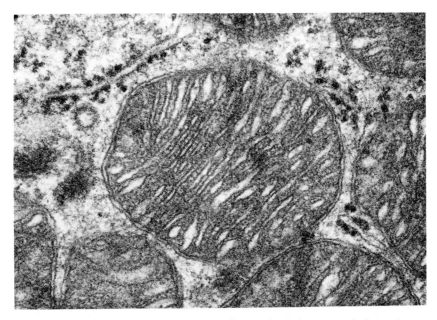

Electron micrograph of a thin section of mitochondria from a rat kidney. A mitochondrion consists of an outer membrane surrounding a series of inner membranes roughly perpendicular to the long axis of the organelle. The electron-transfer reactions of oxidative phosphorylation take place on the mitochondrial inner membranes. Magnification × 73,000. [Courtesy of Eric Schabtach, University of Oregon]

electrons are transported from the oxidizable material to oxygen (the ultimate, reducible electron acceptor) in a pathway involving removal of hydrogen from the former in the first portion and electron transfers to the latter in the second portion. Oxidative phosphorylation is used by all eukaryotic organisms as the ultimate energy source for the formation of ATP. The reactions take place in specialized organelles of the eukaryotic cell called mitochondria. Oxidative phosphorylation is also carried out by many types of bacteria, which lack mitochondria. Indeed, the process of oxidative phosphorylation certainly originated with the prokaryotes, and it has been proposed that mitochondria evolved by way of an ancient symbiosis of a respiring prokaryote with a primitive nonrespiring eukaryotic cell.

Contradictory as it may seem, some prokaryotes, the sulfate- and nitrate-reducing bacteria, can respire in the absence of air. For that purpose they make use of bound oxygen in sulfates and nitrates instead of free oxygen as ultimate electron acceptors. Since sulfates and nitrates were present

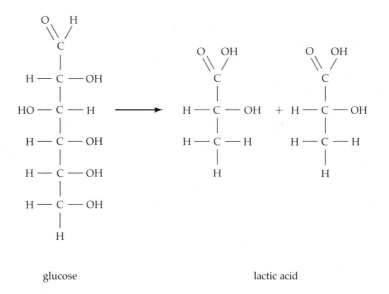

glucose   lactic acid

In the process of fermentation, one molecule of glucose sugar is converted to two molecules of lactic acid through a series of enzymatic reactions. Two molecules of ATP are produced for every molecule of glucose consumed. Respiration begins with the end products of fermentation and further oxidizes them to carbon dioxide and water. The complete process, from glucose to carbon dioxide and water, yields 36 molecules of ATP for each molecule of glucose consumed. Thus respiration represents an enormous gain in energy production over simple fermentation.

in the minerals of the primitive earth, such bacteria may represent an early stage in metabolic evolution, prior to the creation of the oxidizing atmosphere by photosynthetic organisms. There exist still other bacteria, which not only do not respire to derive their energy for the formation of ATP, but also cannot even tolerate the presence of air. Such obligate anaerobic bacteria, for instance *Clostridium*, derive their energy from fermentation. Here a sugar molecule is rearranged chemically to form two lactic acid molecules. In sugar, hydrogen and oxygen are nearly uniformly distributed over the molecule, whereas in lactic acid the hydrogen is concentrated at one (reduced) end of the molecule, and the oxygen is concentrated at the other (oxidized) end. Thus fermentation is in essence an intramolecular oxidation–reduction. The energy yield of this internal rearrangement is rather small, but it produces enough ATP to support the organism. Obligate anaerobes, which live by fermentation of substances that have intramolecular electron donors and acceptors, may represent the early prephotosynthesis stage of evolution.

The earliest photosynthesizers were probably the green and purple sulfur bacteria. These organisms use the energy of sunlight to convert atmospheric carbon dioxide (CO_2) into carbohydrate (CH_2O). They carry a pigment, bacteriochlorophyll, which is raised to an excited state by the absorption of sunlight. In this excited state, the bacteriochlorophyll is oxidized by transfer of an electron to, and hence reduction of, NADP (nicotinamide adenine dinucleotide phosphate) to NADPH. Hydrogen sulfide (H_2S) is then oxidized to sulfur, by returning an electron to, and hence reducing the oxidized bacteriochlorophyll. The energy liberated by that step is used to form ATP, which, together with NADPH, in turn provides the energy for the conversion of carbon dioxide to carbohydrate. It should be noted that this kind of photosynthesis, whose net reaction can be written as:

$$2\,H_2S + CO_2 \overset{\text{light}}{\rightarrow} (CH_2O) + H_2O + 2\,S,$$

does not yield molecular oxygen, and hence cannot have been responsible for the creation of the present atmosphere. This must have been the work of another kind of prokaryote, the cyanobacteria, as well as of eukaryotic algae and plants. In addition to a photosynthetic apparatus similar to that of sulfur bacteria, called photosystem I, the latter have another photosystem, called photosystem II. In this system light is used to excite a different chlorophyll in a different reaction center, which oxidizes (i.e., accepts electrons from) water and thus generates molecular oxygen, according to the net reaction:

$$H_2O + CO_2 \overset{\text{light}}{\rightarrow} (CH_2O) + O_2.$$

In eukaryotic organisms, the photosynthetic generation of ATP and NADPH takes place in specialized organelles called chloroplasts. It is likely that chloroplasts are derived from an ancient symbiosis of a photosynthesizing prokaryote with a primitive, nonphotosynthetic, eukaryotic cell.

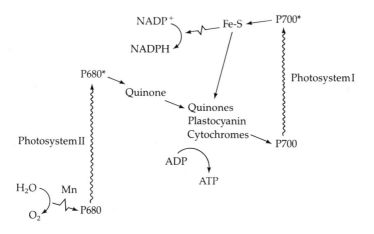

The path of electrons is shown for photosynthesis as it occurs in cyanobacteria and in the chloroplasts of protists and plants. Electrons from water are directed, via a manganese-containing protein (Mn), to a special chlorophyll (P680) of photosystem II. Absorption of light raises the electron to a higher energy and causes it to be funneled into an electron-transport chain leading to the synthesis of ATP. Arriving at the special chlorophyll (P700) of photosystem I, the electron again is raised to a higher energy by light absorption and subsequently transferred to an iron-sulfur center. From there it may return to the electron-transport chain or it may contribute to the reduction of $NADP^+$ to NADPH.

Thus, living organisms have a great variety of ways to derive energy from either intra- or intermolecular reactions, with or without sunlight. All of these processes were originally invented by prokaryotes and are still used today by various types of bacteria. In the course of evolution, some of these processes—namely, fermentation, photosynthesis, and oxidative phosphorylation—were also adopted by eukaryotes.

REFERENCES

Eigen, M. 1971. Self-organization of matter and the evolution of biological macromolecules. *Naturwissenschaften* 58: 465–523.

Margulis, L., and K. V. Schwartz. 1982. *Five Kingdoms: An Illustrated Guide to the Phyla of Life on Earth.* San Francisco: W. H. Freeman.

Miller, S. L., and L. E. Orgel. 1974. *The Origins of Life on the Earth.* Englewood Cliffs, N.J.: Prentice-Hall.

Miller, S. L., and H. C. Urey. 1959. Organic compound synthesis on the primitive earth. *Science* 130: 245–251.

Oparin, A. I. 1968. *Genesis and Evolutionary Development of Life.* New York: Academic Press.

Whittaker, R. H. 1969. New concepts of kingdoms of organisms. *Science* 163: 150–160.

Three

Beginnings of Perception; Species

The unity and continuity of life on earth is manifest in its molecular anatomy. All modern forms of life use nucleic acids as information stores and proteins as agents for the direction of biochemical reactions, with the same processes of transcription and translation mediating the expression of the stored information. The protein and nucleic acid constituents are universal, as is the genetic code, which determines how information stored as nucleotide sequences in long nucleic acid molecules is translated into the amino acid sequences of proteins. Eukaryotes and prokaryotes also share certain special molecules, for instance heme for electron transport, chlorophyll for photosynthesis, ATP for energy storage, and riboflavin for the catalysis of oxidation–reduction reactions and for sensing the presence of light.

The unity and continuity of life is equally manifest in its psychic aspects. Perception in plants and animals is a familiar phenomenon, but the beginnings of perception are also clearly present in microorganisms, in which adaptive behavior demonstrates that they can detect and evaluate signals from the environment and respond appropriately. For example, chemoreception—the ability to sense and respond to changes in the chemical composition of the environment—is manifest in the swimming pattern of chemotactic bacteria. The path of a swimming bacterium corresponds to a random walk: runs of orderly swimming along a straight path are interrupted from time to time by a tumbling motion, resulting in the random selection of a new direction for the next straight run.

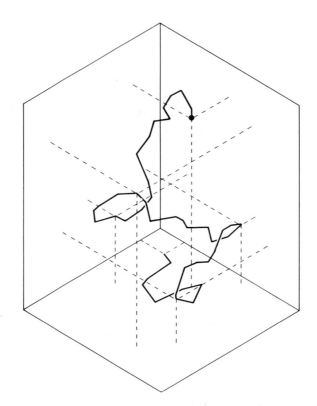

The path of a swimming *Escherichia coli* bacterium tracked for a period of about 45 seconds with a special tracking microscope. While the bacterium was being tracked it executed 40 straight runs and tumbles. The speed of the runs was approximately 20 micrometers per second. The resulting path of motion is a random walk in three dimensions. [After Berg, 1975]

If chemotactic bacteria are in a medium in which there is a gradient of favorable (attractant) or unfavorable (repellent) chemicals, the selection of the new swimming direction following each tumble is still random, but the intervals between tumbles are longer when the path of the straight run is up the attractant or down the repellent gradient. In this way, the overall direction of the random swim becomes biased toward higher concentration of an attractant or lower concentration of a repellent.

The perception of light in prokaryotes is exemplified by the phototaxis, or active avoidance of dark regions in their environment, of photosynthetic bacteria. There are at least two ways in which bacterial phototaxis is accomplished: one of them is a stochastic response consisting of a biased random walk similar to chemotaxis; the other is a deterministic response. Bacteria controlled by the stochastic response, upon sensing that they are swimming down a light gradient, simply stop swimming until Brownian motion gives them a new direction, and then they start swimming again. In this way, the overall path of the random swim is biased in the direction of higher light intensity. Bacteria controlled by the deterministic response are able to swim both forward and backward. If such bacteria sense that they are swimming into regions of lower light intensity, they simply shift into reverse and swim backward into regions of higher light intensity.

Many primitive eukaryotic organisms manifest the deterministic growth response to light called phototropism. The fungus *Phycomyces*, for example, does not resort to photosynthesis as an energy source; however, it resorts to phototropism to guide the growth of the stalk toward the light source and thus places its fruiting bodies at the tip of the stalk in position for optimal dispersal of its spores. The stalk of the fruiting body is actually a cylindrical lens capable of focusing light, which allows the fungus to sense the direction of maximum illumination. *Phycomyces* can also sense gravity, which allows it to grow its stalk in a consistently upward direction (negative geotropism). Finally, *Phycomyces* can detect the presence of a solid surface. Irrespective of illumination, the fungus senses the presence of such a surface at a distance of about a millimeter and grows away from it. Just how *Phycomyces* accomplishes this act of perception is not understood, although it probably involves the emission and absorption of a gaseous or volatile substance either produced by *Phycomyces* or present in the environment.

In the examples of primitive perception considered here, the detection of the signal—chemical attractant or light—involves an adaptation mechanism similar to the dark adaptation of our eyes: the organism sets its level of detection in accordance with the average strength of the stimulus (such as the concentration of chemical or the intensity of light). Thus we have in these single-celled organisms all three components of the perceptive process of higher forms of life: stochastic response, deterministic response, and adaptive response based on immediate past experience. It is a long way, however, from these primitive perceptive processes and their evaluation of environmental signals to the machinery involved in, for example, the decision of a young man to propose marriage to his girlfriend. He responds to her charm with his emotional brain (the midbrain) and his thinking brain (the cerebral cortex). His decision is influenced by his genes, by his imprinting in earliest childhood, by his identity as it detached itself from his mother, by his moral upbringing, by his economic circumstances, and by his surging sex drive.

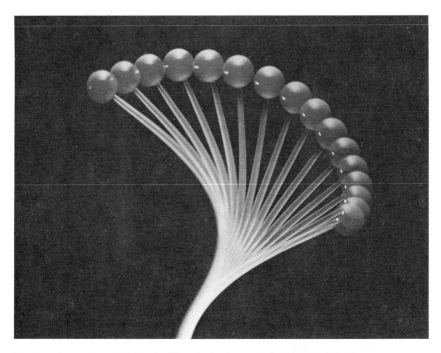

The tropic response of the fruiting body (sporangiophore) of the fungus *Phycomyces*. This stalk, 0.1 millimeter in diameter and up to several centimeters in length, responds with exquisite sensitivity to light, gravity, or the presence of a nearby barrier. Here, in a multiple-exposure photograph with one exposure every two minutes, a sporangiophore is shown bending toward light impinging from the left. The *Phycomyces* sporangiophore, like the human eye, responds to light over an intensity range of about 10^{11}—a remarkable feat for a single fungal cell. [Courtesy of David S. Dennison, Dartmouth College]

Let us trace this long way in order to get a feeling for its continuity. How do we reconstruct the tree of life? How do we identify the common ancestors of the currently living forms? We use the methods of paleontology, that is, digging to find the parts that survived the ages (bones and hard parts of invertebrates, impressions, and petrified structures) and dating them. We date the specimens by a variety of physical techniques and try to establish their relations to each other and to currently living forms. In some cases procedures of this kind can take us very far back, as in some sulfur deposits whose relative content of different sulfur isotopes indicates the biological action of sulfate-reducing organisms a billion years ago. On the whole, paleontological methods are the only ones that give us direct evidence of our ancestors. Much richer, however, is the evidence from comparative anatomy, physiology, and biochemistry of living forms. These methods tell us who is related to whom and how closely. They permit us to infer some properties of actual common ancestors but not those of sidelines that became extinct; no amount of study of present forms would permit us to infer dinosaurs, for example.

Some of the profound differences between prokaryotes and eukaryotes were discussed in chapter 2. These differences arise from the fact that whereas the genetic information carried by a prokaryote fits into a single chromosome, the information carried by a eukaryote does not. Therefore, the higher complexity of eukaryotes made possible by their possession of much more genetic information is attained at the price of much more complicated genetic machinery. Several chromosomes must be enveloped by a nuclear membrane, and mitosis must occur to assure orderly distribution of the chromosomes following their replication. Eukaryotes had also to develop a genetic recombination mechanism more complex than that of bacteria, namely sex, which involves alternating diploid–haploid stages and the fusion of haploid cells to form diploid cells. Even primitive eukaryotes, such as *Phycomyces* and the slime mold *Plasmodium,* undergo this sexual process.

To classify the diversity of extant eukaryotes, the species concept is called on. We no longer define a species as a morphological type, as did Aristotle. Instead, we define a species as a set of individuals that interbreed under natural conditions and produce fertile offspring. This notion of species applies primarily to the sexually propagating higher plants and animals, in that it pertains to a population of interbreeding individuals that are sexually isolated from other species inhabiting the same area. A species can, therefore, be considered as a natural biological unit whose members share a common pool of genes. This does not mean, however, that the population of individuals sharing that gene pool is necessarily genetically homogeneous; the pool may include several variants or alleles of one or more genes. Such genetic heterogeneities present within a species are called polymorphisms.

However, this modern concept of species is not as unambiguous as it may appear. Groups of wild animals sometimes form small, restricted, local breeding units known as demes. Often neighboring demes of a particular type of animal can interbreed, but demes from widely separated geographic areas may have reduced fertility when they attempt to interbreed, and still more distant ones may not interbreed at all. This progressive reduction in fertility upon attempted interbreeding is attributable to the possession of increasingly different chromosomal arrangements of genes by the members of ever more distantly separated demes. Are these widely separated demes members of the same or of different species? Inasmuch as they do not interbreed, they would be assigned to different species, but since they are connected by a continuous path of interbreeding populations, they are considered to belong to the same species after all.

Moreover, the modern concept of species based on the lack of interbreeding is not readily applicable to the admittedly exceptional types of eukaryotic organisms that reproduce without mating, that is, where each member of the species is in any case reproductively isolated. Thus some species reproduce vegetatively (by fission of the parent), parthenogenetically (by development from unfertilized eggs) or hermaphroditically (by self-fertilization). In these cases criteria other than interbreeding have to be called on for classification purposes.

Speciation—the formation of new species—is the process of splitting two subpopulations, initially capable of interbreeding, into two mutually infertile groups. This occurs when one group becomes geographically (or otherwise) isolated from the main population, so that genetic interflow between the two populations ceases. The isolated group does not represent a full spectrum of the genetic polymorphisms present in the gene pool shared by the members of the larger population, thus eliminating some alleles in favor of others from the isolated group (the founder's principle). Moreover, the smaller number of individuals in the isolated group allows new variant genes, or new alleles, to become more rapidly established in the population and thus facilitates its rapid adaptation to a new niche. If the two populations are once more brought into contact after their genetic makeup has diverged, their matings are no longer optimally fertile. Indeed, the hybrid offspring of such matings are often sterile. Since it is now evolutionarily nonadaptive for the two populations to interbreed, it becomes advantageous for both populations to develop biological means for reducing the incidence of ineffective matings. Thus most incipient species erect elaborate barriers that inhibit matings with their precursor species, including specialized sexual features and idiosyncratic patterns of courtship behavior.

Until recent years, only morphological differences in species type could be examined. With the advent of modern biochemical techniques, however, it has become possible to examine differences in protein structure between organisms. This has opened up an entirely novel approach to the determination of the evolutionary relationships between different species. The principle of this approach is that the precise sequence of amino acids making up the (primary) structure of a given type of protein molecule is subject to change by gene mutations. As a result of such a mutation the amino acid normally present at one particular site of the protein is changed to another kind of amino acid. If the individual in which this gene mutation occurred happened to be the founder of an incipient species in the speciation process, then all the members of that new species—as well as all the members of the species that developed from that species—would manifest that particular amino acid substitution in that particular protein. Hence the less closely two species are related (i.e., the more incipient species separate them from a common ancestor species), the more amino acid substitutions would be expected to be found on comparison of the amino acid sequence of a particular type of protein molecule.

One such study of evolutionary relationships within the class of mammals of the vertebrate phylum has resorted to comparison of the amino acid sequences of the ubiquitous electron transport protein cytochrome *c*. Cytochrome *c* is built up of about 100 amino acids, and the precise sequence of these amino acids is subject to mutational substitution at a more or less constant rate, on an evolutionary time scale. Upon examining the amino acid substitutions among the cytochrome *c*'s of various mammalian species, it was found that human cytochrome *c* differs not at all from that of the gorilla and chimpanzee, by one substitution from that of the rhesus monkey, and by nine substitutions from that of the kangaroo. Thus, it follows that on the evolutionary tree, humans are very closely related to the gorilla and the chimpanzee, more remotely related to the rhesus monkey, and much more remotely to the kangaroo. However, if one tries to ascertain which eukaryotic species are most closely related to the prokaryotes by comparing amino acid sequences of prokaryotic proteins functionally equivalent to cytochrome *c* with sequences of diverse eukaryotic cytochrome *c*'s, one finds so little correspondence in sequence in all cases that no relative degree of relatedness can be inferred between prokaryotes and any of the eukaryotes. In other words, the ancestral line of the eukaryotes must have separated from the prokaryote kingdom such a long time ago that the steady accumulation of amino acid substitutions has erased all structural homologies between the cytochrome *c*'s of extant species and those of their remote common ancestor.

REFERENCES

Adler, J. 1976. The sensing of chemicals by bacteria. *Scientific American* 234(4): 40–47.

Berg, H. 1975. How bacteria swim. *Scientific American* 233(2): 36–44.

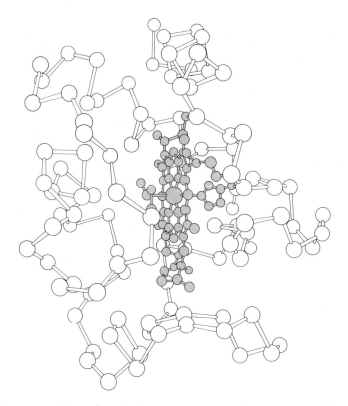

Skeletal representation of a cytochrome *c* molecule, showing in simplified form
how approximately 100 amino acid units are linked together in a continuous
chain that surrounds and grips a heme group. The iron-containing heme plays
an essential role in the electron-transfer reaction mediated by cytochrome *c*.
[After Dickerson, 1972]

Dickerson, R. E. 1972. The structure of history of an ancient protein. *Scientific
   American* 226(4): 58–72.

Dickerson, R. E., R. Timkovich, and R. J. Almassy. 1976. The cytochrome fold
   and the evolution of bacterial energy metabolism. *Journal of Molecular Biology*
   100: 473–491.

Four

Evolution of Genomes

The ultimate determinant of the morphological and behavioral characteristics exhibited by an organism is its ensemble of genes, or its genome, which is, in turn, embodied in the DNA molecules of its chromosomes. Hence, to advance our understanding of the course of evolution, it is instructive to compare the DNA of various organisms. If genome sizes (i.e., the amount of DNA per haploid nucleus) of different organisms are compared, a wide variation is found. The genome size of prokaryotes is about 2 million nucleotide base pairs (bp); that of the lowest eukaryotes (such as fungi) is about 20 million bp; and that of higher eukaryotes ranges from about 200 million to 100 billion bp. Thus, at first sight genome size appears to increase with the complexity of the organism. However, this correlation does not hold within the nearly thousandfold range of genome sizes of the higher eukaryotes, especially not for the multicellular animals (metazoa). Here, within many single taxonomic classes, or even orders, there is a tenfold variation in genome size, with that of the class of amphibia spanning a hundredfold range. The genome size of our own class of mammals is more narrowly distributed within the middle range of the vertebrate phylum and that of our own species *Homo sapiens* falls into the middle of the mammalian range. Thus genome size is a poor index of the degree of evolutionary sophistication of a particular order of higher eukaryotes, since we, the most sophisticated of eukaryotes, have only a middling genome size of 3.5 billion bp. The significance of the wide variation in genome sizes is still unknown.

In any case, it appears that in eukaryotes only a minor fraction of the total DNA included in the measurement of genome size is actually ded-

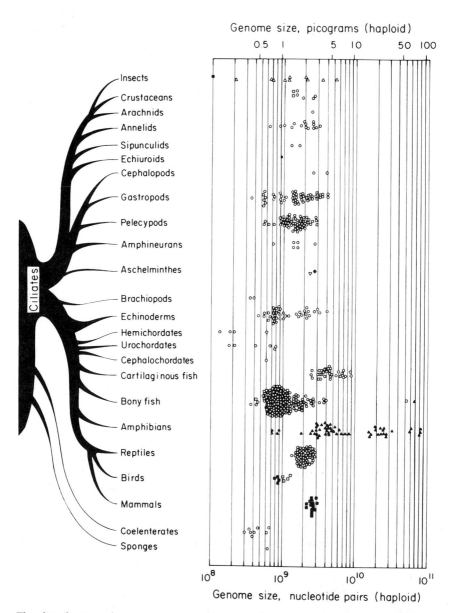

The distribution of genome size in various classes of animals. Each point represents the genome size of a member species of the classes listed on the ordinate according to their phylogenetic relationships. [From Britten and Davidson, 1971. Used with permission.]

icated to the encoding of protein structure. The average protein molecule consists of a polypeptide chain of about 300 amino acids, which (since in the genetic code one amino acid is represented by three successive nucleotide bases) would require about 1000 bp for its encoding. So, if all 3.5 billion bp of the human DNA complement encoded proteins, our genome would specify more than a million different protein molecules. Since this estimate is too high by about a factor of 100, most of our DNA must have some other role.

Some insight into the diversified roles of various parts of the DNA complement is provided by the possibility of dividing genomic DNA sequences into three classes: highly repetitive, middle repetitive, and single copy. The sequences of the highly repetitive class are about 100 bp in length and are present in as many as 10 million copies per genome; those of the middle repetitive class are about 1000 bp in length and present in as many as 100 to 10,000 copies per genome; and those of the single copy class are also about 1000 bp in length and present as a single copy per genome. These classes are defined by the reassociation kinetics of dissociated strands of DNA after the dissociation of the mixture of double-stranded DNA molecules comprising a genome. The principle underlying the interpretation of this test is that the more abundant, (or highly repeated), a particular DNA sequence is in the mixture of dissociated DNA molecules, the more likely it is that complementary strands corresponding to that sequence will encounter one another, and hence the more rapid is their reassociation when dissociated strands of the genomic DNA are allowed to reassociate. Complementary strands of single copy sequences are least likely to meet and hence are the slowest to reassociate. The number of different nucleotide sequences present in the messenger RNA of eukaryotic organisms is generally found to be much less than the number of different sequences present in their respective genomes. This is compatible with the idea that single copy DNA comprises the set of structural genes, that is, those DNA sequences that code for proteins. Some structural genes, however, do occur in multiple copies, such as those in which the structures of histones and immunoglobins are encoded. Moreover, some of the middle repetitive DNA sequences encode the structure of the RNA molecules that form part of the apparatus of protein synthesis, such as ribosomal and transfer RNA. But the function of the bulk of the repetitive DNA is still unknown, although some proposed models give it various roles in the regulation of gene expression.

In prokaryotes, whose much smaller genome consists almost entirely of single copy DNA sequences, the regulation of gene expression is rea-

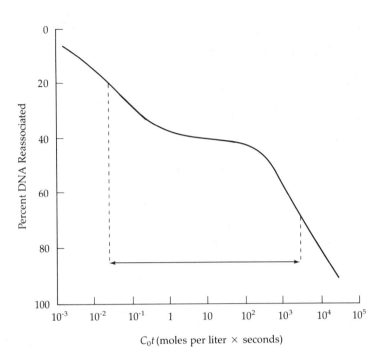

Reassociation kinetics of a representative sample of dissociated mammalian DNA. The percent of DNA reassociated is plotted against the logarithm of the "normalized time" C_0t, where C_0 is the concentration of DNA in the reassociation mixture (in moles/liter) and t the time (in seconds). The reassociation of dissociated strands takes place in two distinct stages, one rapid and one slow. The midpoints of the two stages (dotted lines) are separated by a factor of 100,000. The rapid stage represents the reassociation of repeated sequences of DNA and the slow stage that of single copy DNA. [After Britten and Kohne, 1970]

sonably well understood. Here, groups of structural genes whose expression needs to be regulated coordinately are arranged contiguously on the chromosome. The transcription of such genes into messenger RNA is controlled by a contiguous regulator region of DNA called an operator, and the entire stretch of DNA (operator plus structural genes) is designated as an operon. The regulation of gene expression in eukaryotes is much less well understood, except that it is certain that procedures other than the operon mechanism of prokaryotes must be invoked. Roy Britten and Eric Davidson have proposed one widely discussed model of eukaryotic gene regulation. Their model is based on the observation that in eukaryotes the repetitive DNA sequences are interspersed with the single copy DNA sequences. The model envisages that "batteries" of structural genes are distributed over the genome, each with an identical control region. Expression of a particular battery of genes is turned on or off by response of each of its identical control regions to an "integrating" signal. The integrating signal is, in turn, the product of some other gene, whose expression is itself controlled by the action of yet another integrating signal acting on *that* gene's control region. This type of model makes possible many different ways of turning different combinations of genes on and off in different orders. Thus, the presence of a great deal of "junk" DNA, which does not encode proteins, may be explained as being necessary for communication among genes and for controlling their expression. If this explanation were to account for all the variation in genome size within the vertebrate phylum, it would follow that there is a much more elaborate control of gene expression in amphibia than in mammals.

In the course of evolution, repetitive DNA may arise when a single copy gene is accidentally "Xeroxed" a number of times during normal DNA replication, so that in the progeny genome the single copy gene is replaced by many copies of that gene. In the course of subsequent generations structural rearrangements of the chromosomes disperse the multiple copies throughout the genome, where they might come to have a regulatory function. The members of a given family of repetitive genes need not remain entirely identical in their base sequence; they may develop a limited amount of heterogeneity due to spontaneous point mutations. Once such diversification has progressed so far and the members of the original "Xeroxed" family have become so dissimilar that their complementary strands would no longer reassociate rapidly in the reassociation test, they would no longer be members of the same family of repetitive DNA.

We may now consider the question whether speciation—the splitting of two populations of organisms sharing a common gene pool into two mutually infertile groups—is attributable to a divergence in the character of their proteins (and hence due to a gradual accumulation of point mutations in structural genes) in one or both of the diverging genomes, or to a divergence in the system of the control of gene expression. To answer that question, one must have some knowledge of the rate at which point mutations actually accumulate in the gene pools of natural populations. It is necessary to consider only *neutral* mutations, that is, mutations that result in a change in character that is neither deleterious (so that the mutant gene is not weeded out by natural selection) nor advantageous (so that the mutant gene has no selective edge over the nonmutant version in the gene pool).

Several methods of estimating the "basal" rate of accumulation of neutral mutations all give similar values, namely about 10^{-9} point mutations per bp per year. One method measures the degree of mismatch between single copy DNA sequences of organisms belonging to species known to have diverged within the past 40 million years. (The degree of mismatch of two DNA molecules of slightly different sequence can be assessed by mixing them, dissociating their strands by raising the temperature, allowing reassociation of the dissociated strands by lowering the temperature, and then raising the temperature again and noting the degree of reduction in the temperature at which the imperfectly matched hybrid strands redissociate.) Another method compares the amino acid sequence of a particular type of protein, whose function is unlikely to be critically dependent on the exact amino acid sequence, in a number of related species of known time of evolutionary divergence. One such type of structurally "unconstrained" protein is alpha-fibrinopeptide, which is cleaved from the hemoglobin precursor polypeptide chain after it is initially synthesized in the cell so that the remainder forms the active hemoglobin molecule. The amino acid sequence of that peptide varies greatly from species to species, probably due to its limited biochemical function. Another type of structurally unconstrained amino acid sequence is present in some portions of the electron transport protein, cytochrome c. The portions of the cytochrome c molecule that are near its catalytic center (holding the heme group in place) and those that make contact with cytochrome a and cytochrome b (the neighboring electron transport proteins in the respiratory chain) are structurally constrained and, consequently, highly conserved in evolution. But the remainder of the cytochrome c molecule shows considerable variations from species to species. For instance, as mentioned in chapter 3, the amino acid sequences of the cytochrome c molecules of the kangaroo and the apes differ at nine sites. In fact, a straight line is obtained if the number of amino acid substitutions by which the cytochrome c of various species differs from that of the human species is plotted against the time passed since their evolutionary divergence. The same process of accumulation of neutral mutations also gives rise to genetic inhomogeneities within a single species, as has been demonstrated for various species of sea urchins that diverged 20 million years ago. The basal accumulation rate of one point mutation per billion bp per year is by no means negligible: in the mammalian genome, consisting of about 3 billion bp, three mutations would accumulate each year. Therefore, it is not difficult to understand how a marked degree of genetic heterogeneity develops within an initially homogeneous population over evolutionary time.

But what is the significance of the accumulation of these mutations for the speciation process? Since they are envisaged as neutral in the first place, they seem unlikely to have played a large role in creating the reproductive isolation underlying the formation of species. They merely provide a clock by which the time of divergence can be estimated in retrospect. Thus any point mutations that *were* important for speciation would have had to be of the nonneutral kind, whose rate of accumulation cannot be estimated by the methods used for measuring the basal rate. So, which kind of nonneutral mutations are the important ones as far as evolution is concerned: mutations in structural genes or in DNA sectors concerned with the regulation of gene expression? It seems evident at first sight that a mutation affecting the expression of a "battery" of structural genes would lead to a much more profound difference in the development of the organism, and hence of its adult morphology and character, than one resulting in a change in the function of a single protein.

Allan C. Wilson and his coworkers have compared the histories of frogs and mammals to assess the relative evolutionary importance of these two types of changes. The frogs underwent their major dispersion much earlier than the mammals: about 150 million years ago, compared to about 100 million years ago. Both groups comprise many species: there are about 3000 species of frogs and about 4600 species of mammals. Frogs, however, are all quite similar morphologically and occupy more or less the same niche, whereas mammals are morphologically highly diverse and occupy a wide variety of niches on land, in the sea, and in the air. The broad range in morphological diversity of the mammals is reflected in their assignment to more than a dozen separate orders, whereas all frogs belong to a single order. It must be kept in mind, however, that while species is a biologically grounded concept, higher groupings such as orders and classes are arbitrary (in the sense that they are defined by taxonomic convention) and, in many cases, controversial. As far as the accumulation of mutations in structural genes is concerned, frogs are diversified as much as, or even more than, mammals.

Wilson infers from the fact that frogs show much less morphological diversity than mammals that mutations leading to morphological diversity lead predominantly to changes in the developmental timing and coordination of the expression of batteries of genes. Wilson further conjectures that most such regulatory mutations are not point mutations but rearrangements of chromosome structure. These rearrangements may pertain to only a single gene, as exemplified by the insertion of short, repetitive DNA sequences into single copy sequences, or they may be major aberrations, such as inversions and translocations of substantial parts of a chromosome. A genetic comparison between modern maize and teosinte, the wild grass from which maize was derived, supports this conjecture. Although maize and teosinte are morphologically disparate plants, their genomes differ by only a small number of mutations. If modern maize is crossed with teosinte, the result is a hybrid plant strongly resembling the primitive maize cultivated by North American Indians 7000 years ago, which suggests that the stone age developers of maize selected a few regulatory mutations in the teosinte genome.

Convincing evidence in favor of the conjecture that rearrangements of chromosome structure with their attendant dramatic consequences for the regulation of gene expression are responsible for the generation of morphological diversity is provided by the comparison of the *karyotypes* (i.e., the number, forms, and types of chromosomes carried) of related species. Thus, there are many fewer differences in karyotype among the morphologically homogeneous frogs than among the morphologically diverse mammals. The lesser karyotype diversity in frogs also accounts for the fact that hybrid frogs produced by interspecies crosses are often fertile. In contrast, few species of mammals will even produce hybrid offspring (the mule yielded by a cross of the horse to the donkey is one of the rare cases), and such offspring are almost always infertile (as is the mule), since the structurally disparate parental chromosomes cannot pair properly during meiosis in the ovaries or testes of the offspring.

Chromosomal rearrangements occur frequently in speciation. Major interspecies rearrangements, such as inversions and translocations, may be observed under the microscope by comparing the characteristic pattern of bands shown by chromosomes stained with certain dyes. Minor rearrangements may not be reflected by changes in the chromosomal banding pattern, but their presence can have profound effects on the development of the organism.

Mary Claire King and Wilson have considered the evolutionary relation of chimpanzee and man from this point of view. They find that chimpanzee and human proteins differ in fewer amino acid sequences—there is an overall sequence agreement of 99.3%—than do those of various species of the mouse. By comparison the proteins of different modern human races are much more similar: the small divergence of chimpanzee and human proteins is 20 to 60 times greater than that of the proteins of Black Africans, Japanese, and Caucasians. Despite the very close similarity between the structural genes of chimpanzee and man, there is an obvious morphological disparity between these two species. King and Wilson account for this disparity in terms of the evolutionary

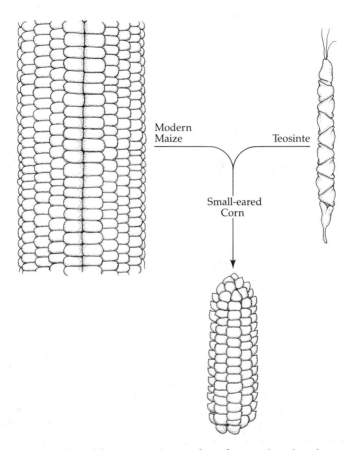

Modern Maize

Teosinte

Small-eared Corn

Crosses between the wild grass teosinte and modern maize give rise to small ears of corn similar to 7000-year-old archaeological specimens found in Mexico and the southwestern United States. [After Beadle, 1980]

accumulation of chromosomal rearrangements rather than of point mutations.

On surveying the karyotypes of primates, one finds that species most often differ by a chromosomal inversion of the type designated "pericentric" (because it includes the centromere at which the chromosome becomes attached to the spindle fiber in cell division), with chimpanzee and human genomes differing by six pericentric inversions. Interspecies matings between primates whose karyotypes differ by pericentric inversions, or even in the total number of chromosomes, may, in some cases, lead to viable offspring. One case is known, for instance, in which a

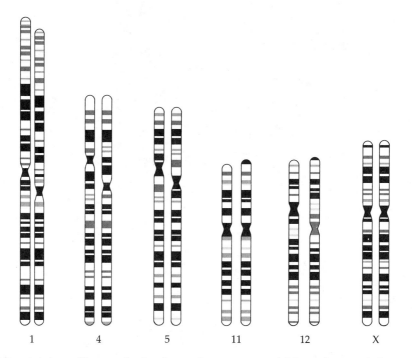

After staining with a particular dye, a chromosome exhibits a characteristic
banding pattern, reflecting its arrangement of DNA. Shown here is a
schematic representation of the banding patterns of several chromosomes from
human (on the left in each chromosome pair) and chimpanzee (*Pan troglodytes*).
Evidently, the chromosomes of human and chimpanzee are not very different
structurally, because for each of the homologous pairs shown the banding
patterns are very similar in both species. Chromosomes 4, 5, and 12 differ
between the two species by pericentric inversions. [After Yunis and Prakash,
1982]

gibbon and siamang of a laboratory colony produced offspring. But such
hybrid offspring are sterile, since their chromosomes will not pair properly during meiotic cell division to form functional sperm or egg cells.
Thus pericentric inversions lead not only to morphological diversification
but also to reproductive isolation of a subpopulation, and hence to
speciation.

The present races of man are typical examples of populations with
partial reproductive isolation. Although, as measured by protein structure, the present races are much more closely related to each other than
any of them is related to the chimpanzee, there do, nevertheless, exist
sufficient protein differences between them so that each race can be said

to constitute a distinct gene pool. The limited genetic interflow to which these distinct gene pools are attributable was more the result of geographical separation and social taboos than of biological restraints, since there appear to be no genetic barriers to interracial hybridization or any hybrid sterility implying incipient speciation.

Some species evolve rapidly; others evolve more slowly. Such differences in the rate of evolution are not attributable to variations in the intrinsic probability of occurrence of genetic changes in individual members of one species or another. That probability is more or less constant across species, for point mutations as well as for rearrangements in chromosome structure. Nor are these differences due to variations in the rate at which unconstrained point mutations are established (i.e., replace the previously extant type) in the *population,* since that rate too is constant across species (at about one mutation per billion bp per year) and, by virtue of its constancy, provides us with an evolutionary clock. Rather, the differences in rate at which the species evolve mainly reflect variations in the rate at which chromosomal rearrangements are established in the population, which in turn is the result of the kind of selective pressure to which the population is subject. On the one hand, the pressure of natural selection will reduce the rate of evolution of a species when environmental conditions are fairly constant and the interbreeding population is large. Here natural selection works against novelty by eliminating most chromosomal rearrangements. An example is provided by the frogs, which did not diversify greatly over a period of 150 million years. On the other hand, the pressure of natural selection will raise the rate of evolution when environmental conditions are in flux and populations are small—for instance, when terrain and climate are changing—and new niches are developing. Here natural selection will work for novelty by favoring the establishment of chromosomal rearrangements that provide the means for occupying a new niche. A prime example of such an acceleration of evolution is the mammalian dispersion (large-scale development of diverse morphological forms) that occurred about 100 million years ago. Specific instances of the invasion of new niches by mammals include the taking to the air by bats and the return to the ocean by cetaceans.

An extreme example of ultrafast evolution is found in the breeding of domestic animals and plants within a time span of a few thousand, or even a few hundred years. In this case, the profound change in the environment is the product of man's activity. In his deliberate breeding efforts man exerts a very strong selective pressure, since the breeder works with small populations and fosters intense inbreeding.

Inbreeding forms a very interesting contrast with outbreeding as a selective force. In nature, many species have adopted special measures to avoid inbreeding. Intense inbreeding vitiates the evolutionary advantage provided by sexual reproduction, which creates new and hopefully adaptive gene combinations from the diversity of alleles, or polymorphisms, present in the gene pool of the species. Moreover, outbreeding often leads to "hybrid vigor," or to the superiority of individuals that carry both variant versions of a gene in their diploid genome over those that carry only one of the two alleles. Indeed it seems that an intensely inbreeding population might as well reproduce vegetatively, that is, by fission of a single parent, rather than going to the trouble of generating biparental offspring sexually. In view of the crucial role of chromosomal rearrangements in generating morphological diversity, however, it is apparent that intense inbreeding can be of considerable advantage in speeding evolution. With inbreeding, when two individuals mate the chance is greatly increased that both will have the same novel pericentric chromosomal inversion in their genomes. In that case, their offspring *will* be fertile, since there is no obstacle to normal pairing in meiotic cell division of two identically inverted chromosomes. With the genesis of a small population of such fertile offspring, a new species will have been established. All the same, while in his cultivation of plants and animals the human breeder enormously speeds up evolution and produces creatures by inbreeding, which are of use to man, these creatures are very incompetent at living in the wild. No corn plant, no sheep could survive in nature without the watchful ministrations of a human caretaker.

REFERENCES

Beadle, G. 1980. The ancestry of corn. *Scientific American* 242(1): 112–119.

Britten, R. J., and E. H. Davidson. 1971. Repetitive and non-repetitive DNA sequences and a speculation on the origins of evolutionary novelty. *Quarterly Review of Biology* 46: 111–138.

Britten, R. J., and D. E. Kohne. 1970. Repeated segments of DNA. *Scientific American* 222(4): 24–31.

Davidson, E. H., and R. J. Britten. 1979. Regulation of gene expression: possible role of repetitive sequences. *Science* 204: 1052–1059.

de Grouchy, J., C. Turleau, and C. Finaz. 1978. Chromosomal phylogeny of the primates. *Annual Review of Genetics* 12: 289–328.

King, M. C., and A. C. Wilson. 1975. Evolution on two levels in humans and chimpanzees. *Science* 188: 107–116.

Myers, R. H., and D. A. Shafter. 1979. Hybrid ape offspring of a mating of gibbon and siamang. *Science* 205: 308–310.

Yunis, J. J., and O. Prakash. 1982. The origin of man: a chromosomal pictoria legacy. *Science* 215: 1525–1530.

Wilson, A. C., G. L. Bush, S. M. Case, and M. C. King. 1975. Social structuring of mammalian populations and rate of chromosomal evolution. *Proceedings of the National Academy of Science USA* 72: 5061–5065.

Five

Evolution of Man

It was in the Precambrian geologic era that the cyanobacteria came into existence, and with them photosystem II. This is the auxiliary photosynthetic system that captures the energy of sunlight for the oxidation of water to produce molecular oxygen, and it was this system that converted the earth's original reducing atmosphere into its present oxidizing condition. The accumulation of molecular oxygen in the atmosphere then enabled other forms of life to adopt a more efficient method of oxidizing and extracting energy from foodstuff. Thus began the rise of metazoa, in the Paleozoic era (600 to 225 million years ago), in whose first period, the Cambrian (600 million years ago), occurred the emergence of marine invertebrates, followed by the first vertebrates (fish) in the second, or Ordovician period (500 million years ago). The first mammals appeared in the Jurassic period (200 million years ago) of the Mesozoic era (225 to 65 million years ago). Manlike creatures—hominids—emerged 3 to 5 million years ago during the Pliocene epoch of the Tertiary period of the most recent, or Cenozoic era (which itself began about 65 million years ago). They came to dominate the Earth during the Pleistocene epoch, which made up the first 2 million years of the Quaternary period of the Cenozoic era. These dates were originally inferred from the geologic characteristics of the strata in which the fossilized remains of the presumed ancestors of man were found and were subject to considerable uncertainty. Modern dating methods, which are based on the relative abundance of the isotopes of carbon, potassium, argon, lead, and uranium in the specimens or in objects found close to them, are considerably more accurate.

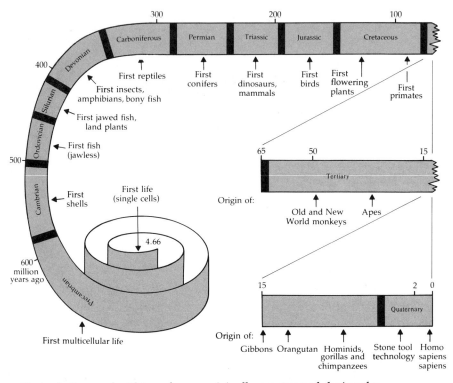

Geologic time scale. This scale was originally constructed during the nineteenth century solely on the basis of fossil evidence. In recent decades, absolute dates of these geological periods have been determined using radioactive-dating techniques. [From Lewin, R., (1984) *Human Evolution*, Blackwell Scientific Publications, Oxford. Used with permission.]

The Pleistocene epoch also saw the latest of the succession of ice ages that have occurred every few million years since the Precambrian era. Ice ages are periods of colder climate attributable partly to changes in the intensity of the radiation emitted by the sun, partly to changes in tilt of the axis of the earth's rotation with respect to the ecliptic (the plane of the earth's revolution around the sun), and partly to changes in the composition and mode of circulation of air in the earth's atmosphere. The Pleistocene ice age was not a continuous period of extreme cold; it was interrupted by three interglacial stages during which a prevailing milder climate melted most of the ice sheets covering our present temperate zones. The most recent glacial stage (designated Würm) ended only about 20,000 years ago. Why these alternations of glacial and interglacial stages occurred during recent geologic times remains unex-

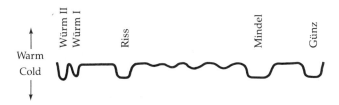

The major glacial periods (with interspersed interglacial stages) of the Pleistocene epoch. The geologic evidence for four separate glacial periods was first found in the Alps. These periods were termed (backward from the most recent) Würm, Riss, Mindel, and Günz. The Günz period occurred about 500,000 years ago. The Riss–Würm interglacial stage probably began 150,000 years ago and lasted about 50,000 years. The Würm period ended, and our present interglacial stage began, about 20,000 years ago.

plained. But there is no doubt that these alternations had a profound effect on the course of biological evolution in the Pleistocene.

The evolutionary divergence of our own order of primates from an arboreal insectivore mammal dates back to the Paleocene epoch, about 70 million years ago. The early primates resembled modern prosimians such as the lemur and the tarsier. One line of anthropoid primates—Old World monkeys, apes, and man—diverged from the prosimians about 45 million years ago. The other line of anthropoid primates—the New World monkeys—may have diverged from the prosimians even earlier, but not before continental drift had eliminated the land bridge linking South America with Africa (which were already separated 65 million years ago). The general morphological resemblance of the families of New World and Old World monkeys is rather remarkable, since their common prosimian ancestor, who must have lived prior to the separation of New and Old Worlds, was unlike either of the modern monkey families. Evolutionists thus consider the resemblance of New World and Old World monkeys as an instance of parallel evolution, in which two groups of initially very similar creatures evolve independently in the same direction.

The separation between the apes and the Old World monkeys may have occurred about 30 million years ago. *Aegyptopithecus*, a fossil primate of the Oligocene epoch, probably lived at about the time of this separation, although it is not known whether it is representative of a time before the divergence or a time after. Distinctly apelike fossils occur during the early Miocene epoch; these are the *Proconsul* and *Dryopithecus* genera. They were animals about the size of baboons and are believed to be

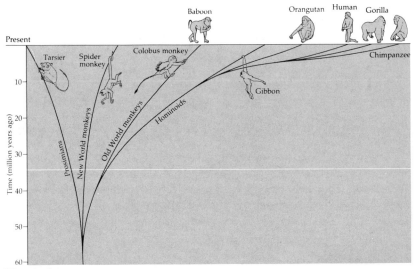

Primate family tree.

A primate family tree. [From Lewin, R., (1984) *Human Evolution*, Blackwell Scientific Publications, Oxford. Used with permission.]

common ancestors of the modern great apes—orangutans, gorillas, and chimpanzees—as well as man. Just how and when the human ancestry diverged from that line is still the subject of controversy. Many evolutionists used to consider the fossils assigned to the extinct genus *Ramapithecus*, dating back 8 to 15 million years, to be those of the very first protoman. However, if one interprets the very high degree of structural similarity of human and chimpanzee proteins in terms of the molecular evolutionary clock, one reaches the conclusion that the human and chimpanzee lines must have diverged much more recently than the appearance of *Ramapithecus*, possibly about 5 million years ago.

There is a general agreement that fossils assigned to the genus *Australopithecus* are distinctly human. *Australopithecus* was first described by Raymond Dart in 1925 as being "of importance because it exhibits an extinct race of apes intermediate between living anthropoids and man." The most ancient specimen of *Australopithecus*—an unusually complete, 3-million-year-old, fossilized human skeleton called "Lucy"—was found by Donald C. Johanson near Hadra, Ethiopia, in 1974. Johanson assigned "Lucy" to a separate *Australopithecus* species and, since Hadra is located in the Ethiopian region of Afar, designated that species *A. afarensis*. It is conjectured that by this time, 3 million years ago, *A. afarensis* walked upright, more or less like modern man. *A. afarensis* gave rise to a line of

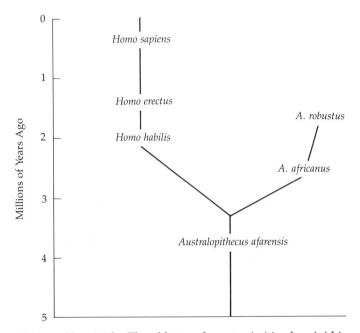

The evolution of hominids. The oldest and most primitive hominid is considered to be *Australopithecus afarensis* (Lucy), who was ancestor to all others. D. C. Johanson reasons that increased development of molar teeth was a late Australopithecine phenomenon, and the types that display it are assigned to a separate phyletic branch. The most heavily molarized *A. robustus* is at the end of that branch. The molar teeth of the members of the genus *Homo* are essentially unchanged from those of their ancestor *A. afarensis* and have been assigned to a phyletic branch of their own, with the increasingly advanced *H. erectus* and *H. sapiens* evolving out of *H. habilis*, who was the first tool maker. The controlled use of fire was developed by *H. sapiens*. [After Johanson and Edey, 1981]

several other *Australopithecus* species, including *A. africanus* and *A. robustus*. *A. africanus* seems closer to modern man than the much larger *A. robustus*, in that the former is inferred to have eaten a diet that included meat and to have been a maker and user of simple tools, in contrast to the latter whose diet was largely tough vegetable matter and who did not use tools.

A transition between *Australopithecus* and modern man is exemplified by the tool-making *Homo habilis*, who came on the African scene a little more than 2 million years ago. Finally, with the appearance of *Homo erectus* about 1.5 million years ago, we reach the era in which modern man emerged. *Homo erectus* is the generally accepted name of a group of

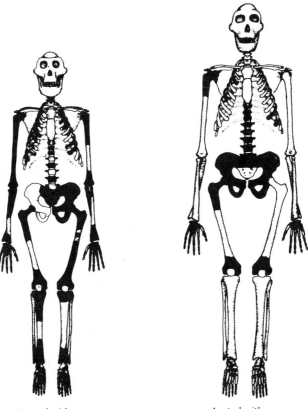

Australopithecus
afarensis

Australopithecus
africanus

Comparison of four hominid skeletons. The parts of each skeleton actually found are shown in black. The skulls of all three fossil skeletons should actually be shown in black also, but this has not been done to avoid obscuring the facial features. *A. afarensis* was about 3.5 feet tall and weighed about 50 pounds; *A. africanus* was about 4.5 feet tall, and *A. robustus* about 5.5 feet tall. *A. robustus* was heavily built and is not considered to have been an ancestor of modern man, whose skeleton is shown at right for comparison. [Drawings by Luba Dmytryk-Gudz from *Lucy: The Beginnings of Humankind.* © 1981 Donald C. Johanson and Mailand A. Edey]

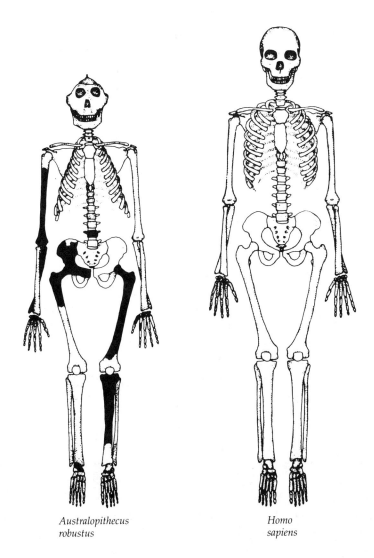

Australopithecus robustus

Homo sapiens

human races that are now recognized as comprising a single species, although formerly they were considered as separate species on the basis of the findings of single fossil bones or teeth. This group includes Java Man (the first specimen of *H. erectus* found in Java, in the 1880s), Heidelberg Man, and Peking Man, which date back 300,000 to 1.3 million years. A likely route of expansion of *H. erectus* has been inferred from the estimated ages of fossil finds in the various localities. That route would have taken *H. erectus* north from his presumed site of origin in Eastern Africa to the Mediterranean and/or the Indian subcontinent. From there he would have turned west and east, to leave his remains found in Hungary, Germany, Spain, and Morocco, and in China and Indonesia.

One of the reasons for the great uncertainty in age estimations of the fossilized precursors of man is the incompleteness of their skeletons. Often jaws and teeth are the only remnants, since these are the bones most resistant to decay. More complete skeletons are obtained only under fortuitous circumstances, for instance when remains have been protectively encased in the mud of lake shores. Fortunately teeth and jaws are of special evolutionary significance, in that they can provide information regarding the diet and general life-style of the defunct primate. Thus a comparison of the teeth and jaws of modern chimpanzees with those of *A. africanus* reveals the presence of a well-developed canine tooth in the former but not in the latter. The large, protruding canine teeth of the chimpanzee are useful for tearing fibrous foodstuff or for fighting, but not for chewing. The chimpanzee's dentition is thus adapted to the niche of fruit eater in the forest. By contrast, the small canines and more heavily developed molar teeth of *A. africanus* are well-suited for chewing seeds but not for tearing. This change in the structure of the teeth and jaw may be correlated with our ancestors' emergence from the forest and move to the grasslands. These changes in the structure of jaw and teeth were accompanied by alterations in the general bone structure of the head. In the progression from chimpanzee through *H. erectus* to *H. sapiens*, there is manifest an increase in the size of the skull, a decrease in the amount of bony arch over the eye, and the appearance of a projecting chin.

Predating the changes in teeth and jaw structure in the human line were morphological changes in the bones of feet, legs, and pelvis. These skeletal modifications are presumably related to the development of upright walking and the corresponding alterations in balance and musculature accompanying the move from forest to grasslands. These modifications are a distinctly human development, since no other primates walk upright. Behavioral developments accompanying the emergence of upright posture included the formations of small bands of running individuals, who preyed upon small animals, scavenged the kills of other predators, or roamed the grasslands gathering seeds and nuts. Louis Leakey has conjectured that the eating of meat by the protohumans began with their scavenging the remains of the kills of big cats, thus competing with the hyenas for the leftovers. Leakey has attempted to recreate such scavenging forays in the modern African savannah. Using only the resources

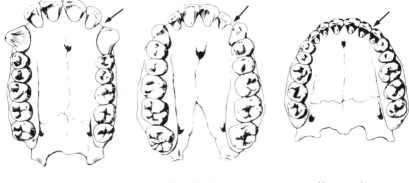

Chimpanzee   *Australopithecus*   *Homo sapiens*
                    afarensis

Comparison of dentition in the upper palates of an ape (chimpanzee), *Australopithecus afarensis* and a human of the genus *Homo*. *A. afarensis* dentition is a mixture of human and ape characteristics. The incisors are relatively large, like an ape's, and there is a gap (arrow) between the canine and incisor. Such a gap is uncommon in later hominids. [Drawings by Luba Dmytryk-Gudz from *Lucy: The Beginnings of Humankind*, © 1981. Donald C. Johanson and Mailand A. Edey]

presumed available to the ancient hominids, he managed to fend off the hyenas and obtain parts of the carcasses of animals killed by other beasts of prey. He believes that scavenging occupied a long period preceding the practice of hunting with tools. According to Leakey, the first hunting tool to be developed was the bola, a weapon consisting of two stones tied together with a thong.

After the move to the grasslands, the next phase of man's development began with his migration northward during interglacial periods and occupation of caves during glacial periods. Moving into the caves had an important effect on human development, since it required the eviction of other animal inhabitants by such methods as stone throwing and organized shouting. The debris of animal bones found in these caves reveals, furthermore, that their human inhabitants had begun to hunt by that time. Such hunting, as well as competition with and defense against bears and leopards, brought about the development of stone tools of varying refinement. Occasional use of fire in caves, presumably for cooking, occurred as far back as 700,000 years ago, but the regular use of sustained fire may date back only 40,000 years, to the last glacial period. It is important to remember that the use of sustained fire requires

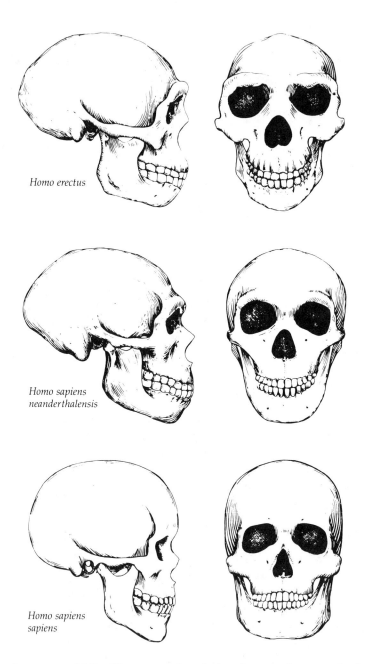

Homo erectus

*Homo sapiens
neanderthalensis*

*Homo sapiens
sapiens*

Over the course of 1.5 million years of evolution, humans have acquired a higher and rounder skull (encasing a larger brain), a decrease in the amount of bony arch over the eyes, and a distinct chin. [Drawings by Luba Dmytryk-Gudz from *Lucy: The Beginnings of Humankind*, © 1981. Donald C. Johanson and Mailand A. Edey] a great deal of planning and foresight, in that ashes must be banked, combustibles gathered and stored, and the fires continuously tended.

It was nutritionally more efficient for man to increase the proportion of meat in his diet, particularly during the glacial periods. Meat is richer in calories than most vegetables and its proteins are richer in the essential amino acids required by man. Meat is also a less seasonal food, especially in the northern latitudes. As meat came to constitute a larger proportion of their diet, humans made the technical and social advances necessary to improve hunting techniques and thus hunt larger mammals. We will consider the relationship of language and organized hunting in chapter 19.

The first known burials of the dead occurred 100,000 years ago in the Neanderthal culture. The Neanderthals (*H. sapiens neanderthalensis*) ranged over Europe, Africa, and Asia, forming a variety of different races. They were apparently much more advanced morphologically and cranially than they are popularly conceived to have been. The popular misconception of the Neanderthals originally arose because the first Neanderthal bones found near Düsseldorf in 1856 were those of an aged, arthritic individual, not at all representative of his time or species. The European Neanderthals were exterminated about 40,000 years ago by modern man, designated *Homo sapiens sapiens*. The origin of *H. sapiens sapiens* was a mystery for many years; the prevailing opinion today is that he was simply one of many races, belonging to a highly diverse and cosmopolitan group that included the Neanderthals. The extermination of the European Neanderthals by modern man has its historical analog in the virtual extermination of the American Indian by the invading European settlers 39,500 years later; here, too, one race destroyed another of the same species, in order to take its land.

It therefore appears that in giving an account of human evolution, one cannot construct a simple phylogenetic tree; rather one must postulate a network of populations, which separated only to recombine later. As was pointed out in chapter 3, geographical isolation of an incipient species need not be irreversible. The isolated population may retain a residual cross-fertility with its ancestor population, and upon restoration of contact between the two populations, the two divergent gene pools may be reunited. The early hominids lived in local pockets of small populations, dispersed over large areas of low population density, as small widely separated bands roaming through Europe, Africa, Asia and Australia. (Populations of hominids reached Australia by way of a land bridge from Southeast Asia, uncovered as the levels of the oceans dropped during a glacial stage.) There was relatively little reproductive contact among these dispersed populations, which therefore developed into separate races, with separate gene pools.

Let us recapitulate the significant landmarks of the history of human evolution. First, the habitat changed from forest to grassland, while the erect stature developed (about 3 million years ago). Second, stone tools came into use at the beginning of the Pleistocene (about 2 million years ago), followed by many refinements in tool-making during the various stages of the Stone Age. (It is to be noted that some human populations are *still* living in the Stone Age, 5,000 years after most races passed beyond it.) Third, there was a northward migration during the Günz–Mindel or pre–Günz interglacial stage. The harsher northern conditions led to the hunting of larger mammals, with its attendant social organization, including a division of labor, under which the women continued to gather foodstuff while the men hunted. Presumably this new life style also included setting up camps, which would have required more elaborate planning and more sophisticated ideation than previous modes of human existence. This higher level of sophistication developed in the middle Stone Age, during the dominance of the Neanderthals, and led to such rituals as burial of the dead, which provided anthropologists with better and more abundant skeletal remains. Most importantly, the domestication of plants and animals 10,000 years ago brought about the rise of civilization. Deliberate domestication of wild species by late Stone Age man created genetic changes in plants and animals in a few centuries that would have taken millions of years under natural selection. Domestication therefore constituted a fantastic biological experiment whose success profoundly altered man's relation to nature.

REFERENCES

Ciochon, R. L., and R. S. Corruccini, eds. 1983. *New Interpretation of Ape and Human Ancestry.* New York: Plenum Press.

Dart, R. A. 1925. *Australopithecus africanus: the man ape of South Africa. Nature* 115: 195–199.

Johanson, D. C., and M. A. Edey. 1981. *Lucy—The Beginnings of Mankind.* New York: Simon and Schuster.

Johanson, D. C., and T. D. White. 1979. A systematic assessment of early African hominids. *Science* 203: 321–330.

Lewin, R. 1984. *Human Evolution—An Illustrated Introduction.* New York: W. H. Freeman and Co.

Pilbeam, D. 1984. The descent of hominoids and hominids. *Scientific American* 250(3): 84–96.

———. 1970. *The Evolution of Man.* London: Thames and Hudson.

Siever, R. 1983. The dynamic earth. *Scientific American* 249(3): 46–55.

Washburn, S. L. 1978. The evolution of man. *Scientific American* 239: 194–208.

Weiner, J. S. 1971. *Man's Natural History.* London: Weidenfeld and Nicholson.

Six

Evolution of the Brain

In our quest for understanding how the capacity to know truth and reality arose in an initially nonsentient universe, the evolution of the human brain is obviously of central importance. To a first approximation, the brain may be regarded as a computer for processing information inputs brought to it from sensory receptors and for commanding motor outputs executed by the muscles, as well as for carrying out numerous higher functions, such as cross-correlating inputs from different sensory modalities (for instance, hearing and vision), learning, and symbolic manipulations. Later we will see that in an epistemological context that view of the human brain may not be fully adequate.

One of the few available methods of reconstructing the evolutionary origins of the brain is to compare the nervous systems of various living species, considering them as representatives of successive evolutionary stages. For that purpose we suppose that the nervous systems of present-day simpler organisms resemble those of the ancestral, now extinct, archetypes from which the more complex organisms later evolved.

The basic cellular component of the nervous system is the *neuron*, a type of cell that generates and processes electrical signals. The typical neuron consists of a *soma*, which contains the cell nucleus, and of thin extensions, or processes, emerging from the soma. Among these are an *axon*, by means of which the neuron reaches out to contact and connect with other cells of the nervous system, and *dendrites*, which provide the neuron with sites at which it can be contacted by, and receive input from,

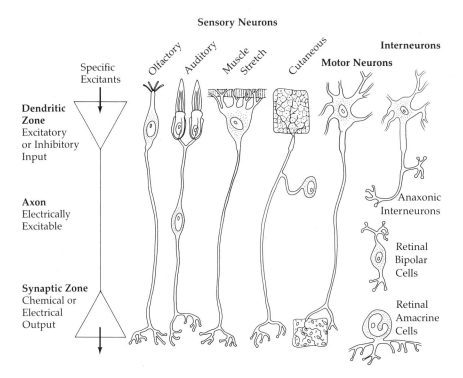

Sensory Neurons

Olfactory · Auditory · Muscle Stretch · Cutaneous

Interneurons

Specific Excitants

Motor Neurons

Dendritic Zone
Excitatory or Inhibitory Input

Axon
Electrically Excitable

Anaxonic Interneurons

Retinal Bipolar Cells

Synaptic Zone
Chemical or Electrical Output

Retinal Amacrine Cells

Diagram of a variety of sensory neurons, motor neurons, and interneurons, arranged to bring out the basic agreements in functional and structural features. The position of the soma, or nucleated mass of cytoplasm, does not have a constant relation to the functional geometry in terms of impulse origin. [After Bullock, Orkand, and Grinell, 1977]

the axons of other neurons. The capacity to generate and process electrical signals is a cellular property of great evolutionary antiquity, since even ciliated protozoa use the generation and processing of electrical signals to control the direction of their active movement. Being single-celled organisms, ciliated protozoa do not, of course, have a nervous *system*. However, as soon as we ascend the metazoan branch of the phyletic tree and reach the first true metazoa, the jellyfish, we encounter a nearly full-blown nervous system in possession of the structural and functional features of the nervous systems of higher animals. In particular, jellyfish, which originated more than 500 million years ago, have the three specialized cell types characteristic of nervous tissue: motor neurons, sensory neurons, and interneurons, which mediate between sensory and motor neurons. Furthermore, the connections made between these elements of the jellyfish nervous system consist of *synapses* at which, as in all higher organisms, an intercellular transfer of electrical signals is

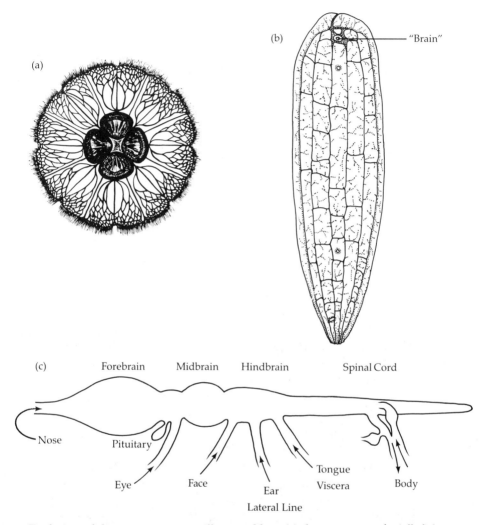

Evolution of the nervous system illustrated by (a) the nerve net of a jellyfish [After Bullock and Horridge, 1965; originally drawn by G. J. Romanes in 1885] (b) the nerve cords and simple "brain" of a flatworm [After Bullock and Horridge, 1965; originally drawn by Y. Delage in 1886.] (c) an outline of the vertebrate nervous system with its tripartite brain and specific cephalic neural inputs [After Shepherd, 1983]

accomplished by chemical transmitter molecules. That is not to say, however, that the nervous system of the jellyfish is not more primitive than that of more complex animals: the nerve net formed by the interconnections of the three types of jellyfish neurons is quite unsophisticated, in line with the limited behavioral repertoire of these simple animals. Another difference is that jellyfish neurons are dispersed throughout the body tissues, rather than being concentrated in special centers. This dispersed nerve net provides a high degree of local autonomy, in the sense that any part of the animal is capable of carrying out a complete stimulus–response reaction.

At the next stage of metazoan evolution are the flatworms, represented by modern tapeworms and planaria. The flatworms were the first animals with a longitudinal body axis, specialized head and tail ends, and symmetric right and left sides. Flatworms represent an important advance in the design of the nervous system, namely *centralization*. Rather than being widely dispersed throughout the tissues, flatworm neurons are concentrated in clusters, or *ganglia*, in the interior of the body. Moreover, the circuitry of the nervous system is more differentiated, especially in that the feature of *labeled lines* has made its appearance. Labeled lines are like call-bell signals in the butler's pantry of the old manor house; they allow identification of the source of the signal reaching the pantry—drawing room, dining room, or master bedroom—by virtue of the particular line over which the signal arrives, that is, which bell is ringing. Use of neurons for labeled lines made possible the development of a nearly limitless variety of sophisticated stimulus–response circuits in the nervous system that can govern complex behavioral repertoires.

In addition to centralization and labeled lines, the flatworm adumbrated another key feature of the nervous system of higher metazoa, namely *cephalization*. This term designates the evolutionary trend of displacing more and more of both functional responsibilities and mass of nervous tissue frontward into the head, or cephalon, with increasing organizational and behavioral complexity. The cephalic agglomeration of ganglia then led to the formation of the organ designated as "brain." The adaptive value of cephalization derives from the general tendency of bilaterally symmetric animals to move in the direction of their longitudinal axis, with the mouth in the forward position. Thus it is with their heads that such animals first encounter most changes in their environment to which a rapid response may be required. For that reason, the head is the preferred site for installation of sensory receptors, particularly of those receptors capable of sensing the environment at some distance from the animal, such as eyes, ears, and noses. Hence the ganglia whose neurons are to process these sensory data and eventually convert them into commands to the effectors are similarly installed in the head, to place them as near as possible to their input receptor neurons. The brain sends these commands to, and receives additional sensory input from, the hind part of the body through one or more rearward-coursing nerve cords. The structure of the nervous systems of all higher metazoa can be considered as mere modification or elaboration of that original flatworm plan.

The centralization and cephalization process reached its pinnacle with the appearance of the vertebrates. The rapid locomotion possible with a rigid body skeleton made life much more eventful and increased the need for better and faster processing and conversion into behavioral output of sensory data gathered by the cephalic sensory organs. The central nervous system of vertebrates comprises a tripartite brain—forebrain (or cerebrum), midbrain, and hindbrain—which communicates with the rest of the body via the spinal cord. The olfactory receptors of the nose report their sensory data to the cerebrum; the visual receptors of the eye report to the midbrain (of which, embryologically speaking, the retina is actually a part); and the acoustic receptors of the ear report to the hindbrain. Superimposed on the hindbrain is the cerebellum, an organ where complex sensorimotor coordination takes place.

The evolutionary development of the various classes of vertebrates was accompanied by variations on this central ground plan of the tripartite brain. One of the most significant of these modifications is that the brain grew larger as larger animals with more complex behavioral repertoires made their appearance, culminating in the behaviorally most sophisticated vertebrate class of mammals. However, in assessing the "intelligence" of different species of vertebrates or of different specimens of the same species, sheer brain size cannot simply be correlated with behavioral sophistication, since brain size depends on body size. To appreciate this aspect of the relation between brain and body size of vertebrates let us consider H. J. Jerison's plot of the logarithm of the brain weight in grams against the logarithm of body weight in kilograms, for numerous species of vertebrates, including fish, reptiles, birds, and mammals. A striking correlation is apparent in this plot between body weight and brain weight, namely, that animals with larger bodies have larger brains. If the set of points plotted for the lower vertebrates (fish and reptiles) is considered separately from that plotted for the higher vertebrates (mammals and birds), then the points of each set can be connected via a straight line of slope 2/3. Inasmuch as this is a log–log plot, this value of the slope of the straight line indicates that brain weight is proportional to body weight to the 2/3 power. Since the surface area of a sphere is proportional to the 2/3 power of its volume, and hence its weight, this relation would imply that for animals with bodies of roughly spherical shape, brain size increases proportionally with body surface area.

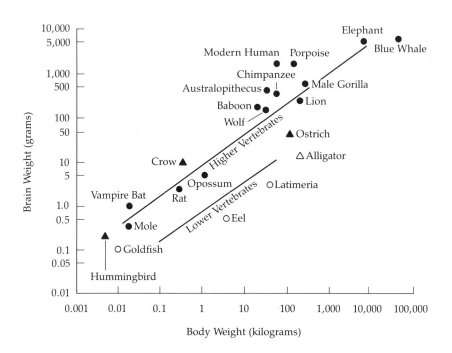

The relation of brain weight and body weight, plotted on logarithmic coordinates. Open circles and triangles represent fish and reptiles; closed symbols, birds and mammals. The two oblique lines show that, at a given body weight, the brain of higher vertebrates is larger than in lower vertebrates. The slope of both lines is 2/3, indicating that brain weight is proportional to the 2/3 power of body weight. [After Jerison, 1973 and Sarant and Netsky, 1981]

Why should brain weight increase proportionally with body surface area? Before trying to answer this question, it is necessary to enquire how the increase in brain size is actually achieved. The brain is a highly complex organ, with many distinct structures, tissues, and cell types that have characteristic functions. This complexity makes it difficult to evaluate the significance of differences in brain size between two different species, say rat and bear. Do brain size differences represent differences in the numbers of nerve cells, in the sizes of cells, in the volume of intercellular spacings or in the amount of non-neural brain tissue? The answer appears to include all these possibilities. Jerison believes that the proportionality between brain size and body surface area can be attributed to the need for a larger body surface to be innervated by more sensory and motor nerve cells, which in turn require more connecting neurons to process their transactions. This explanation does not seem so plausible, however, since it is not obvious why, as implied, the body surface of the elephant should require the same absolute density of innervation as that of the mouse. Perhaps the close correlation between brain weight and surface area of the body is not attributable to the dependence of one of these parameters on the other at all, but rather to their joint dependence on some third "hidden" evolutionary parameter. (Editors' Note: Harvey and Bennet (1983) have reported that, in the case of mammals, brain weight is more nearly proportional to the 3/4 power of body weight than to its 2/3 power. Hence brain weight would have to depend on some parameter other than surface area, such as the rate of basal metabolism, which happens to vary with the 3/4 power of body weight. But why brain weight should be related to metabolic rate is no more obvious than why it should be related to body surface area.)

Although on the log–log plot the brain–body weight points for lower vertebrates and higher vertebrates both fall on straight lines with a slope of 2/3, the line connecting the brain–body weight points of lower vertebrates intercepts the ordinate at body weights about ten to twenty times higher than the corresponding intercept of the line connecting the points of higher vertebrates. This means that fish and reptiles have ten to twenty times smaller brain sizes with respect to their body surface area than do mammals and birds. That general difference between the vertebrate classes can be expressed quantitatively by the "encephalization quotient," or EQ, which is defined as 0.12 times the ratio of brain weight over body weight to the 2/3 power. (The factor 0.12 has been chosen so that for an "average" mammal, EQ = 1.) The lower vertebrates have an EQ of about 0.07, compared to the higher vertebrates, whose EQ is about 0.7. The points registering the brain weight of primates lie significantly above the general mammal–bird line, corresponding to EQs between 1.2 and 2. The highest deviation from the mammalian line occurs with man and dolphin, which have EQs of about 7. (Editors' Note: Perhaps the EQ of mammals should be redefined as the ratio of brain weight to body weight to the 3/4 power. However, this redefinition would not require any substantive changes in the following discussion.)

Thus rather than sheer brain size, it is the EQ that appears to provide a rough index to what we intuitively assess as the relative intelligence of various vertebrate species. The limited sophistication of the lower vertebrates, such as fish, amphibians, and reptiles, is reflected in their very low EQ, compared to the tenfold higher EQs of the obviously more intelligent birds and mammals. And the still higher EQ of the primates, with the EQ of man scoring 100 times higher than that of the reptiles,

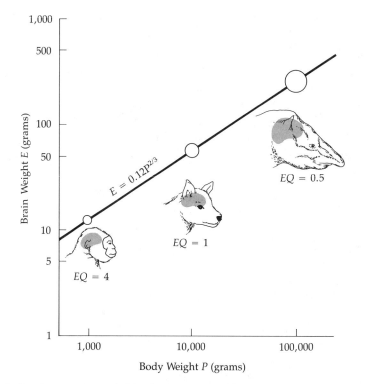

Encephalization quotients (EQ) of a "smart" monkey, an "average" dog and a "stupid" tapir. [After Jerison, 1976]

provides further support for the apparent correlation between EQ and intelligence. We leave open the question whether the anomalously high EQ of the nonprimate dolphins confirms claims of their high intelligence or raises doubts about the inferred relation between EQ and intelligence. In any case, EQ values provide one of the few means for assessing the intelligence of extinct vertebrate species, since cranial capacity (and therefore brain weight) and body size (and therefore body weight) can often be estimated from fossilized remains. Such estimates show that the EQ of ancient reptiles falls within the same range as the EQ of modern reptiles. This indicates that the popular opinion that lack of intelligence caused the extinction of the dinosaurs is not warranted. By contrast, ancient birds and mammals show consistently lower EQs than modern members of their classes. The EQ of mammals remained at the level of about 0.2 for more than half of the nearly 200 million years of their existence before it began to rise to its present values. The EQ of the

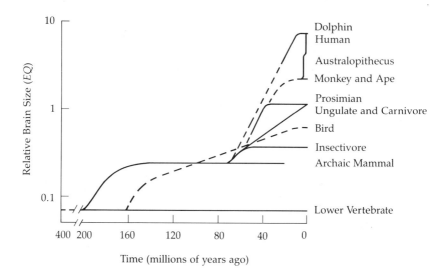

Rate of evolution of grade of encephalization (EQ) in different vertebrate groups and at different times. Brain size actually varies within groups too, so the curves are somewhat arbitrary. In the case of cetaceans, the highest grade attained is plotted to emphasize that the cetaceans that reached the dolphin grade did so long before the primates reached even an australopithecine grade; the recent and rapid evolution of the hominid brain is notable. The dotted lines indicate gaps in the fossil data. [After Jerison, 1976]

protohuman *Australopithecus* is estimated to have been about 3: intermediate between that of modern man (EQ = 7) and modern apes (EQ = 2).

The EQ is, of course, only a very rough guide for making interspecies comparisons of the intelligence of various classes of vertebrates, since their brains differ in more ways than total weight. For such EQ differences to be really meaningful, they require comparison of the relative sizes of various parts of the brain, and of the various cell types within these parts. For instance, such a comparison between rat and mouse brains would be of special interest, since these species have similar lifestyles and morphology but large differences in body and brain weights. If we compare the brains of birds and mammals with the brains of fish, amphibians, and reptiles, we note that in the higher vertebrates cerebellum and cerebrum have expanded considerably relative to midbrain and hindbrain. As for the cerebellum, it has not only expanded greatly in relative size (and cell number) but also increased in its histological complexity in the course of the evolution from fish to mammals. The basic three-layered structure of the cerebellar cortex has remained the

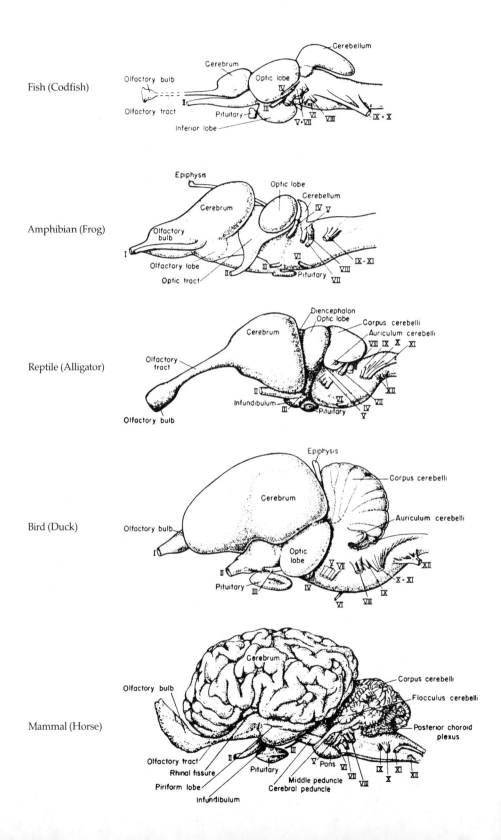

Fish (Codfish)

Olfactory bulb
Cerebrum
Optic lobe
IV
Cerebellum
Olfactory tract
I
Pituitary
III
VI
V·VII
VIII
IX + X
Inferior lobe

Amphibian (Frog)

Epiphysis
Optic lobe
Cerebrum
Cerebellum
IV V
Olfactory bulb
I
Olfactory lobe
II
III
VI
IX - XI
VIII
VII
Optic tract
Pituitary
VII

Reptile (Alligator)

Diencephalon
Optic lobe
Corpus cerebelli
Cerebrum
Auriculum cerebelli
VIII IX X XI
Olfactory tract
II
XII
Infundibulum
VI
VII
III
IV
V
Pituitary
Olfactory bulb

Bird (Duck)

Epiphysis
Corpus cerebelli
Cerebrum
Auriculum cerebelli
Olfactory bulb
I
Optic
lobe
II
V
VII
XII
Pituitary
III
IV
VI
VIII
IX
X + XI

Mammal (Horse)

Cerebrum
Corpus cerebelli
Olfactory bulb
Flocculus cerebelli
Posterior choroid plexus
Olfactory tract
II
III
V Pons
VI
IX XI XII
Rhinal fissure
Pituitary
VII
X
Piriform lobe
Middle peduncle
VIII
Cerebral peduncle
Infundibulum

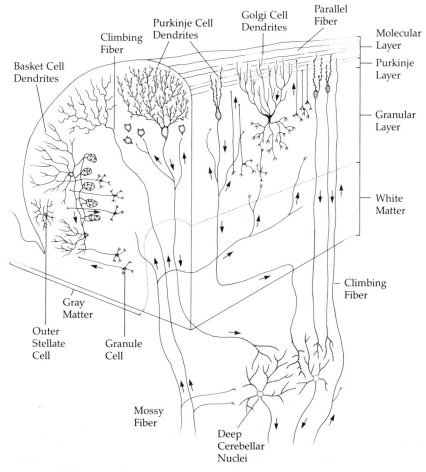

Basket Cell
Dendrites

Climbing
Fiber

Purkinje Cell
Dendrites

Golgi Cell
Dendrites

Parallel
Fiber

Molecular
Layer

Purkinje
Layer

Granular
Layer

White
Matter

Climbing
Fiber

Gray
Matter

Outer
Stellate
Cell

Granule
Cell

Mossy
Fiber

Deep
Cerebellar
Nuclei

▲ The principal types of neurons in the mammalian cerebellar cortex and their interconnections. Upward pointing arrows indicate the two types of input axons (climbing fibers and mossy fibers). The mossy fibers innervate granule cells and Golgi cells in complex synaptic structures, called glomeruli. The granule cell axons then rise toward the surface of the cerebellum, where they branch to form parallel fibers that excite Purkinje cells, Golgi cells, basket cells, and stellate cells. The Purkinje cell axons (marked by downward pointing arrows) constitute the only output from the cerebellar cortex. [After Bullock, Orkand, and Grinnell, 1977]

◀ Comparison of representative brains from different classes of vertebrates. Each roman numeral designates the root of a cephalic nerve. [From *The Vertebrate Body*, Shorter Version, Fifth Edition, by A. S. Romer and T. S. Parsons. Copyright 1978 by W. B. Saunders Company. Copyright 1956, 1962, and 1971 by W. B. Saunders Company. Reprinted by permission of CBS College Publishing.]

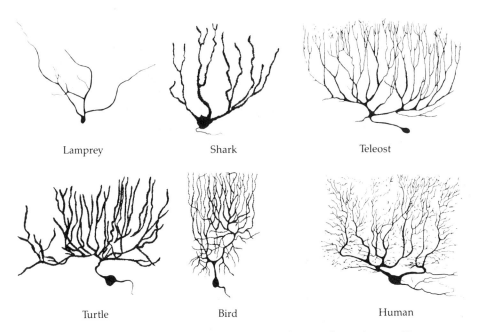

Lamprey   Shark   Teleost

Turtle   Bird   Human

Purkinje cells in the cerebellar cortex in various classes of vertebrates. [From Nieuwenhuys, 1967. Used with permission.]

same: an inner layer of small granule cells, a middle layer of large Purkinje cells, and an outer layer of Purkinje cell dendrites and the granule cell axons that make synaptic contacts with them. But the architecture of the Purkinje cell, which appears to be the central integrative element of the cerebellum, has become ever more elaborate, developing from the modest bush of a few dendrites in the shark to the fantastically ramified dendritic tree in man. This evolutionary elaboration of Purkinje cell dendrites was accompanied by a progressive increase in the number of granule cells that contact each Purkinje cell, and hence in the overall ratio of the number of granule cells to Purkinje cells in the cerebellar cortex. Thus the ratio of granule cells to Purkinje cells has risen at least tenfold in mammalian evolution, from about 300 in the rat to about 3,000 in man, an indication of the ever-increasing complexity of the information delivered by the granule cells to each Purkinje cell for processing. To aid in that processing, an additional type of nerve cell—the basket cell—made its appearance in the outer layer of the cerebellar cortex in the course of vertebrate evolution, beginning with the reptiles.

The cerebrum—especially its outer covering, or *cerebral cortex*—has expanded enormously in mammals, not only in volume but also, and even more so, in surface area, by an elaborate system of infoldings. It

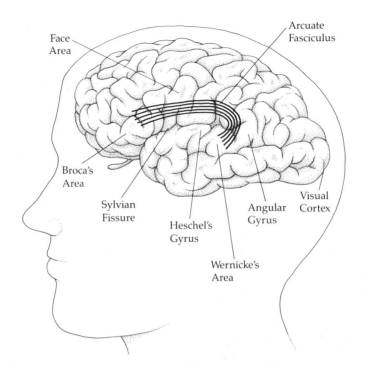

The primary language areas of the human cerebral cortex. They are thought to be located in the left hemisphere, because only rarely does damage to the right hemisphere cause language disorders. Broca's area, which is adjacent to the region of the motor cortex that controls the movement of the muscles of the lips, the jaw, the tongue, the soft palate, and the vocal cords, apparently incorporates programs for the coordination of these muscles in speech. Damage to Broca's area results in slow and labored speech, but comprehension of language remains intact. Wernicke's area lies between Heschl's gyrus, which is the primary receiver of the auditory stimuli, and the angular gyrus, which acts as a way station between the auditory and visual regions. When Wernicke's area is damaged, speech is fluent but has little content and comprehension is usually lost. Wernicke's and Broca's areas are joined by a nerve bundle called the arcuate fasciculus. When it is damaged, speech is fluent but abnormal, and the patient can comprehend words but cannot repeat them. [After Geschwind, 1972]

has become a six-layered sheet of billions of nerve cells, of which differ-ent areas are dedicated to the processing and association of particular sensory inputs, such as touch, smell, hearing, and sight, and to the generation and integration of particular motor functions. This develop-ment culminated in the most elaborate of all cerebral cortices, namely that of the human brain. The human cerebral cortex has some unique features that set it apart from those of other mammals, even from the cerebral cortex of our closest evolutionary relative, the chimpanzee. One of the most important of these human-specific features is the presence of two cortical areas dedicated to the production of speech. These are designated as Broca's and Wernicke's areas, and are interconnected via a tract of nerve fibers, the arcuate fasciculus. Neurologists concerned with the diagnosis of patients afflicted with aphasia (the inability to speak) often attempt to classify this disorder in terms of damage to, or disconnection of, one or the other of these two areas. Another speech-related area of the human cerebral cortex is the angular gyrus, which is concerned with decoding rather than production of speech. Although many of the functions of the cerebral cortex are distributed symmetrically over its two bilateral hemispheres, the speech production areas are present on only one side (usually, though not invariably, in the left hemisphere).

Complex nervous system and complex mind evolved together in animals. Why not in plants? Plants, too, respond to signals of various modalities with fantastic sensitivity. Plants, too, have to coordinate these signals. They, too, have complex mating behavior and circulation of body fluids. But plants differ from animals as Germany does from France—by having much less centralization. Germany was dismembered and continued to thrive. France without Paris and Paris without France are unthinkable.

REFERENCES

Bullock, T. H., and G. A. Horridge. 1965. *Structure and Function of the Nervous Systems of Invertebrates.* San Francisco: W. H. Freeman.

Bullock, T. H., R. Orkand, and A. Grinnell. 1977. *Introduction to Nervous Systems.* San Francisco: W. H. Freeman.

Geschwind, N. 1972. Language and the brain. *Scientific American* 226(4): 76–83.

Harvey, P. H., and P. M. Bennett. 1983. Brain size, energetics, ecology and life history patterns. *Nature* 306: 314–315.

Jerison, H. J. 1976. Paleoneurology and the evolution of mind. *Scientific American* 234(1): 90–100.

———. 1973. *Evolution of the Brain and Intelligence.* New York: Academic Press.

Kuffler, S. W., J. G. Nicholls, and A. R. Martin. 1984. *From Neuron to Brain.* 2d ed. Sunderland, Mass.: Sinauer Associates.

Nieuwenhuys, R. 1967. In *The Cerebellum,* edited by C. A. Fox and R. S. Snider. New York: Elsevier.

Sarant, H. B., and M. G. Netsky. 1981. *Evolution of the Nervous System.* Oxford: University Press.

Shepherd, G. M. 1983. *Neurobiology.* Oxford: University Press, New York and Oxford.

Weiner, J. S. 1971. *Man's Natural History.* London: Weidenfeld and Nicholson.

Seven

Vision

Let us now consider the evolution of a specific part of the human brain, namely its visual system. The pathway of visual perception begins at the eye, which consists of a reasonably good lens and the retina, on which the light refracted by the lens forms an image of the visual field. The retina is a three-layered sheet of nerve cells, of which the outer layer (i.e., that furthest away from the incident light) consists of about 100 million *photoreceptor cells*. In the human retina there are two different kinds of photoreceptors, the *rods* and the *cones*, which have different functions.

The cones are specialized to process daylight, that is, to function under conditions of high luminance. They predominate in the center of the retina, the *fovea*, where the optics of the lens provide the highest visual acuity. The cones of many animals, moreover, form subclasses with respect to the particular wavelength of light to which they are most sensitive. In the primates there are three types of cones, each maximally sensitive to red, green, or blue. Thanks to these three subclasses of cones, we are among the animals endowed with color vision. The rods are specialized to function at night, that is, under conditions of low luminance. They predominate in the periphery of the retina, where visual acuity is low. There is only one class of rod with respect to the wavelength of maximal light sensitivity. Thus rods alone cannot provide for color vision, which is why at night all cats look gray.

The absorption of light by a photoreceptor cell produces an electrical signal, whose strength increases with the intensity of the light falling on

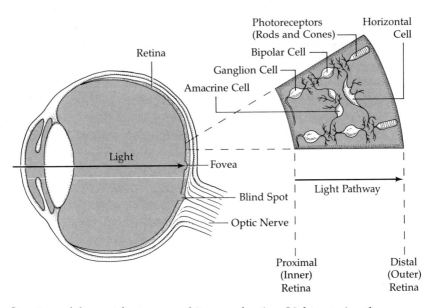

Structure of the vertebrate eye and its neural retina. Light entering the eye must first travel through the proximal layers of the retina before reaching the photoreceptors. [After Kandel and Schwartz, 1981]

the receptor. At this first stage of vision, the light–dark pattern of the visual image is thus transformed into a two-dimensional pattern of electrical activity in the retinal receptor mosaic. The processing of that electrical pattern begins with the transmission (via synapses) of the signals generated by several adjacent photoreceptor cells to another type of cell, the *bipolar cell*, located in the middle layer of the retina. Thus each bipolar cell receives sensory input from a small fraction of the total area of the retinal receptor mosaic and responds by generating another pattern of electrical signals. Next, the signals generated by several adjacent bipolar cells are transmitted (again via synapses) to a third type of cell, the *retinal ganglion cell*, which is located in the innermost layer of the retina (i.e., that struck first by the light entering the eye through the lens).

Since there are about a million retinal ganglion cells, each ganglion cell receives the sensory input collected by about 100 of the 100 million photoreceptor cells. The set of photoreceptors that provides input to a single ganglion cell (designated as the *receptive field* of that cell) occupies a circular area of the retinal receptor mosaic. As functional analyses of retinal ganglion cells, first carried out by Stephen Kuffler in the early 1950s, showed their role is not so much to make a *sum* of the intensity of light

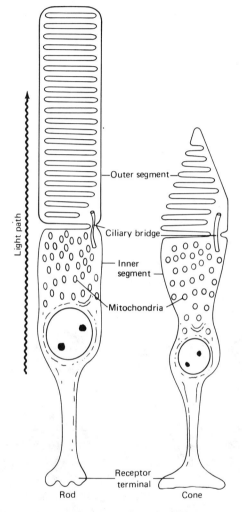

Structure of photoreceptors. Both rod and cone cells are differentiated into inner and outer segments connected by a ciliary bridge. The inner segments of both cell types contain the nucleus and most of the biosynthetic machinery and are continuous with the receptors' terminals. The membranous discs in the outer segments of rod cells (unlike those in cone cells) are not connected with the plasma membrane. [Reprinted by permission of the publisher from *Principles of Neural Science*, by E. R. Kandel, and J. H. Schwartz, eds. p. 215. Copyright 1981 by Elsevien Science Publishing Co., Inc.]

that strikes each receptive field as it is to compute the *contrast* in illumination that exists between two concentric areas of the field, a central circular area and its surrounding annular area. Here we encounter the first example of "abstraction" in the processing of sensory input: the

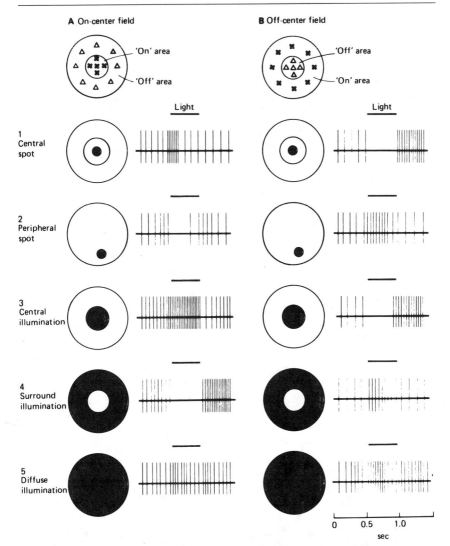

Responses of on-center and off-center retinal ganglion cells to different types of illumination (X = excitatory zone, Δ = inhibitory zone). A. An on-center cell responds best to a spot of light shone onto the central part of its receptive field (1, 3). Illumination (bar above records of neutral firing) of the surrounding area with a spot (2) or an annulus (4) of light reduces or suppresses the discharge and causes a response when the light is turned off. Diffuse illumination of the entire receptive field (5) elicits a relatively weak discharge because center and surround oppose each other's effects. B. A cell with off-center receptive field has its spontaneous firing suppressed when the central area of its field is illuminated (1, 3) and accelerated when the light is turned off. Light shone onto the surround of an off-center receptive field area excites (2, 4). The light stimulus is indicated in gray or black. [Reproduced by permission of the publisher from *Principles of Neural Science*, by E. R. Kandel and J. H. Schwartz, eds., p. 239. Copyright 1981 by Elsevier Science Publishing Co., Inc.]

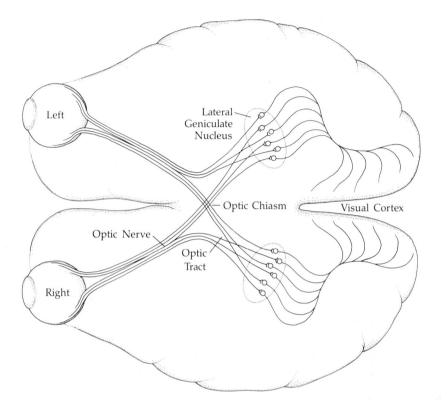

Visual pathway is traced schematically in the human brain, seen here from below. The output from the retina is conveyed, by ganglion cell axons bundled in the optic nerves, to the lateral geniculate nuclei; about half the axons cross over to the opposite side of the brain, so that a representation of each half of the visual scene is projected on the lateral geniculate nucleus of the opposite hemisphere. Neurons in the geniculate nuclei send their axons to the striate visual cortex. [After Hubel and Wiesel, 1979]

information about the distribution of light intensities at 100 million points of the retinal image gathered by the photoreceptor cells is reduced by the retinal ganglion cells to information about the light contrast present within a million small, circular areas of the image.

The axons, or nerve fibers, of the million retinal ganglion cells leave the eye as a bundle called the *optic nerve,* through which the information about the distribution of light contrast in the visual field travels to the brain for further processing. The optic nerves from right and left eyes meet at the *optic chiasm,* whereupon half of the million nerve fibers from each eye project to the opposite side and the other half project to the same side of the brain as that on which their eye of origin is located. The fibers that project to the opposite side come from retinal ganglion cells whose receptive fields lie in the nasal half of the retina (the half next to the nose); those that project to the same side come from the temporal half of the retina (the half next to the temples). The destination of the optic nerve fibers on either side of the brain is a part of the midbrain designated as the *lateral geniculate nucleus (LGN)*. There are two mirror-symmetric LGNs on the left and right sides of the midbrain. Each is an oblong structure extending along the transverse axis of the brain. The nature of this partially crossed projection is such that information gathered by both eyes about the left half of the visual field, which forms an image on the nasal half of the left retina and on the temporal half of the right retina, converges on the LGN of the right side of the brain; information gathered about the right half of the visual field, which forms an image on the nasal half of the right retina and on the temporal half of the left retina, converges on the LGN of the left side of the brain. In other words, the left side of the brain "sees" only the right visual field and the right side "sees" only the left visual field.

Each optic nerve fiber transfers the electrical activity pattern of its retinal ganglion cell to one or more nerve cells of the LGN. These LGN cells, in turn, send their nerve fibers in a bundle to the hind (or occipital) part of the cerebral cortex, designated as *visual cortex*, which is dedicated to the further processing of the visual input. The LGN nerve fibers enter the visual cortex, and make synaptic contacts with cortical nerve cells, in an area called V-1, area 17, or striate cortex. (The nomenclature of brain anatomy is blessed with a redundancy of terms that mean the same thing and are evidently designed to please the experts and confuse the neophytes. Here we will refer to the area of LGN fiber entry as area 17.) The distribution of the synaptic contacts made by the incoming LGN fibers with their target nerve cells in area 17 is such that in the projection from retina to visual cortex, the topological coherence of the image of the visual field has been preserved. That is to say, although the shape of area 17 is very different from that of the retina, adjacent points in the visual image are nevertheless "seen" by adjacent points on the visual cortex.

From area 17, there are further projections to other areas of the visual cortex, designated as areas 18 and 19, where the topological coherence of the visual image is still preserved. From areas 18 and 19, the visual input is passed on to yet other cortical areas for further processing, but in these further areas, the visual input retains less of its topological coherence. The reason for this loss is probably that by the time the visual input leaves areas 18 and 19, the essential information regarding the spatial relationships of various components of the image has already been extracted from it, and its further processing concerns such higher level abstractions as the shape, color and identity of objects in the visual field.

These connections from one area of processing visual input to the next have been traced by several anatomical methods. One of them consists of creating local lesions in the nervous system—that is, destroying nerve cells in specific regions—and then searching for areas in which degenerating nerve fibers are manifest. Since nerve fibers die if the cells of which they are a part have been destroyed, the presence of degenerating nerve fibers reveals a target area of the nerve cells lying in the region of the local lesion. For instance, lesioning a patch of the most nasal part of the nasal retina of the left eye results in a patch of degenerating nerve fibers in the area of the right LGN nearest to the body midline. Another method of tracing the processing of visual input involves local injection of a radioisotope-labeled amino acid into some region of the nervous system. The nerve cells of that region take up the labeled amino acid, incorporate it into the proteins they synthesize, and transport some of the labeled protein along their nerve fibers to the synaptic terminals. The target areas of these terminals can then be identified by virtue of the radioactivity they emit. For instance, injection of the most nasal part of the retina of the left eye results in a patch of radioactive synaptic terminals in the area of the right LGN nearest to the body midline.

A third method is the converse of the second. Here the location of the cells of origin of nerve fiber terminals is located by local injection of the enzyme horseradish peroxidase into some region of the nervous system. The synaptic terminals located near the site of injection take up the enzyme, which is then transported along the fibers to the cells themselves, where the presence of the enzyme can be visualized by special histological staining procedures. For instance, injection of the area of the right LGN nearest to the body midline with horseradish peroxidase results in a patch of stain in the most nasal part of the retina of the left eye. Finally, the connections can also be traced by electrophysiological methods, by local passage of electrical current into some region of the nervous system via an inserted stimulating electrode. The nerve cells in that region are excited by the current and produce electrical impulses, which travel along their nerve fibers to the synaptic terminals. The target areas of these terminals can then be identified by their impulse activity, as registered by a recording electrode. It must be emphasized, however, that tracing the connections of a nerve network does not automatically provide an understanding of the nature of its function.

Important insights into the functional aspects of the network of the visual system have been obtained by presenting various visual stimuli to experimental animals, such as cats and monkeys, and recording with electrodes inserted into their brains the electrical activity evoked by these stimuli in individual nerve cells of the visual cortex. Such experiments were pioneered by David Hubel and Torsten Wiesel in the 1960s. First of all, they found that individual nerve cells in area 17 of the cerebral cortex receive visual input from a precisely circumscribed area of the visual field, which is larger than the area "seen" by individual retinal ganglion cells. Moreover, most of these cortical cells are binocular, in the sense that the visual input from the circumscribed area of the visual field reaches them through both eyes, that is, through the temporal retina of the eye on the same side of the body and the nasal retina on the other side. Second, Hubel and Wiesel discovered that individual cortical nerve cells respond only to particular light and dark patterns that appear in the circumscribed area of the visual field, while ignoring other stimulus patterns. One type of cell responds only to straight line edges of light and dark contrast that have a particular orientation with respect to the body axes of the animal. Other cell types respond only to edges of light and dark contrast of a particular orientation that move in a particular direction and with a particular speed across the relevant part of the visual field. Thus the cortical nerve cells of area 17 perform a further abstraction of the visual input. While the retinal ganglion cells extract information from the activity of the photoreceptor mosaic about the light contrast within individual small, circular areas of the image, the cortical cells in area 17 abstract information about the light contrast along sets of many such small, circular areas arranged along straight lines of particular orientations.

The role of the cortical cells discovered by Hubel and Wiesel is accounted for by a theory of visual perception of shapes proposed by David Marr in the 1970s. The starting point of Marr's theory of perception lies in the commonplace experience that a real scene and an artist's sketch of that scene evoke similar percepts in the viewer, despite the fact that they produce very different retinal images. This fact suggests that the artist's sketch corresponds in some way to an intermediate stage of the process by which the percept is extracted from the image of the real scene. Accordingly, Marr envisages that perception begins with a transformation of the retinal image into what he calls the *primal sketch*. The idea underlying both design and interpretation of the primal sketch is the tacit knowledge of the percipient that contour outlines, and hence the forms, of objects in the visual surround are represented by the areas in the image where there is an abrupt change in light intensity. So, to make

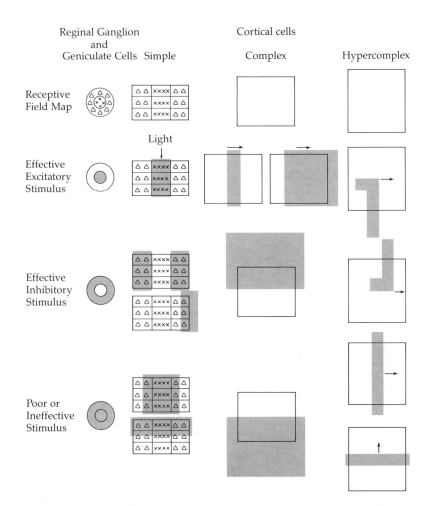

Summary of the receptive field properties of neurons in the retina and lateral geniculate nucleus and those in the striate cortex. Retinal ganglion and lateral geniculate cells respond mainly to brightness contrast; simple and complex cortical cells respond to shapes, lines, edges, and boundaries. X = excitatory zone; Δ = inhibitory zone; gray area = light stimulus. Arrows indicate direction of stimulus movement. [Reproduced by permission of the publisher from *Principles of Neural Science*, by E. R. Kandel and J. H. Schwartz, eds., p. 246. Copyright 1981 by Elsevier Science Publishing Co., Inc.]

explicit the presence of contour outlines, which are merely implicit in the image, it is first necessary to describe the way in which the light intensity changes from place to place in the image. This description is the primal sketch.

In order to generate the primal sketch, the image has to be subjected to just the same kind of light contrast analysis that is carried out by the neurons of area 17 of the visual cortex. Marr assigns to these neurons the function of measuring the rate of change of light intensity along a given direction. Hence, by simultaneously scanning the entire image, the ensemble of these cortical neurons extracts from the image the overall pattern of spatial variation in light intensity. In the primal sketch, as in the artist's sketch, each line represents the position and orientation of a change in light intensity in the image. The primal sketch thus makes explicit the position, directions, magnitudes, and spatial extents of light intensity gradients present in the image. According to Marr's theory, the next stage in the visual perception process, probably carried out by neurons in cortical areas 18 and 19, determines which of the lines of the primal sketch actually correspond to contour outlines of objects.

We saw in chapter 3 that the perception and processing of sensory information provided by visible light must be of great antiquity. It is manifest even in prokaryotes, such as the photosynthetic bacteria, which actively move toward a source of light. Specialized photoreceptor cells date back to the jellyfish stage of evolution of the metazoan nervous system, which processes the sensory information they provide to distinguish day from night. The aggregation of several photoreceptors into a pair of cephalic visual organs, or eyes, accompanied the development of the flatworm nervous system. Flatworm eyes detect not only variations in the intensity of light but also the direction of its source and thus mediate the behavioral tendency of flatworms to swim toward the dark. Flatworm eyes lack a lens, however, and thus cannot provide a visual image of the surround. The basic plan of the vertebrate camera eye, which has a lens that projects an image onto the three-layered retina, arose no later than the time of the appearance of fish. Moreover, the retinas of fish already possess both rods and cones, bipolar cells, and retinal ganglion cells, which send the already abstracted visual input to the midbrain via the optic nerve for further processing. In fish, amphibians, and reptiles, however, the projection from retina to midbrain is completely crossed, with optic nerve fibers from right and left eyes going exclusively to left and right sides of the brain respectively. In these lower vertebrates, the midbrain is the final destination of the visual input. From there it is integrated with other sensory inputs for conversion into commands appropriate for motor outputs. With the development of the greatly expanded cerebral cortex in mammals and its enormously increased capacity for carrying out complex information processing, the old midbrain termini of the optic nerve fibers took on the function of relay sta-

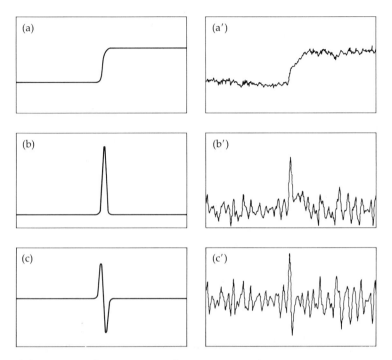

Spatial derivatives of an image emphasize its spatial variations in intensity. The left part of the illustration describes a sharp edge between two even shades of gray. The intensity along a path across the edge changes abruptly from one value to another (a). The first derivative of the intensity is the rate at which intensity changes (b). Toward the left or toward the right there is no change; the first derivative therefore is zero. Along the edge itself, however, the rate of change rises and falls. The second derivative of the intensity is the rate of change of the rate of change (c). Both derivatives emphasize the edge. The first derivative marks it with a peak; the second derivative marks it by crossing zero. The right part of the illustration describes an edge more typical of the visual world, where shades of gray are often nonuniform and edges not perfectly sharp. The intensity contour (a') and its first and second derivatives (b', c') are "noisy." The edge must be smoothed before derivatives are taken. [After Poggio, 1984]

tions, through which the partially processed visual input is sent on to what became the visual areas of the cortex.

In reviewing the sensory history of the mammalian line that led to the primates, and eventually to man, we note that it is characterized by a transition from an olfactory and tactile mode of life to a visual mode. This transition was attended by a change of placement of the eyes in the head, from the lateral position they occupy in horses and cows, which

provides a nearly panoramic view of the surround, to the frontally positioned eyes of carnivores and primates, which look forward and jointly
focus on the same limited visual field in front of the animal. The early
mammals of 200 million years ago had laterally positioned eyes, and
probably depended rather little upon their vision, except for the detection
of predators. Accordingly, only a relatively small area of their cerebral
cortex was dedicated to the processing of visual input. By contrast the
earliest primates of 55 million years ago had frontal eyes and were heavily
dependent on vision. Their cerebral cortex bulged in the rear to provide
a larger cortical area dedicated to processing visual input and thus accommodate the animal's increased dependence on vision. The movement of
the eyes from the side to the front of the head was also accompanied by
a change in the crossover pattern of the optic nerve fibers at the optic
chiasm. In the early mammals with their lateral eyes, there remained the
nearly complete crossover of the visual projection from right and left
eyes to left and right parts of the midbrain respectively, characteristic of
the visual systems of lower vertebrates and also of horses and cows.
With the development of frontal eyes, however, and the increasing overlap of the part of the visual field seen by both eyes, the crossover at the
optic chiasm became increasingly incomplete until, with the nearly complete binocular overlap of the field of carnivores and primates, only the
optic fibers from the nasal half retina and none from the temporal half
retina cross over.

The main change in life-style associated with the movement of the eyes
from the side to the front of the head was the change in sustenance from
grazing to predation on other animals. As an example of the use of frontal
eyes in predation by a lower primate, we may consider the tarsier as it
attacks a lizard sitting on a tree branch. Until the lizard is in the proper
position for being attached, the tarsier sits quietly in place. When it sees
the lizard moving, it focuses on the lizard, estimates position and velocity
of the prey, coordinates spatial vision and motion, jumps, and seizes the
prey. This ability to prey upon small animals gave a selective advantage
to frontal, focal vision. First, to seize the prey the predator must face it
and hence look to the front. For that purpose, frontal eyes provide an
image of much better optical quality than lateral eyes, because frontal
eyes see to the front along the optical axis of their lens, whereas lateral
eyes can see to the front only along the side of a wide angle with their
optical axis, which causes large optical aberrations. Indeed, to minimize
such aberrations even in its frontal eyes, the primate visual system pays
special attention to the part of the image that falls on the central part of
the retina, or fovea. Accordingly, a disproportionately large area of the

visual cortex of the primate brain is dedicated to the processing of the foveal visual input. Second, the ability to focus with both eyes on the same object gives the predator an opportunity to make stereoscopic estimates of both direction and distance of the prey. To maximize the utility of binocular stereoscopy, good hand–eye coordination by the brain is required.

Frontal vision was acquired at a price, namely loss of the ability to see behind the head and thus secure early warning of the approach of an enemy or predator from the rear. The primates compensated for this loss in two different ways suited to two different life-styles. One way consisted of the development of extremely good sound localization, in order to hear an approaching source of danger. This solution was adopted by the prosimians, such as the lemur, and by carnivores with frontal vision, such as cats and dogs. The other way, which was adopted by the anthropoid primates including man, consisted of the development of a complex social organization, which included facial alarm signals and a vocabulary of warning calls. (In support of the inference of such a vocabulary, it may be noted that some species of monkeys have three distinctly different calls, one to warn of snakes, another to warn of predators on the ground, and yet another to warn of predators in the air. The advantage of a vocabulary of calls is that it tells the fleeing monkeys what type of evasive action to take before they themselves can see the cause of alarm.) The logical weakness of this speculative explanation of the origin of the development of meaningful vocalizations among the primates, however, is that it is not clear why it was necessary to evolve a complex social system just to provide a warning of the approach of danger from the rear, when a third eye in the back of the head might have served the same purpose, as it does in spiders and some other creatures. Possibly in mammals a third eye would require too much additional area of visual cortex, for which there might not be sufficient room or which is indispensable for other cerebral functions. Or perhaps additional eyes simply did not happen to evolve before social defense had already become effective. After all, defensive social behavior systems had their early start in such relatively simple forms as herding, with more complex behavior patterns following later.

There is an anatomical difference between the two types of primates that adopted the alternative solutions to the dangers entailed by frontal vision. The prosimians (with exception of the tarsier) share with other mammals (including cats and dogs) the feature of a split upper lip, whose two halves are firmly attached to the maxillar bone of the upper jaw. The technical name for such a split immobile upper lip is *strepsirhine* (from the Greek for "twisted nose"). By contrast, the anthropoid primates, including man, have a continuous upper lip, which is attached to the upper jaw in such a way that it can be moved. The technical name for such a continuous, movable upper lip is *haplorhine* (from the Greek for "half nose"). The haplorhine lip allows facial expressions, such as smiles, frowns, and the baring of teeth in threats, which cannot be generated with the strepsirhine lip. Thus the grimace is a hominid and not merely a human attribute. Good vision is needed to derive the social benefits of the haplorhine lip, since it is important not only to produce meaningful facial expressions but also to perceive and interpret them correctly.

Among the mammals, primates also developed the most effective color vision, which proved enormously useful in spotting edible colored fruits among green leaves. Moreover, the evolutionary increase in the size of primates increased their food requirements, making it necessary for them to develop a visual–spatial memory for the location of food sources such as fruit trees.

REFERENCES

Allman, J. 1977. Evolution of the visual cortex in the early primates. *Progress in Psychobiology and Physiological Psychology* 7: 1–53.

Hubel, D. H., and T. N. Wiesel. 1979. Brain mechanisms of vision. *Scientific American* 241(3): 150–162.

———. 1977. Functional architecture of macque monkey visual cortex. *Proceedings of the Royal Society of London* B 198: 1–59.

Kandel, E. R., and J. H. Schwartz, eds. 1981. *Principles of Neural Science.* New York: Elsevier.

Kuffler, S. W., J. G. Nicholls, and A. R. Martin. 1984. *From Neuron to Brain,* 2d ed. Sunderland, Mass.: Sinauer Associates.

Marr, D. 1982. *Vision.* San Francisco: W. H. Freeman.

Poggio, T. 1984. Vision by man and machine. *Scientific American* 250(4): 68–79.

Eight

Perception

One might naively imagine that visual perception amounts to the conscious mind looking at the image on the retina. This is obviously not so; between retina and consciousness there are many processing steps that progressively boil down the information provided by the pattern of neuronal excitation in the retina. We will now move to yet more abstract levels of the perception process, which illustrate some general principles of adaptive brain evolution. These levels reflect the capability of the human cerebral cortex to filter and process the visual input to give "objective," observer-independent information about an object being observed. This capability was not worked out by neurophysiologists with their electrodes but "psyched out" by perceptual psychologists. It is manifest in numerous perceptual constancy phenomena, of which we will discuss three examples. In each of these phenomena the perceptual apparatus of the cortex extracts objectified information from the visual input.

1. The first example is the constancy of the perceived color of an object, irrespective of the color of the illuminating light. We perceive that an object has the same color, whether we see it in the bluish light of morning, in the reddish light of evening, or in the yellow light of a fire or of an incandescent lamp. (One of the rare situations in which the perceptual apparatus for color vision is grossly fooled is that of a scene illuminated by a monochromatic light source, such as the yellow sodium lamps used for lighting streets and highways. Monochromatic light is, of course, highly unnatural and was not present in the environment while the human

perceptual apparatus evolved.) Thus, under natural conditions, the real color of an object is perceived regardless of the color of the illuminating light. This is possible because what we actually perceive as the color of an object is its property of absorption and reflection of the red, green and blue components of polychromatic light, *in relation to other objects in the scene.* This abstraction of the color of an object from its relative absorbance and reflectance of the spectral components of the illuminating light is performed preconsciously, by the intuitive use of the concepts of "white" (meaning light in which all spectral colors are equally represented) and "complementary color" (meaning a member of the color pairs red and green, or blue and yellow, whose mixture is perceived as white light). In 1925, Ewald Hering proposed that to assess the color of various objects in a scene, the perceptual apparatus surveys the whole field of vision and defines one object as white, that is, as reflecting equally all colors of the visible spectrum. The light reflected from all other objects is then interpreted relative to the spectral composition of the light reflected by the white object. To make that interpretation, the perceptual apparatus can be thought of as adding phantom light of a color complementary to that of the illuminating light so that the object defined as white is actually perceived as white. For instance, if the illuminating light is predominantly red, the perceptual apparatus adds phantom green light to it, which makes a white object look white rather than red. The addition of phantom light of complementary color to the actual light source then provides not only for the perception of the white object as white but also for the reasonably accurate perception of the real colors of all other objects.

2. The second example of a perceptual constancy phenomenon is the invariance of the perceived position of an object during voluntary head or eye movements. As a person shifts the gaze or turns the head, the image of the objects in the visual surround moves on the retina. This movement is not, however, perceived as a motion of the objects; they are correctly perceived as being stationary. This perceptual compensation for the motion of the image is so completely automatic that it is not even consciously registered as a motion of the head or the eyes. It is not registered because the change in position of the image of the objects on the retina is filtered out by the perceptual apparatus. A simple experiment reveals how this filtering process works. If you close one eye and jiggle the other with your fingers, stationary objects are perceived as jiggling. Since in this experiment your eye is moved passively (rather than actively by contraction of your head or eye muscles), the result

shows that the normally perceived constancy of spatial position during a voluntary movement is the result of your movement being taken into account by your perceptual apparatus. Another experiment reveals that what is taken into account here is not the actual occurrence of the voluntary movement itself, but the *command* to the muscles to perform it. In this experiment the muscle that would carry out the movement is temporarily paralyzed by injection of a drug. Under these conditions, where the intention to move the eye but not its motion can occur, command of an eye movement causes the stationary image of an object to be incorrectly perceived as a movement of the object. Here the perceptual apparatus proceeds as if the eye *had* been moved voluntarily and adjusts the fixed position of the image to compensate for the intended movement. To inform the perceptual apparatus that a command for a head or eye movement has been issued, a duplicate of the nerve impulse pattern directed from the brain to the motor neurons that command contraction of the appropriate muscles is simultaneously sent to the relevant cerebral neurons. It is this "efference copy" of the command that allows for compensation of the movement of the retinal image. The idea of the role of such an efference copy in providing for the brain a quantitative expectation of the change in sensory input resulting from the animal's own movements was first proposed by Erich von Holst in the early 1950s. There is now neurophysiological evidence that eye movement commands do influence neurons in the visual cortex in a manner consistent with von Holst's efference copy proposal.

3. The third example of a perceptual constancy phenomenon is the invariance of the perceived size of an object regardless of the distance at which it is seen. When an object is moved toward the eyes, the size of its retinal image increases, yet the object is not incorrectly perceived as increasing in size. The perceptual apparatus accomplishes this compensation by evaluating distance information according to the principles of perspective. A variety of clues are available to the perceptual apparatus regarding the distance of the object. For instance as the object approaches, the curvature of the eye lens increases (by action of the ciliary muscles) to keep the retinal image of the object in focus, and if both eyes are to stay trained on the approaching object, their optical axes must increasingly converge (by action of the two sets of extraocular muscles). Either of these clues can be provided by an "efference copy" of the command to the eye muscles. But if both eyes remain trained on a stationary distant object, the images cast on their retinas by the approaching object will

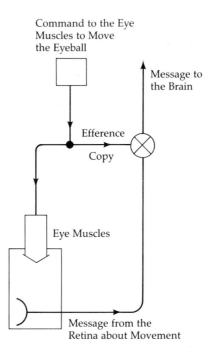

Command to the Eye
Muscles to Move
the Eyeball

Message to
the Brain

Efference

Copy

Eye Muscles

Message from the
Retina about Movement

Block diagram illustrating von Holst's hypothesis that the cerebral command
for an eye movement is added, in the form of an efference copy, to the eye's
report of perceived motion. According to this hypothesis, this operation
determines whether the perceived motion is interpreted as a result of the
percipient's own movement, or of the movement of the perceived object or
visual surround. [After Hassenstein, 1971]

become increasingly disparate (parallax). This third clue can be provided
by nerve cells in the visual cortex that are especially dedicated to com-
puting the binocular disparity of retinal images, to subserve the stereoscopic depth perception made possible by the evolution of frontal eyes.
On the basis of these clues about the closeness of approach, the perceptual apparatus adjusts the perceived size of the retinal image to yield the
correct view that an object of constant size is coming closer.

It is to be noted that all the processes mentioned here as being responsible for perceptual constancy phenomena involve preconscious operations. Hence it might be said that sensations as such do not have access
to consciousness. The processes by which percepts are abstracted from
the sensory input cannot be introspected by the percipient. This point
is often overlooked when physicists discuss the nature of reality, since

they tend to equate sensation in the sensory organs with what is presented to the consciousness. The conscious mind has no access to raw data; it obtains only a highly processed portion of the input. From the evolutionary viewpoint, such processing is enormously adaptive, since it allows the mind to cope with the real world. For instance, Donald McKay suggests that voluntary movements of the eyes are really preconscious questions about the world: if upon moving the eyes the images of objects move, the perceptual apparatus infers that the objects are in reality stationary. All these processes serve to abstract information free of the vagaries of the sensory organs and thus allow us to construct an objective world from our sensations.

The abstraction of constancy of object color, position, and size from the retinal image represents only a very low level of the entire process of perception. The next higher level is that of constancy of abstraction of form. That is, when an object is seen under changing conditions, its perceived form remains the same even though entirely different sets of sensory receptors are stimulated at different times. The variability of the object's aspects simply does not reach the consciousness. What is abstracted is the form of the object, irrespective of the particular part of the sensory system that provided the information about the object. This capacity for abstraction of form from diverse bits of information, such as the illumination and the angle from which an object is seen, is what certain psychologists call *Gestalt* perception, namely the ability to see an object as a whole. This capacity is a precondition to forming the category of object, which, as we shall soon see, is one of the early concepts that the developing intellect of the infant produces.

How is it that the mind perceives an object as a whole, and the world as only one real world, in view of the fact that the brain consists of two hemispheres? Or to put this question in another way, how do the two hemispheres give rise to a single mind? From our previous discussion, we know that the right half of the visual field projects to the left visual cortex, and the left half of the visual field to the right cortex. A similar crossed pathway also obtains for the projection of the acoustic field to the auditory cortex and for the projections from the bilateral motor areas of the cortex, which issue their commands to the musculature on the opposite side of the body. The existence of two halves of the brain is not in itself surprising, since the human body is, on the whole, bilaterally symmetric. However, the two halves of the body must communicate, because they behave in a coordinated manner.

It might be thought that this coordination or integration of the two halves would take place in an organ that is unique rather than bilaterally

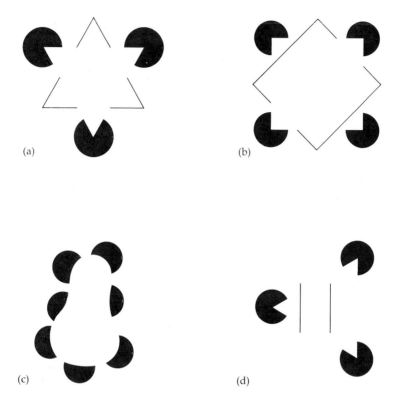

(a)

(b)

(c)

(d)

Gestalt perception is an active contribution of our perceptive apparatus to the interpretation of these figures. In each case, structures are seen that are not actually present. They are called subjective contours. When the contours are examined closely, they disappear. One subjective contour even appears to pass under another that intersects with it (b). Optical illusions demonstrate that subjective contours have the same functional effect as real contours, as indicated by the Ponzo illusion shown in (d). Although both vertical lines are the same length, the effect of the subjective triangle is to make the line on the left appear longer. [After Kanizsa, 1976]

symmetric, reflecting the unity of the mind. René Descartes took this line of reasoning early in the seventeenth century. In the course of his anatomical explorations of the brain, Descartes discovered the pineal body—a single organ lying near the center of the brain—and designated it as the seat of the mind. Modern investigations have shown the inadequacy of the theory of the unity of the mind in general and of its seat in the pineal body in particular. As for the pineal body, it appears to function, not as the seat of the mind, but as a component of the biological clock that controls the daily rhythms of physiology and behavior.

No, in our quest for the mind, we must focus on the cerebral cortex, which is the organ of consciousness and of language. Do consciousness and language refer to the same function? Certainly not, for otherwise we would never be at a loss for words to express our thoughts. But can we be conscious of something that would be impossible for us to verbalize? Here the work on *lateralization* of various cortical capabilities has revolutionized our insights. Normally the two halves of the cortex are so intimately integrated that investigation of their individual function is very difficult. Some years ago, however, surgeons introduced an operation for patients with severe epilepsy. In this operation the *corpus callosum*, a massive strand of nerve fibers connecting the two hemispheres, is severed. Superficial observation of such patients after their operation indicated, very surprisingly, that they seemed to have suffered no loss at all of their normal perceptions, their motor activities, or their speech. But more refined studies by Roger Sperry of "split brain" patients revealed a fantastic situation: visual, auditory, or tactile inputs can be so designed as to reach only one of the hemispheres, and when this is done the other hemisphere literally does not know about it. This can be tested by asking the patient to identify—say, by touch with the right hand, controlled by the left hemisphere—an object seen in the left half of the visual field, and thus with visual input leading to the right hemisphere. The patient cannot do it, even though the verbal instruction is given to both halves of the brain. Even more strikingly, it turns out that the right half is incapable of verbalizing what it "knows," even though this knowledge is clearly present, since the right half is able to use it for solving complex mental tasks.

How is this astonishing result to be explained? As we saw in chapter 6, the cortical areas dedicated to the production of speech are present on only one side (usually the left), rather than symmetrically distributed over both hemispheres. When the corpus callosum is cut, the left hemisphere, which contains the speech production centers, has no idea of what is being presented to the right. Nevertheless, while the right hemisphere cannot produce speech, it is capable of a great deal of mental processing on its own. The cerebral dichotomy goes so far that the patient may show an emotional response, say by a smile, when seeing a picture with the right brain, but is asked *why* he or she smiles, the verbalizing left brain can only admit ignorance. These great discoveries show that we have *two* minds under one roof, two minds normally so well integrated that their separation is inapparent: they talk to each other via the corpus callosum, and then talk to the outside world with one voice, controlled by the left mind.

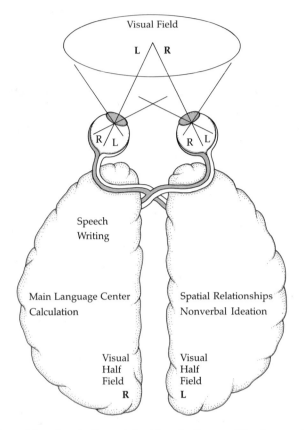

Lateralization of function in the cerebral hemispheres of the human brain. The left hemisphere (in the majority of individuals) is specialized for language comprehension, speech, and computational abilities. The right hemisphere is specialized for spatial constructions and nonverbal ideation, and also possesses simple verbal abilities. These lateralized functions can best be demonstrated in individuals in which the neural connections (via the corpus callosum) between the two cerebral hemispheres have been severed in the surgical treatment of severe epilepsy. [After Sperry, 1968]

Does the right hemisphere, the nonspeaking hemisphere, have consciousness? It certainly has a mind, in the sense that it can hear and understand speech and rationally answer questions, not by speech, but by solving problems. Whether one wants to call this consciousness is a matter of terminology, and terminology in this area is not settled at present. In any case, the unity of the mind in normal persons is evidently the result of an interhemispheric consensus mediated by the corpus callosum. We will now strive to take a broader view of human perception and consider the relevance of these neuropsychological findings for epistemology, that is to say, for the philosopher's quest for understanding how we come to know what we know.

Until quite recently, it was one of the basic misconceptions of philosophers that the mind deals with primary sense impressions and that the individual learns to make the abstractions that form the basis of perception. For instance, according to the empiricism of the early eighteenth century, as formulated mainly by David Hume and the French encyclopedists, the mind at birth is a clean slate on which there is gradually sketched a representation of the real world, built on cumulative experience. This representation is orderly, or structured, because, thanks to the principle of inductive reasoning, we can recognize regular features of our experience and infer causal connections between events that habitually occur together. This viewpoint rejects as a logical absurdity the possibility of innate or a priori knowledge of the world, that is, knowledge possessed prior to having experienced the world, which was a central feature of the seventeenth century philosophy of rationalism advocated by Descartes. In the latter part of the eighteenth century, however, Immanuel Kant demonstrated that empiricist philosophy and its rejection of the possibility of a priori knowledge is grounded on an inadequate understanding of the mind and its relation to reality. Kant pointed out that sensory impressions can become experience, that is, gain meaning, only after they are interpreted in terms of the a priori categories—such as time, space and object—that we bring to, rather than derive from, experience. Tacit resort to propositions whose validity is similarly accepted a priori, such as "Some A are B; therefore all A are B" (induction) or "The occurrence of a set of conditions A is both necessary and sufficient for the occurrence of B" (causation by A of B), allows the mind to construct reality from that experience. Kant referred to these a priori categories and propositions of cognition as "transcendental," because they transcend experience and were thought by him to be beyond the scope of scientific inquiry.

But is it not strange that if, as Kant alleges, we bring such categories as time, space, and object, as well as the notion of causality, to sensation a priori, that they happen to fit the real world so well? Considering all the bizarre ideas we might have had prior to experience, it seems nothing short of miraculous that our a priori ideas happen to be those that fill the bill. The way to resolve this dilemma opened when Charles Darwin put forward the theory of natural selection in mid-nineteenth century. But few philosophers or scientists seemed to have noticed this until Konrad Lorenz drew attention to it in the 1940s. Lorenz pointed out that the empiricist argument that knowledge about the world can enter the mind only through experience is valid if we consider only the *ontogenetic* development of man, from fertilized human egg to adult person. But once we also take into account the phylogenetic development of the human brain through evolutionary history, it becomes clear that persons can know something of the world innately, prior to and independent of their own experience. After all, there is no biological reason why such knowledge cannot be passed on from generation to generation via the ensemble of genes that determines the structure and function of our brain. For that genetic ensemble came into being through the process of natural selection operating on our remote ancestors. According to Lorenz, "experience has as little to do with matching of the a priori with reality as does the matching of the fin structure of a fish with the properties of water." In other words, the Kantian notion of a priori knowledge is not implausible at all. Rather, Kant's claims of the "a-priori-ness" of such categories as space, time, and object, as well as of causality, as transcendental components of cognition almost hit the nail on the head. These ideas are indeed a priori for the individual, but they did not fall from heaven; they are matters of evolutionary adaptation, designed for survival in the real world.

It appears therefore that two kinds of learning are involved in our dealing with the world. One is *phylogenetic* learning, in the sense that during evolution we have evolved very sophisticated machinery for perceiving and making inferences about a real world, of which the preconscious neurophysiological abstraction processes acting on visual input, the perceptual constancy phenomena associated with vision, and the interhemispheric consensus of our two minds reached via the corpus callosum are but a few examples. They show that, collectively and across history, the human species has learned to deal with signals coming from the outside world by constructing a model of it. In other words, whereas in the light of modern understanding of evolutionary processes, we can say that the individual approaches perception a priori, this is by no means true when we consider the history of mankind as a whole. What is a priori for individuals is a posteriori for the species. The second kind of learning involved in dealing with the world is *ontogenetic* learning, namely the lifelong acquisition of cultural, linguistic, and scientific knowledge.

Thus we see the world through multiple pairs of glasses: some of them are inherited as part of our physiological apparatus, others acquired from direct experiences as we proceed through life. In a sense, the discoveries of science help us to see what the world is like without some of these pairs of glasses. As Konrad Lorenz has put it, every step of knowledge means taking off a pair of glasses—but we could never dispense with all of them.

REFERENCES

Campenhausen, C. von. 1981. *Die Sinne des Menschen*. Stuttgart: Thieme.

Geschwind, N. 1978. Specialization of the human brain. *Scientific American* 241(3): 180–199.

Hassenstein, B. 1971. *Information and Control in the Living Organism*. London: Chapman and Hall.

Hubel, D. H., and T. N. Wiesel. 1970. The period of susceptibility to the physiological effects of unilateral eye closure in kittens. *Journal of Physiology* 206: 419–436.

Kanizsa, G. 1976. Subjective contours. *Scientific American* 243(4):48–52.

Lorenz, K. 1941. Kant's Lehre vom apriorischen im Lichte gegenwärtiger Biologie (Kant's doctrine of the a priori in the light of contemporary biology). *Blätter für Deutsche Philosophie* 15: 94–125. In *General Systems*, ed. Bertalanffy and Rapoport, vol. 7, pp. 23–35. Ann Arbor: Society for General Systems Research, 1962.

———. 1959. Gestaltwahrnehmung als Quelle wissenschaftlicher Erkenntnis (Gestalt perception as a source of scientific knowledge). *Zeitschrift für Experimentelle und Angewandte Psychologie* 6: 118–165. In *Studies in Animal and Human Behaviour*, vol. 2, pp. 281–322. Cambridge: Harvard University Press, 1971. Also in *General Systems*, ed. Bertalanffy and Rapoport, vol. 7, pp. 37–56. Ann Arbor: Society for General Systems Research, 1962.

McKay, D. M. 1971. Voluntary eye movements are questions. *Bibliotheca Ophthalmologica* 82: 369–376.

Purves, D., and J. W. Lichtman. 1985. *Principles of Neural Development*. Sunderland, Mass.: Sinauer Associates.

Sperry, R. W. 1968. Mental unity following surgical disconnection of the cerebral hemispheres. *The Harvey Lectures* 62: 293–323.

———. 1982. Some effects of disconnecting the cerebral hemispheres. *Science* 217: 1223–1226.

Wiesel, T. N., and D. H. Hubel. 1963. Single cell responses in striate cortex of kittens deprived in one eye. *Journal of Neurophysiology* 26: 1003–1017.

Nine

Cognition

The evolutionary interpretation of the Kantian viewpoint that the "a-priori-ness" of such fundamental categories as space, time, object, and causality is the result of phylogenetic learning does not necessarily mean that the perceptual and cognitive apparatus of which these epistemological tools are the product is already present in the mind, full blown, at birth. On the contrary, it can hardly be present at birth, since the human brain is obviously undergoing a substantial postnatal development, making new connections and modifying the neural network all the while. Moreover, that postnatal development is the result of a constructive interaction between the gene-directed synthesis of proteins relevant for the genesis of the nervous system (the information for which is what is actually passed on hereditarily) and the environment. That is to say, the distinction between phylogenetic and ontogenetic learning is not as obvious as we might have made it seem at the close of the preceding chapter. What is learned phylogenetically is not how to enter the world with ready-made adaptive concepts but how to have the brain so interact with the world before, during, and after birth that it is certain to develop adaptive rather than maladaptive categories of thought.

One of the clearest neurophysiological and neuroanatomical demonstrations of the (phylogenetically learned) postnatal interactions of the environment with the developing perceptual apparatus was provided by the work of Hubel and Wiesel with cells in area 17 of the visual cortex. They showed that the network of connections of the cells of the adult cortex that respond specifically to straight edges of light and dark contrast of a particular orientation is not complete at birth, but is shaped postnatally by early visual experience. Such shaping has been demonstrated to occur in kittens for several weeks after birth. In the new-born kitten, as in the adult cat, the majority of the nerve cells in area 17 are initially binocular, that is, respond equally well to visual input to either eye. If one eye of the kitten is sutured closed for the first three months of life, so that the visual cortex receives visual input only through the other open eye, then after the visually deprived eye is reopened, the previously binocular cells will respond only to input from the nondeprived eye. The cortex no longer processes visual input from the deprived eye, which, as far as perception is concerned, has become permanently blind. If, however, the kitten's eye is sutured closed only after the first three months of life and left closed for as long as a year, upon reopening the deprived eye full vision is immediately restored to it. Hubel and Wiesel concluded from these findings that during the first three months of the kitten's life its visual cortex passes through a "critical period," during which normal vision with both eyes is required for the maintenance of binocular connections to the perceptual apparatus. The human visual cortex evidently undergoes a similar critical period, as can be inferred from the fact that whereas an adult who loses vision in one eye because of occlusion of the lens by a cataract immediately regains sight upon operative removal of that optical obstruction, an infant born with a congenital cataract will be permanently blind in the deprived eye unless the cataract is removed during early childhood.

The existence of a critical period of susceptibility of a part of the young brain to deprivation or abnormal experience is quite general in the animal kingdom. Examples have been found in birds, where one of the most dramatic cases is the neonatal "imprinting" discovered by Konrad Lorenz for the "following response" of chicks. Newly hatched birds of many species will follow the first object they see after hatching that moves, clucks, and has a reasonable odor. Anything will do, from a cylinder with stripes of light to a human being. In a natural context such imprinting serves for the chick's lifelong identification of the mother bird, but in artificial situations the chick will accept as "mother" anything that grossly simulates the motion and some other aspects of the mother bird. Here the critical period lasts for only a few hours after hatching. In other bird species acquisition of a specific song occurs during a critical period for nestlings. If the chick is deprived of an opportunity to hear this song during that period, it will never learn it in later life.

Thus it seems that the critical period is the time in life when a particular neuronal subsystem matures, and proper use of the system during that time is essential for its normal development. But what functional significance can be attributed to the critical period of binocular connections in the visual cortex? Whereas the value of imprinting a mother image or a specific song on a young bird is not difficult to fathom, it seems less obvious why the binocular connections converging on the neurons in the visual cortex should not be permanently wired and retain, independent of later visual experience, the functional character they possess at birth.

On further reflection, a solution can be readily found for this teleological riddle. For this purpose, we direct our attention to the congruence of the circumscribed areas of the visual field that are reported to a given cortical binocular cell from each of the two retinas. To provide for the sharp binocular vision of the frontal eyes of cats and humans, this congruence has to be very exact. But where the image of a particular area of the visual field will focus on the retina of each eye depends on the physical optics of that eye, particularly on the precise structure and orientation of its lens. It would be nothing short of miraculous if the genes could direct the innate development of an absolutely perfect functional congruence of two entirely independent structures and tune, in advance of any visual experience, the retinal neuronal connections to any structural idiosyncracies. Accordingly, it appears that the congruence of the two areas of the visual field seen by the binocular cells of the visually naive cortex of the newborn is not nearly as perfect as it is in the adult and that the visual inputs during the critical period tune the system by selecting the appropriate pathways from an overconnected network. The rule by which this selection appears to proceed is that only those binocular connections that bring coherent and synchronous electrical signals to the same cortical cell are allowed to survive the critical period.

Thus at birth the system is overconnected, in the sense that individual binocular cortical cells receive inputs from an area of both retinas covering large and only partly overlapping areas of the visual field. Under these conditions vision is, of course, completely blurred. But during early visual experience, only those points of the two retinas on which the same point of the visual field *does* happen to come into focus would send a synchronous signal pattern to a given cortical cell. Other retinal points that are initially connected to that same cortical cell but that happen to see different points of the visual field do not send synchronous signals, and hence their connections would gradually wither. Thus blurred vision would eventually cease and the exact binocular congruence of the input to individual cortical cells would become established. However, if one eye is sutured closed during the critical period, it does not send any signal pattern to the cortex at all and hence its connections to all cortical cells would wither.

The conclusions drawn from these studies on the visual cortex may be extended to provide some general understanding of the brain. First, ontogenetic learning can be regarded, not as a fringe benefit, but as a necessary adjunct to any complicated nervous system, since once a certain degree of complexity of organization has been attained, the genes cannot direct the innate development of the nervous system to functional perfection. Second, the experiential rather than innate perfection of the complex nervous system proceeds by selective survival of pathways from an innately overconnected network. That is to say, only those functions can be learned ontogenetically for which the corresponding neuronal pathways already exist in the brain, thanks to phylogenetic learning.

It should be noted, however, that not all complex functions of the nervous system arise in the experience-dependent manner. For instance, when young birds "learn" to fly, it seems as if they are flapping their wings for practice. But if one places a young bird in a tube in which it cannot practice flying for several weeks, upon release it flies as well as a bird of the same age that was not so confined. Thus the neural network responsible for generating the flight movement matures postnatally in a genetically determined, autonomous manner, of which the practice of flight is a nonessential component.

In the light of these insights gained into the postnatal perfection of complex nervous systems we can now turn to the ontogenetic development of the human brain and examine how its cognitive functions, including the Kantian a priori categories, arise in the mind of the infant and the child. For this purpose we turn to the studies begun by Jean Piaget in the 1920s. In designing IQ tests to be administered to French schoolchildren, Piaget noticed that children are consistent in the sort of incorrect answers they give to certain questions: the answers are not randomly wrong but have a systematic character. He concluded that this consistency of error must represent qualitatively different structures of intellect present at different stages of cognitive development. In trying to identify these structures, Piaget evolved a theory about the process by which the most basic categories of thought arise. He concluded that the mind is not a passive apparatus for handling sensory input, according to some fixed pattern of signal flow, but that it actively transforms the input by means of exploratory action. Piaget's approach was to look upon human intelligence as a strategy of active construction of reality, rather than as a passive receiver and processor of information from the world. However, although human intellectual activities are unavoidably emotion laden, Piaget avoided the study of the affective component of mental operations and concentrated entirely upon cognitive capabilities and their development in ontogeny.

This area of research is a gold mine for epistemological exploration, one that was overlooked for millenia by philosophers. Traditionally philosophers have discussed only knowledge and truth as possessed by the adult human mind, without considering to any great extent that their origins lie in the mind of the infant. Admittedly, in the first half of the eighteenth century, Jean-Jacques Rousseau (after whom the Geneva institute of which Piaget became director was named) had recognized that "nature wants children to be children before men. . . Childhood has its own seeing, thinking, and feeling." But it was only at the turn of this century that psychologists, especially James Baldwin, began to make a systematic assessment of the cognitive capacities of the infantile mind and of the stages by which it matures to the adult condition. Even after Piaget took up this line of investigation, another quarter century had to pass before his findings made any significant impact on epistemological thought.

Piaget did not consider to any great extent whether the postnatal development of cognitive structures occurs autonomously (i.e., is genetically determined) or heteronomously (i.e., is learned from experience, or even training). In any case it would be difficult to distinguish these alternatives operationally since children deprived of normal experiences might develop abnormally in either case. Children so deprived might be unable to unfold their genetically determined developmental program properly since, as we saw in the examples of frontal binocular vision and imprinting, phylogenetic learning may include the anticipation of particular patterns of postnatal sensory input. Therefore, it would be necessary to use highly abnormal experimental conditions to determine the degree to which a cognitive function is autonomously preprogrammed or heteronomously dependent on specific ontogenetic learning experiences.

Fortunately, in the context of discussing the development of the human mind it is unimportant whether our adult notions about the world and ourselves are determined by the genes or implanted in the mind by experience. It is sufficient to recognize that the cognitive categories of the mind constitute a set of adaptations to the real world. That real world is the world of the middle dimensions, constituted of things that are more-or-less directly accessible to our sensory apparatus. It is not surprising therefore that, as we shall see in later chapters, many of these notions must be discarded or modified when science moves beyond these middle dimensions to the very small and the very brief, as it does when considering the structure of the atom and of its nucleus, or to the very large and the very long, as it does when considering the structure of the universe and its evolution.

At this point of our inquiry, we are interested in the evolution and the development of these notions, not because we want to know the mechanisms by which the brain generates them (which is the subject of neurophysiology) or the mechanisms by which the capacity of the brain to generate them arises (which is the subject of neuroembryology), but because we are interested in the fact that they arise step by step, in an integrated fashion. We are interested in this stepwise process because we want to explore whether there are any possible alternatives to the common categories by which we construct reality. As described by Piaget, the ontogenetic maturation of the mind begins with the development of notions of space, time, and objects, followed somewhat later by the development of the ideas of causality, logic, sets, and numbers. These categories of cognition arise during different developmental periods:

1. The first such period is the sensorimotor period (from birth to 2 years of age), during which infants construct the concepts of object, space, and causality.

2. The second period is the preoperational period (from 2 to 5 years of age), during which children's thought processes begin to use symbols, either in the form of mental images, developing out of imitation, which become more and more internalized, or in the form of words, as symbolic representations of objects and events. Furthermore, one object may be taken as a symbol for another object, as for instance in imagery-play or make-believe. Children also begin to reason from memory and analogy during this period.

3. During the next, or concrete operational period (from 5 to 10 years of age), children can perform mental operations on objects concretely present: they can classify, construct hierarchical structures, begin to understand ordinal relations (seriation), comprehend the equivalence of sets, and make effective use of imagery. Late in this period, the concept of conservation of continuous properties, such as quantity, weight, and volume, makes its appearance.

4. The last stage is that of formal operations (from 10 to 14 years of age) in which the real world is conceived of as a subset of possible worlds. Propositional thinking, with assertions and statements that can be true or false, becomes possible.

Each of these periods can be subdivided into a number of stages characterized by different intellectual structures.

One of the most striking of Piaget's conclusions is that although the age at which individual children reach one or another of these periods and stages can vary greatly, the sequence of the stages is invariant. That the order of the stages is always the same must mean that the beginning of one stage presupposes the completion of the development characteristic of all preceding stages. Each stage is integrated within itself, according to an equilibrium of all elements that comprise the child's cognition. Piaget's usage of the word "equilibrium" is not in the usual mechanical or chemical sense. He intends it to convey the idea of a dynamic steady state between the two major antithetical aspects of cognitive performance, namely accommodation and assimilation. Accommodation to new situations means changing an existing mental or behavioral technique to adapt it to the specific characteristics of new objects and new relationships, thus taking into account novel aspects of reality. It is a way of being realistic, taking life as it comes. Assimilation, the counterforce to accommodation in the equilibrium, means fitting novel aspects of reality into old behavioral and cognitive schemes rather than changing them. It is a way of being autistic or of shaping reality according to one's own preconceived notions. For instance, according to a very simple example of this equilibrium, infants have a method of grasping objects. If given a novel object to grasp, they perform both assimilation, by including the object in the mental class of things that are graspable, and accommodation, by modifying their grasping technique to suit a novel object. It is a particular position of the equilibrium between the two antithetical cognitive forces that characterizes each stage of cognitive development. The equilibrium becomes upset in play, dreams, and make-believe, where autistic assimilation occurs without accommodation to reality. In the upset of the equilibrium during these activities, objects may be commanded to do certain things, which leads to symbolization: one bends the object playfully to represent something that it is not. The equilibrium also becomes upset during imitation, but in the opposite direction: imitating a model is nothing other than accommodation of the self to the reality of the world. This also applies to imagery, since a mental image is an internalized imitation of reality.

In the first, or sensorimotor, period of cognitive development, in which the space, time, and object concepts are constructed, hand–eye coordination is developed. During their first month of life infants may move their arms, but they cannot appreciate that the hand they see is their own. The grasping reflex is already present, and infants may intend to grasp an object that they see. This intent can cause an increase in the amplitude and speed of hand motion, but the hand may not necessarily move in the right direction. Later infants are able to grasp an object they see, not by aiming a hand directly at the object, but by reaching the object by trial and error. This sequence constitutes a mutual assimilation of tactile and visual spaces. It is succeeded by the coordination of sight and sound and by the ability to follow a moving object. Thus is vision accommodated to motion.

Some of Piaget's observations on his small children, which led him to these conclusions, were described by him in the following protocols, as published in his book *The Construction of Reality in the Child* (1954). (The numbers at the beginning of each protocol designate the age of the subject in years, months, and days). The first observation demonstrates that by the age of 6 months and 3 days the infants are able to follow a moving object.

> At 0;6(3) Laurent, lying down, holds in his hand a box five centimeters in diameter. When it escapes him he looks for it in the right direction (beside him). I then grasp the box and drop it myself, vertically, and too fast for him to be able to follow the trajectory. His eyes search for it at once on the sofa on which he is lying. I manage to eliminate any sound or shock and I perform the experiment at his right and at his left; the result is always positive. (Observation No. 6)

The next step in the development of the object concept is the beginning of the capacity for remembering objects while they are out of sight.

> At 0;8(30) Lucienne is busy scratching a powder box placed next to her on her left, but abandons that game when she sees me appear on her right. She drops the box and plays with me for a moment, babbles, etc. Then she suddenly stops looking at me and turns at once in the correct position to grasp the box; obviously she does not doubt that this will be at her disposal in the very place where she used it before. (Observation No. 18)

The following observation is particularly interesting because it shows that infants' initial object concept is clearly not what we as adults conceive to be an object.

> At 0;10(18) Jacqueline is seated on a mattress without anything to disturb or distract her (no coverlets, etc.). I take her parrot from her hands and hide it twice in succession under the mattress, on her left, in A. Both times Jacqueline looks for the object immediately and grabs it. Then I take it from her hands and move it very slowly before her eyes to the corresponding

place on her right, under the mattress, in B. Jacqueline watches this movement but at the moment when the parrot disappears in B she turns to her left and looks where it was before, in A. (Observation No. 40)

At this stage of development, the notion of an object is such that all objects have a permanent place. Accordingly an object does not persist when moving from one place to another. Furthermore, when an object disappears from view, infants expect it to be at the place where it was first seen: it has gone back to the place where it belongs. Within the next few months, however, infants come to believe in the continued existence of objects.

> At 1;1(18) Lucienne is seated on a bed, between shawl A and cloth B. I hide a safety pin in my hand and my hand under the shawl. I remove my hand closed and empty. Lucienne opens it at once and looks for the pin. Not finding it, she searches under the shawl and finds it . . . (Observation No. 63)

Thus, thanks to the belief in the permanence of the object, infants are able to search for it when it is not present.

Finally, by the end of the sensorimotor period, the concept of the permanent object has been elaborated further and consolidated.

> At 1;7(23) Jacqueline is seated opposite three object-screens. A, B and C (a beret, a handkerchief, and her jacket) aligned equidistant from each other. I hide a small pencil in my hand saying "Coucou, the pencil." [The child had previously found it under A] I hold out my closed hand to her, put it under A, then under B, then under C (leaving the pencil under C); at each step I again extend my closed hand, repeating "Coucou, the pencil." Jacqueline then searches for the pencil directly in C, finds it and laughs. (Observation No. 65)

Infants now have mental images of objects and are able to fathom complex, even invisible, spatial displacements of any object. They have entered the second, or preoperational, period of cognitive development, which lasts from about 2 to 5 years of age.

By this sequence of steps infants gradually acquire the notion of a permanent object with continued existence under various transformations. As we will see in later chapters, it is just this aspect of permanence of the object notion that has to be discarded in the study of quantum mechanics, since it does not apply to such microscopic things as electrons. Experience, therefore, accommodates our concepts only to the middle dimensions of the reality of our everyday life.

It is, however, still a long way from the concept of an object and its permanence to the concepts of cardinal number. A cardinal number designates a particular class of equivalent sets—for example, "five" and "seven" designate two different classes of pairable sets—without implying a serial relation between these classes—that is, without implying that "seven" comes after "five." Although the concept of ordinal number, by which objects or entities are ordered serially, can arise only after the concept of cardinal number has been grasped, the former is not necessarily implied logically by the latter. Thus children pass through a stage in which they have no notion that when going from one cardinal number to another, one must pass all intervening cardinal numbers—that is, in going from "five" to "seven" one must pass through "six." We will return to the number concept in chapter 11, when we discuss in detail how mathematicians deal with it.

Mastery of the number concept is an accomplishment of the third, or concrete operational, period of cognitive development. Grasping the concept of number requires the child to understand the notion of the equivalence of sets, a notion that children do not understand in their preoperational period. If asked to order sticks of varying lengths according to length, children in the preoperational period are generally unable to do so, although they may produce some kind of fictitious (though clearly not random) ordering. A 5- to 7-year-old child may be able to order the items of the set but only with difficulty. Moreover, the child cannot establish the equivalence between sets, as for instance between one set containing large sticks and another set containing an equal number of small sticks. All such tasks fail because children are distracted by space relations among the elements of a set, such as size or shape, with which the developing number concept is always in conflict. The following protocol taken from Piaget's *Child's Conception of Numbers* (1964) is instructive in this regard. It describes the response of a child aged 4 years, 7 months to Piaget's placing six sweets in a row and telling him that they belong to his friend Roger.

> "Put as many sweets here as there are there. Those . . . are for Roger. You are to take as many as he has." (He made a compact row of about ten, which was shorter than the model.)—"Are they the same?"—"Not yet" (adding some)—"And now?"—"Yes"—"Why?"—"Because they're like that" (indicating the length).

The child evidently failed to use the notion of equivalence of sets, matching items one by one; instead he used length as the standard of comparison.

At that age even if a child were forced to match the items of two sets one by one, the child would not understand set equivalence. Piaget asked the child to put one flower in each of ten vases. The following protocol describes the procedure he used to test whether the child realizes that the set of flowers was numerically equivalent to the set of vases.

> The flowers were taken out and bunched together in front of the vases. [That is, they formed a shorter row than did the vases.] "Is there the same number of vases and flowers?"—"No"—"Where are there more?"—"There are more vases"—"If we put the flowers back into the vases, will there be one flower in each vase?"—"Yes"—"Why?"—"Because there are enough." (The vases were closed up and the flowers spaced out.)—"And now?"— "There are more flowers."

Evidently, even after the child himself had established a one-to-one correspondence between flowers and vases, he failed to conserve the idea of the numerical equivalence of the two sets. In other words equivalence, and therefore cardinal number, is not yet understood at this stage. Only between the ages of 5 and 7 do children reach the stage where they can attain the concept of the cardinal number. This is shown by the following protocol.

> "Take the same number of pennies as there are there [there were six in set A]." He made a row of six under the model, but put his much closer together so that there was no spatial correspondence between the rows. Both ends of the model extended beyond those of the copy. "Have you got the same number?"—"Yes"—"Are you and that boy [referring to the hypothetical owner of set A] just as rich as one another?"—"Yes"—(The pennies of the model were then closed up and his own were spaced out.)—"And now?"— "The same."—"Exactly?"—"Yes"—"Why are they the same?"—"Because you've put them closer together."

At this stage children evidently use vicariant (arbitrary) ordering of sets and are capable of disregarding dissimilarities between similar objects. By now, the concept of cardinal number is most certainly present.

Early in the concrete operational period, however, children still lack the concept of relative sizes of sets. If at that early stage a child is given six flowers—three yellow and three of other colors—and asked which set is greater, the set of flowers or the set of yellow flowers, the child will reply "they are the same," even though one set contains six items and the other only three. The child cannot quantify class inclusion relations yet. But later in the concrete operational period there comes a moment at which children realize that a set contains more items than its subset.

At this point they have gained the ability to handle hierarchical structures, that is, sets comprised of subsets, such as the set of "flowers," which includes various kinds, or classes, of flowers. Upon gaining the ability to conceive of hierarchical structures, children also have access to the notion of ordinal number. They are now equipped with the two most powerful conceptual tools for dealing with the quantitative aspects of the real world.

REFERENCES

Ginsberg, H., and S. Opper. 1979. *Piaget's Theory of Intellectual Development.* 2d ed. Englewood Cliffs, N.J.: Prentice Hall.

Piaget, J. 1954. *The Construction of Reality in the Child.* New York: Basic Books.

———. 1964. *Child's Conception of Number.* Atlantic Highlands, N.J.: Humanities Press.

Ten

Causality, Time, Space

In the preceding chapter, we considered Piaget's system of dividing the development of cognitive capabilities into various periods and stages and traced some of the stages of the first, or sensorimotor, period. In these stages the concept of object is developed, where by "object" we mean an entity that has permanence, whether it is visible or invisible and whether it is moving or stationary. We saw how the object concept arises in the context of infants' structuring of the space of their surroundings, by coordinating and assimilating spatial relations of their visible, touchable, and movable worlds. At the onset of this development, only that part of the world is so structured and apprehended by the nascent object concept that is immediately reachable by the infants' appendages or mouth. The rest of the world remains an infinite firmament.

We contrasted these early developmental concepts with those that are constructed only much later, in the concrete operational period (ages 5 to 10), such as the concept of number. The development of the number concept has nothing to do with learning to recite strings of numbers in their proper order, but consists of grasping the idea of the equivalence of sets. Once that idea has been grasped children are able to pair two sets, such as sets of pennies and candies, or of vases and flowers, without being distracted by the disparate features of their elements. This development occurs at such a late stage because preoperational children (before the age of 5) find it very difficult to perform the mental operation of pairing disparate objects. They can concentrate on one object, but have great trouble in trying to establish relations between objects. In particular, children are confused by the task of abstracting objects from their situational context, particularly if the objects are arranged differently in space. The idea of conservation of number of objects irrespective of their spatial arrangement is not comprehended by preoperational children, who simply do not have the required cognitive apparatus.

We now turn to the development of another concept studied by Piaget, namely that of causality. Causality has been an important subject of philosophical debate since antiquity. Beginning with Newton, however, the nature of causality also became a topic of concern to physicists, in that Newton's postulation of forces acting at a distance, such as gravitational attraction, seemed to run counter to the intuitive notion that a cause and its effect ought to be contiguous. The role of the causality concept in physical theory became more controversial still with the advent of modern physics, particularly, as we shall see in later chapters, upon the appearance of the relativity and quantum theories early in the twentieth century. By causality we mean the idea that there is a necessary, although often hidden, connection between an earlier and a later event, between cause and effect. This idea is closely tied to the notion (which is definitely not primitive) that the entire universe is embedded in a common space and time. Whence does this idea come? Early in the eighteenth century, David Hume said that the idea of such a necessary connection arises from the feelings, rather than the reason, of the individual. Hume further asserted that the extrapolation from past experience to the future cannot be logically justified.

Hume's critique of the logical basis of the causality concept was addressed by Kant, who argued that causality, though not of demonstrable logical validity, is another of the a priori categories, like time, space, and object, that are a precondition of all experience. Thus, since the causality category is used for creating experience, it cannot be acquired by, or inferred from, experience. According to this view, the human mind simply cannot conceive of a world in which the future is *not* determined by the past. The Kantian view of causality was inspired by Newtonian physics and its application to celestial mechanics, whose success made it seem obvious that the world is governed by deterministic laws: given the initial conditions and Newton's laws of motion, the trajectories of the celestial objects are uniquely determined. This viewpoint was to be dealt a blow by the development of the theory of relativity, because in situations to which that theory applies, notions of what is past and what is future must be modified. Here the finding by one observer that event A preceded event B is ambiguous, since a second observer moving relative to the first might find that event B preceded event A. Accordingly, the first observer might infer from his measured order of these events that A is the cause of B, whereas the second observer might infer from his data that B is the cause of A. However, in this case both observers would be wrong, since, according to relativity theory, an inversion of the order of two events can be registered only if they are *not* causally connected. This follows from the (seemingly incontrovertible) proposition that if the earlier event A is the cause of the later event B, some signal must be exchanged between A and B. Because the signal—whatever its nature—cannot propagate faster than light (see chapter 15), the minimum measurable time interval between A and B is zero, which would be registered by an observer himself traveling at the speed of light from A to B. All other observers would find that the cause preceded its effect.

As we shall see in chapter 16, when we will undertake an in-depth exploration of modern physics, the quantum theory and its uncertainty principle put a definite limit on the definability of the past or future state of any system, and therefore also on the applicability of the intuitive causality concept.

Let us examine what Piaget's approach can tell us about the genesis of the idea of causality in the infantile mind. Piaget argues that the notion of cause and effect first arises during the sensorimotor period (from birth to 2 years of age), and has two roots. The first of these roots Piaget identified as dynamism, or efficacy, which means that children are vaguely aware that their own intentions and volitions are somehow responsible for what happens. They discover that in order to make a rattle rattle, they must move themselves in some way, such as wriggling, although they are not directly aware in a reflective way in what way they achieve the effect causally and have no concept of wriggling. All the same, they are aware that there is a connection between the wish for the sound of the rattle and its occurrence. The second root of causality is observation of the regularity of events that are contiguous in *time*. The mother's unfastening of her dress and the availability of milk are events that are contiguous in time but not in space. This awareness of the regularity of interconnected events is reached much earlier than the development of the space concept. Unfortunately, much of Piaget's evidence for these conclusions is anecdotal, as opposed to experimental, and may therefore be questioned on the grounds that it is uncontrolled and unrepeated.

Children's notion of causality is peculiarly different from an adult's, and continues to be peculiar from an adult's point of view up to the age of 6 to 10. The children think that anything can cause anything, whether the requirements of the adult notion of causality, such as continuity of cause and effect in time and space, are met or not. Thus, the notion of complete determinism in the external world, as propounded by eighteenth-century physicists, is not yet present in the minds of children aged 6 to 10.

Indeed, the root nexus in the infantile mind between will and event, where the will can be mine or that of others, including gods and demons, is often carried over into adulthood. In this view of causality there need be no physical connection between will and event, as there is not in the case of the cause–effect relation commonly designated as magic. The adult idea of a deterministic universe can be regarded as a hardened version of the other infantile root nexus, the connection between temporally contiguous events. This latter view of causality is closely tied to the developments of the categories of space and time and of a universal space and time frame enveloping the whole of the perceived world. We shall now turn to that process.

The categories of time and space do not arise automatically in the infantile mind. The notion of the whole world being embedded in one universal flow of time is reached only at a comparatively late stage of development, along with the notions of an all-pervading space providing unique places for the world's objects and of motion as the change from one place to another of an object in the universal flow of time. Children's inability to grasp these notions is illustrated by the following experiment:

Suppose a child under 5 (i.e., still in the sensorimotor period) is confronted with two objects that start and stop moving at the same time and at the same speed and is asked: (1) Have the objects started at the same time? (2) Have they moved at the same speed? (3) Have they moved the same distance? (4) Have they stopped at the same time? The child will generally respond correctly to all these questions. But if the test is repeated with one of the objects moving faster than the other, the child will still respond correctly to questions 1, 2, and 3 but will reply incorrectly to question 4 that the faster moving object stopped later, despite answering correctly questions 2 and 3 that the faster moving object moved at a greater speed and for a longer distance. Piaget concludes from this result that at this early stage speed is an intuitive primary kinetic category based on the ordinal succession of points traversed in space and time, without separate consideration of the actual distances moved or time intervals taken. Here intuition about time, especially about the notion of simultaneity, is derived from, rather than underlying, the assessment of speed. Thus children under 5 are unable to conceive that two objects might start at the same time and stop at the same time, while one of them has traversed more space. They can focus on the different displacements of the two, but they cannot embed those displacements in a common time frame. At this stage they see any chain of events as having its own private time.

Children's lack of access at this stage to the concepts of universal time and space is also the root of their peculiar notions about causality, since they lack the empirical basis for discovering the temporal and spatial connectedness of events and hence the alleged compulsion to postulate a universal causal nexus between them. To illustrate the development of causal explanations of physical phenomena in the infantile mind, consider the uniform, straight-line motion of objects. According to the principles of Aristotelian physics, such motion requires a continuously acting cause. If the cause ceases to exist, the object stops moving. According to the concept of momentum of Galilean physics, however, only a change in velocity requires a cause, since the momentum of an object will perpetuate its motion in the absence of any cause. Both explanations envisage a deterministic world (i.e., only one straight-line motion in a given context), but Aristotelian and Galilean theories make different assignments to the necessity for cause in the same phenomenon. The decision about which is the more reasonable theory—Aristotelian or Galilean—must be based on evidence garnered from the particular context of the phenomenon. A motile bacterium would certainly believe in the Aristotelian theory, since it lives in a world where viscous forces dominate inertial forces by an enormous factor. That is to say, the drag exerted on the bacterium by the viscosity of the water through which it moves vastly exceeds any inertia that the bacterium may have while moving. Even though a bacterium swims at high speed in relation to its body size, covering 30 times its body length in 1 second (which, on the scale of an automobile, would correspond to a speed of about 300 miles/hour), its forward motion stops within a fraction of its body length (say within a foot or so, on the automobile scale) as soon as its flagella stop moving. Thus, the empirical evidence would lead the bacterium to conclude that continuing motion requires a continuously acting cause.

To probe their capacity to provide a causal explanation of uniform linear motion, Piaget often asked children between the ages of 4 and 10 what makes clouds move. He reported that on the basis of the answers given, he was able to distinguish definite stages in the development of causal thought. In the first stage children think that as people walk, the clouds move with them; in other words, the motion of the person causes the clouds to move in some magical manner. In the second stage, reached

(a)

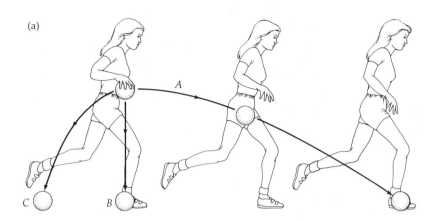

(b)

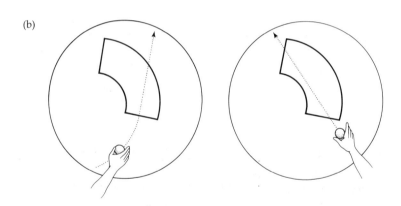

Two demonstrations that Galilean theories are not obvious to naive, physical intuition. [After McClosky, 1983]

a. According to Galilean physics, a ball dropped by a running person continues to move forward at the same speed as the runner. The forward motion of the ball, due to its momentum, combines with a steadily accelerating downward motion due to gravitational force to produce a parabolic trajectory (A). Intuitive beliefs about the motion of objects do not always correspond with this analysis. When college students were asked where a ball would land if it were dropped by a walking person, 45% of them knew that because of its Galilean momentum the ball would travel forward as it fell; 49% thought that, as envisaged by Aristotelian physics, the ball would fall straight down and land directly under the point where it was released (B); and 6 percent thought the ball would move backward as it fell (C).

by the age of 5 or 7, children think that clouds are moved by the sun and moon, that is, by command, not physical force. Finally, 8-year-olds usually think that the wind moves the clouds, and the wind is in turn created by the clouds. This circular causal chain is a very Aristotelian view of physics.

How does the child develop the concept of space? The dogma that Piaget attempted to establish was that the order in which children acquire spatial concepts is exactly the reverse of the order in which mathematicians acquired them historically. The branch of mathematics concerned with spatial relations is geometry, and the objective of most geometric analyses is to demonstrate the equivalence of shapes. Mathematicians first grasped the *metric* aspects of space in the fourth century B.C., upon the development of Euclidean geometry. Metric geometry depends mainly on the concepts of length of a line and width of an angle. Here the equivalence of figures is based on an equality of their contours with regard to these parameters. For example, two circles of equal diameter are metrically equivalent (i.e., congruent). The *projective* aspects of space were grasped next, in the nineteenth century. Projective geometry depends mainly on the concept of the straight line as the basis of spatial relationships. Here the equivalence of figures is based on the notion of perspective, or on the possibility of transforming one figure into another by projecting its contour onto the contour of another via a set of straight lines. For example, any two circles are projectively equivalent. The topological aspects of space were grasped last, in the twentieth century. *Topo-*

---

b. Some persons interact with moving objects as if the objects could be given circular impetus. A 90-degree segment of a ring was painted on a table, and experimental subjects were given a small "puck" with a ball bearing that would enable it to roll smoothly across the table. The subjects were asked to push the puck up to one edge of the ring segment and release it; the task was to make the puck cross to the other side of the segment without touching the curved sides. At the left is the strategy used by 25% of the subjects: they moved the puck in an arc, apparently in the (non-Galilean) belief that the object would continue to travel in a curved path as it moved through the ring segment. This strategy invariably failed, as illustrated by the broken line, which represents the path of the puck after it was released. The correct strategy, shown at the right, was applied by 67% of the subjects: they aimed the puck to take advantage of its straight-line trajectory after it was released. The remaining 8% of the subjects tried other unsuccessful strategies.

logical geometry depends mainly on the identification of qualitative features inhering in shapes, such as continuity as opposed to separation and openness as opposed to closure, as well as on counting the number of such features present. Here the equivalence of figures is based on the notion of homeomorphy, that is, the possibility of transforming one figure into another by a simple continuous deformation of its outline without any tear or overlap. For example, a circle and a square are topologically equivalent.

Piaget claimed that in cognitive development topological aspects of space are grasped first, projective aspects second, and metric aspects last. This claim was eventually put to a rigorous test by two Canadian psychologists, M. Laurendeau and A. Pinard, who studied a cohort of children over a 10-year period. As the children matured from the age of 2 to the age of 12, five standardized tests designed to measure and establish the acquisition of the topological, the projective, and the metric aspects of spatial concepts were given at regular intervals under well-controlled conditions. Their results show that while Piaget's dogma appears to be well-founded in some respects, in other respects it stands on less firm ground.

The first of the five tests, a *stereognostic*, "touch-and-tell" test, probes the child's capacity to recognize objects and distinguish shapes. This test consists of three sections and requires the ability to coordinate tactile and visual sensations. The first section examines the child's ability to recognize by touch, without seeing them, individual items of a set of eleven common objects, such as a comb, a key, a spoon, a pair of scissors, and a button. As a criterion of recognition the child is asked to identify the touched object verbally, or to point to its pictorial representation on a chart containing pictures of all eleven test objects. The second section examines the child's ability to distinguish the topological as well as metric (Euclidean) features of abstract geometric shapes. The child is shown one of two duplicate sets of twelve different shapes cut out of hard cardboard and made to touch samples from the second. The child is then asked to identify the shape he or she touched in the second set of shapes. Some shapes of the set differ topologically: a disk with one hole in the center and another disk with two holes, or a closed ring and an open ring. Other shapes are topologically equivalent but differ in their metric aspect: a regular star, an irregular star, a Greek cross, a circle, a rectangle, and a square. The third section is similar to the second, except that it is more restricted in scope, being intended to examine the child's ability to distinguish topologically equivalent (homeomorphic) abstract shapes on the basis of differences in their metric features. Here the twelve abstract

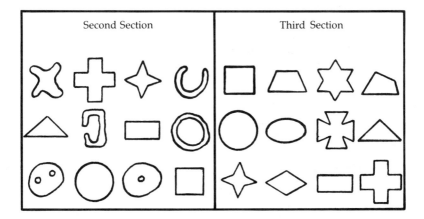

The abstract geometric shapes used in the second and third section of the stereognostic, touch-and-tell recognition test. Dimensions are proportional to that of the circle, whose diameter is 7.5 cm. Among the shapes of the second section, some differ topologically while others are topologically equivalent but differ in their metric aspects. The shapes of the third section are all topologically equivalent and differ only in their metric aspects. [From Laurendeau and Pinard, 1970. Used with permission.]

shapes in the two duplicate sets, such as a circle, a square, a Maltese cross, a Greek cross, a trapezoid, and a rhombus, differ only metrically.

In scoring the answers to this test, account was taken not only of the number of correct or incorrect answers, but also of the nature of the errors made. The results could be interpreted in terms of the passage of the infantile mind through four stereognostic stages. In stage 0, children refuse to participate in, or are unable to understand the test, or if they do participate, they do not demonstrate that they can recognize even common objects. Of the children tested more than half had passed out of stage 0 by the age of 2, and all were beyond it by the age of 3. In stage 1, children can recognize common objects but not geometric shapes. More than a fourth of the children had reached that stage by the age of 2, with the typical age of accession for stage 1 lying between ages 2 and 3. In stage 2, children can distinguish abstract geometric shapes on the basis of their topological features and can also distinguish between cur-vilinear and rectilinear contours. None of the children had reached this stage by the age of 2; the typical age of accession lies between the ages of 4 and 5. Finally, in stage 3, children can distinguish abstract geometric shapes on the basis of their metric (Euclidean) features. None of the children had reached that stage by age 3; the typical age of accession for this stage lies between the ages of 7 and 10.

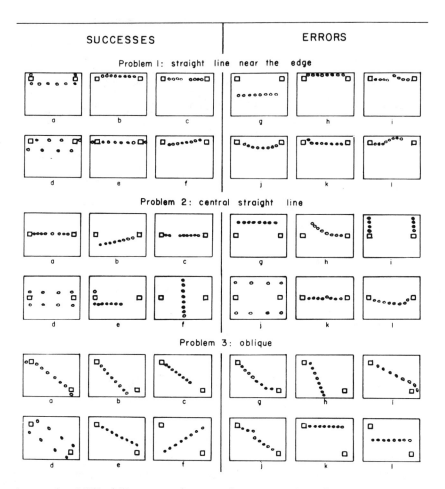

A test of a child's ability to use the mental representation of projective geometry. Subjects were asked to solve three problems. In each case, the two small squares indicate the position of the miniature houses on a rectangular piece of plywood. Subjects were instructed to construct a straight line of eight lampposts connecting the two houses. This figure shows examples of responses considered to be successes and errors in the solution of each of the three problems. [From Laurendeau and Pinard, 1970. Used with permission.]

The second of the five tests is intended to probe children's ability to use the mental representations of projective geometry, by asking them to construct straight lines. The test consists of presenting to the child a board on which two "houses" (squares) are placed. The child receives eight lampposts and is asked to construct a straight "street" between the two houses, by forming the lampposts into a straight line that connects the two houses. The houses are placed in three different positions, so that the straight line connecting them correctly would run near the edge of the board, or through the center of the board, or obliquely across the board. The nature of the wrong answers shows how much difficulty children have in constructing a straight line. As in the case of the first test, the results of the second test could be interpreted in terms of four stages. In stage 0, children refuse to participate, are unable to understand the test, or are unable to construct even a curved or twisting line connecting the houses. Here too, more than half the children tested had passed out of stage 0 by the age of 2, but as judged by this test not until the age of 5 were all of them beyond it. In stage 1, the children are able to connect the houses in a topologically correct manner, but the connecting lines are never straight. The typical age of accession of this stage lies between the ages of 2 and 3. In stage 2, the children are able to connect the houses with straight lines, if the connecting lines are parallel to the edge of the board, but not if the lines have to be oblique. The typical age of accession for this stage lies between the ages of 3 and 5. Finally, in stage 3, the children are able to construct straight connecting lines even if the lines have to be oblique. The typical age of accession for this stage lies between the ages of 5 and 8. The result of this second test thus lends further support to Piaget's dogma, by showing that stage 2 of stereognosis (ability to distinguish topological features and to distinguish curvilinear from rectilinear contours) is reached before stage 3 of straight-line construction which, in turn, is reached before stage 3 of stereognosis (ability to distinguish metric features).

The third of the five tests is intended to assess the capacity for localization of topographical positions on duplicate maps. It seeks to verify the topological character of the child's first spatial representations. In this test, the child is presented with two duplicate versions of a miniature landscape. The landscape consists of a road and a railroad track, which cross near the center and divide the landscape into four sections of differing shapes and sizes. The landscape also includes five toy houses that are easily distinguishable by size or color. The examiner places a toy man at a series of spots on one of the duplicate versions of the landscape and asks the child to place another toy man in the exactly corresponding spot on the other version. The test has two sections. In the first, the duplicate landscapes are placed side by side; in the second, they are rotated by 180 degrees with respect to each other. In the second section, the task is, of course, more difficult. A spread in the ability to perform this task, as characterized by four successive stages, is observed from ages 3 to 12.

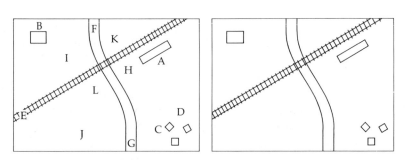

Miniature landscapes of the localization of topographical positions test. The rectangular figures represent the houses; the letters indicated in the left-hand landscape designate the successive positions that the examiner asks the subject to locate in the right-hand landscape. [From Laurendeau and Pinard, 1970. Used with permission.]

As before, in stage 0, children refuse to cooperate or do not understand the instructions. In stage 1, children make many errors in placement, and the nature of the errors indicates that the children are seeking purely topological solutions for the position of the man (i.e., the neighborhood of his placement), while completely ignoring its projective and metric aspects. In stage 2 (typical age of accession: 3 to 6 years), children are able to establish the spatial orientation of the placement of the toy with respect to their own bodies, as expressed by such projective relations as left–right and before–behind. Finally, in stage 3 (typical age of accession: 7 to 10 years), children free themselves of their own point of view and locate the correct placement.

The fourth test is intended to probe the child's ability to differentiate between right and left. This distinction is an integral part of the projective representation of space about which many adults remain confused, and which quite definitely depends on the use of language. The test is divided into three sections. In the first section the examiner sits next to the child and asks the child to point out his or her own right hand, left leg, right ear, left hand, right leg, and left ear. In the second section, the examiner sits opposite the child and asks the child to point out these same appendages on the examiner, in a different order. In the third section, the examiner places three objects on the table, and questions the child about their relative right–left locations, both while the objects can still be seen and after they have been removed from the child's view. The results of this test are interpreted to mean that after the children have passed out of the noncooperation, noncomprehension stage 0, they reach stage 1 (typical age of accession: 4 to 6 years), in which the terms *left* and *right* refer to body parts located on the same side and to the position of external objects relative to their bodies. But they cannot apply these concepts to spatial relations between external objects. Upon reaching stage 2 (typical age of accession: 6 to 8 years), the children can apply the concepts of right and left to relations between external objects, but the designation of which side is which still refers to their own bodies, i.e., is still subjective. Only upon reaching stage 3 (typical age of accession: 9 to 11 years) are the children able to provide an objective assignment of the designations of sideness to external objects, with reference to the body of another person.

The fifth test assesses the children's ability to coordinate perspective. The subjects are presented with a board on which are placed three cones of different colors and sizes, representing mountains. They are also shown a set of nine sketched scenes, which reproduce nine different perspectives in miniature of the mountainscape. [Two of them are impossible, given the actual positions of the mountains.] The examiner asks the children two types of questions. For the first type, the examiner places a toy man in various places on the board and asks (for each place) which of the sketched scenes corresponds exactly to the little man's perspective. For the second type of question, the examiner points to one of the sketched scenes and asks from which place on the board the toy man would see it. This test requires a mental operation of a very high order: namely, putting oneself mentally in a different place, and forming a conception of space in one's mind in order to be able to identify another person's point of view.

The results of this fifth test are also interpreted in terms of four stages. After the children pass out of stage 0 of noncooperation or noncomprehension, they reach stage 1 (typical age of accession: 6 to 8 years) of complete egocentrism. Here the children almost always choose the sketched scene corresponding to their own position rather than that of the toy man in response to the first type of question. Similarly, in response to the second type of question, they place the toy man in the position on the board that corresponds to their own perspective rather than to the sketched scene to which the examiner points. Upon reaching stage 2, the stage of "partial decentration" (typical age of accession: 8 to 12 years), the children show the beginnings of the capacity to conceptualize a perspective other than their own. However, they are not yet entirely free of the egocentrism of the preceding stage, and their answers to both types of questions reflect a continual oscillation between egocentric and "decentered" behavior. Only upon reaching stage 3 of "operational coordination" do the children master all the projective relations involved in

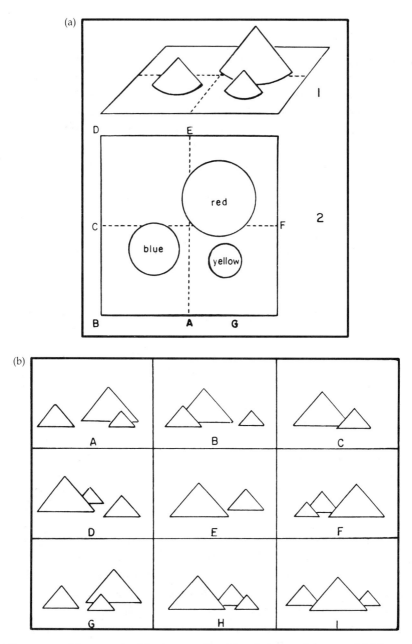

Placement of "mountains" in the coordination of perspectives test. (a) The three cones (representing mountains) are seen from the front in 1 and from above in 2. (b) A set of 9 pictures, showing various perspectives of the mountain scene, from which the subject is asked to choose the correct one in this test. The capital letters A, B, C, D, E, F, and G indicate the positions in panel a for which the correspondingly lettered picture in panel b represents a correct representation of the perspective view. The toy man is successively placed at positions F, C, and B. Drawings H and I are impossible views. [From Laurendeau and Pinard, 1970. Used with permission.]

this test. They are able to recognize the picture that corresponds exactly to the toy man's perspective and their explanations contain explicit references to all the left–right and before–behind relations that define the positions of the mountains, each in relation to the other two, and all three in relation to the toy man. By the age of 12, only 40% of the children tested had actually reached stage 3, which indicates the difficulty of the intellectual task required by this test.

Taken as a whole, the results of Laurendeau and Pinard's tests appear to support Piaget's dogma that children acquire their spatial concepts via an orderly procession of stages, in which the acquisition of topological notions precedes the acquisition of projective notions, which, in turn, precedes the acquisition of metric notions. But when the implications of that dogma are examined in more detail, the agreement between observations and theory is much less satisfactory. In particular, the results do not confirm Piaget's original claim that there is a *general* "topological" period in the development of children's spacial concepts—that is to say, a period during which their representation of space is obtained exclusively from the qualitative relations—such as neighborhood, enclosure, or continuity—inherent in each object or particular configuration. Similarly the results do not confirm another key notion of Piaget's, namely that there is a *general* period of "egocentrism" during which children are unable to differentiate subject from object and confuse the infinitely varied aspects presented to the subject by the external world. As is evident from the data presented here, the age of accession to each of the developmental stages is different for each of the tests. That is to say, whether children have or have not transcended the "topological" or the "egocentric" period depends on the nature and difficulty of the task with which they are confronted. These data are complemented by the findings of other investigators who have similarly found that the stage of cognitive development—"preoperational", "concrete operational", and "formal operational"—to which a child is assigned varies with the nature and familiarity of the task, the manner in which it is presented by the experimenter, and the kind of language in which it is couched.

How *could* a child be in one general stage of cognitive development in one context and in another stage in another context? To overcome the threat posed by these empirical findings to the logical structure of his theory, Piaget and his followers have invoked the idea of *décalage*. *Décalage* envisages the possibility that accession to a particular stage of cognition may occur sooner in some situations than in others, thus raising doubts about the structural integrity of each stage. The notion of *décalage* may be correct, but it greatly weakens the predictive power of Piagetian developmental theory.

Nevertheless, there can be little doubt that our spatial concepts develop in childhood by way of an adaptation to the world in which we live. Thus it appears that the concepts of projective geometry are an adaptation to a visual surround in which light propagates in straight lines and that the concepts of metric (Euclidean) geometry are an adaptation to an environment rich in rigid objects. In fact, Einstein had already reached similar conclusions, although he did not express them in terms of evolutionary adaptations. He thought that geometric notions arise in the child as individually learned ideas, upon seeing light propagated in a straight line and experiencing rigid bodies with fixed shapes. Einstein was not aware of Konrad Lorenz's proposal that ideas could also be learned by a species in evolution. Certainly the cognitive capability that permits man to analyze space in geometric terms must, to a large extent, be evolutionarily derived. We will explore the space–time–causality scheme of thought in more detail when we take up physics, but before we do so, we shall consider mathematics and logic.

REFERENCES

Laurendeau, M., and A. Pinard. 1970. *The Development of the Concept of Space in the Child.* New York: International University Press.

McCloskey, M. 1983. Intuitive physics. *Scientific American* 248(4): 114–123.

Eleven

Numbers

To conduct our inquiry into the nature of truth and reality, we adopted the point of view that cognition constitutes an evolutionary adaptation of the human species for dealing with the real world. We saw that the concepts with which we structure our experience and hence come to know the world are derived as much from the genes with which evolution has endowed our species as they are from our individual human experience. Moreover, these concepts are inextricably intertwined. We will now examine these adaptive concepts more closely, to try to understand their epistemological relation to the real world. We begin with the numbers, the keystones of the edifice of mathematics.

We will encounter various kinds of numbers. The simplest and most fundamental kind of number is represented by the *natural* numbers, such as 1, 2, 3, which are used for counting objects. A second kind comprises the *integers*, which include the natural numbers, as well as zero and negative numbers, such as $-3, -2, -1, 0, 1, 2, 3$. The third kind is the *rational* numbers, which include the integers as well as all numbers, such as ½ and ⅔, that are expressible as ratios of integers. The theory of integers and rational numbers is usually called arithmetic, while the branch of mathematics known as analysis addresses the theory of yet other kinds of numbers. One of those other kinds, the *real* numbers, comprises rational numbers as well as *irrational* numbers, such as $\sqrt{2}$ and π (the ratio of the circumference of a circle to its diameter), which are not expressible as ratios of integers. The analytical relation between rational and irrational numbers was clarified by Richard Dedekind in 1858 in the following way.

Dedekind considered the real numbers as points on a line, and he cut this line at a point corresponding to the number x. Dedekind's cut at x divides the *rational* numbers on the line into two sets, such that every rational number in one set (the L-set) is less than any rational number in the other set (the R-set). Then x is itself a rational number if x is either the largest rational number of the L-set or the smallest rational number of the R-set. But if x is an irrational number, then the L-set has no largest and the R-set has no smallest rational number. For instance, if Dedekind's cut is made at $x = \sqrt{2}$, then the L-set comprises all positive rational numbers whose square is less than 2, of which there is no largest, and the R-set comprises all positive rational numbers whose square exceeds 2, of which there is no smallest. Analysis is concerned also with *complex* numbers, each of which is described by a pair of real numbers (indicative of a displacement in a plane), of which one, the "imaginary" member of the pair, is multiplied by $\sqrt{-1}$ and then added to the other.

As we saw in chapter 9, the concept of natural number arises in children as they gain the ability to perform the concrete operation of construction of equivalent sets. In this operation the elements of one set are paired off with the elements of another set: candies here with candies there, dolls with umbrellas, flowers with vases, and so on. To perform this operation it is necessary to be able to disregard the identity of individual objects, as reflected in their shape, their size, their quality, and especially their spatial arrangement. This ability, taken together with the ability to order objects according to their spatial relations, suffices for mastery of the operations on which the theory of numbers is based.

Once the equivalence and the ordering of sets has been grasped during the concrete operational period, the addition $a + b = s$ is understood as the union of two sets, a and b, and the subtraction $s - a = b$ as the reversal of this operation. The commutative rule of addition, $a + b = s = b + a$, becomes manifest by interchanging the relative position of the two sets, whose elements are arbitrarily ordered. The transitive rule of equivalence, i.e., that if $a = b$ and $b = c$, then $a = c$, is similarly manifest. However, negative numbers are not yet understood in the concrete operational period. Subtraction as the reversal of addition is therefore a formal rather than concrete operation. Similarly, the multiplication $a \times b$ may be understood in terms of the concept of sets, as the union of b equivalent a sets. It is also easy to see why multiplication is commutative; $a \times b = b \times a$ since both sides of the equation correspond merely to two different ways of ordering the same set.

The ordering of sets to handle numbers is closely linked to spatial concepts. But such ordering does not necessarily invoke either metric

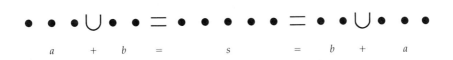

$$a \quad + \quad b \quad = \quad s \quad = \quad b \quad + \quad a$$

The commutativity of addition.

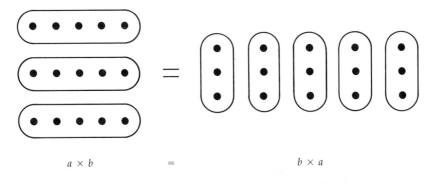

$$a \times b \quad = \quad b \times a$$

The commutativity of multiplication.

Euclidean or projective geometry, since it does not call for a firm order. Only a very loose ordering is required to concede the rule of commutativity, although there is a limit to how loose the ordering can be. For instance, a blind fish that lives in a fluid environment and cannot see straight lines might have some difficulty conceiving of even the loosest ordering and consequently might not accept the rule of the commutativity of multiplication. Ordering sets might also be troublesome for the mouse, which has poor vision, depends primarily on tactile and olfactory cues, and lives in a topologically restricted environment, such as underground burrows. In such a non-Euclidean and complicated space the mouse would have difficulty evolving the number concept and theories concerning the handling of numbers. In any case, as Konrad Lorenz pointed out, it is possible to imagine that other rational beings might not quantify their world by means of numbers in the same way that we do.

One can also arrive at the distributivity rule $a(b + c) = ab + ac$ via spatial concepts. For this purpose, one forms the union of the multiplicative sets $a \times b$ and $a \times c$ and shows that they can be transformed by

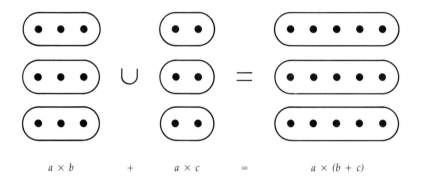

$$a \times b \qquad + \qquad a \times c \qquad = \qquad a \times (b + c)$$

The distributivity rule.

a concrete operation into $a \times (b + c)$. Finally, spatial concepts also lead to the associative rule $(ab)c = a(bc)$, although in this case a three-dimensional representation of the sets is required to show their equivalence.

These equivalence rules about numbers are accepted as being valid for all positive integers, that is to say for an infinite set. However, there are hazards in accepting an equivalence rule for an infinite set. It seems quite innocuous to accept such a rule as long as we are working with fives and threes, but might it not get us into trouble once we start considering very large numbers? We will take up the problems arising from dealing with infinite sets in the next chapter.

Let us now consider the operation that is the reverse of the multiplication of integers, namely factoring. To ask whether an integer is decomposable into factors amounts to asking whether the set corresponding to that integer can be viewed as a union of several (i.e., two or more) sets containing more than one element per set. Empirically we find that some integers can be so decomposed and others cannot. The nondecomposable integers are called *prime numbers*: 2, 3, 5, 7, 11, and so forth. This set of numbers seems very erratic and clearly thins out as one considers larger and larger numbers.

Many questions can be asked about primes. One such question is whether the set of prime numbers is finite. Is there a largest prime number p_n? The answer is "no," as is shown by the following indirect proof found in Book IX of Euclid's *Elements*, Proposition 20. Assume that there is a largest prime number p_n. Then form the product of all the prime numbers and add 1 to this product. The resulting number,

$$N = p_1 p_2 p_3 \ldots p_n + 1,$$

is not divisible by any of the prime numbers equal to or smaller than p_n, since N divided by any of them leaves a remainder of 1. Thus either N is a prime number larger than p_n, or, if N is not a prime number, then there must exist a prime number larger than p_n and smaller than N that divides N without remainder. The initial assumption that there is a *largest* prime p_n is therefore false, and hence the set of prime numbers is infinite. (It is not known for certain whether Euclid is the originator of this brilliant proof, since Euclid was essentially a compiler of the mathematics known at his time, and earlier sources have been found for many of the propositions in his books. However, according to B. L. van der Waerden, no earlier source has been located for this particular proof.)

How good is this proof actually? If someone presented a number p_n claiming it to be the largest prime number, how would we go about disproving this claim empirically? First, we must show that p_n is indeed a prime number. If it is, and we construct N, as in the proof, we may find that N is not in fact, a prime number after all. The number $p_6 = 13$ is the smallest prime for which this is the case: $2 \cdot 3 \cdot 5 \cdot 7 \cdot 11 \cdot 13 + 1 = 30031$, which is divisible by 59 and 509, which *are* prime numbers. All that we can be certain of is that there must exist another prime number between the putative largest prime number p_n and the number N. So even after constructing N, we must perform a search for the extant prime number that is larger than the putative largest, but the search may now be performed within the finite set of numbers ranging from p_n to N. As of March 4, 1971, the largest known prime number was $2^{19937} - 1$, a number with 6002 decimal digits. (Editors' note: By the end of 1983, five larger prime numbers of the form $2^m - 1$ had been found, the largest being $2^{132,049} - 1$, which has 39,751 decimal digits.)

Another question that can be asked about prime numbers is whether the sequence of numbers, which we will call E (for Euclid), where E_k is the product of the first k primes plus 1, comprises a finite number of prime numbers. In other words, even if there is no largest prime number p_n, is there a largest number E_n that is a prime? We already saw that $E_6 = 2 \cdot 3 \cdot 5 \cdot 7 \cdot 11 \cdot 13 + 1 = 30031$, being decomposable into 59×509, is the first E number in the sequence that is not a prime. The largest *known* prime in this sequence is $E_{11} = 200,560,490,131$. Beyond that, up to E_{60}, the sequence contains no other primes. (Editors' note: Since Delbrück gave these lectures, three more Euclid primes have been found: E_{75}, E_{171}, and E_{172}.) Whether there is a largest prime in the E sequence remains for the number theorists of the future to determine.

Let us continue considering the *composite numbers*, as decomposable (i.e., nonprime) numbers greater than 1 are called. If we decompose a

E_1 $= 2 + 1 = 3$ (prime)
E_2 $= 2 \cdot 3 + 1 = 7$ (prime)
E_3 $= 2 \cdot 3 \cdot 5 + 1 = 31$ (prime)
E_4 $= 2 \cdot 3 \cdot 5 \cdot 7 + 1 = 211$ (prime)
E_5 $= 2 \cdot 3 \cdot 5 \cdot 7 \cdot 11 + 1 = 2{,}311$ (prime)
E_6 $= 2 \cdot 3 \cdot 5 \cdot 7 \cdot 11 \cdot 13 + 1 = 30{,}031 = 59 \times 509$
E_7 $= 2 \cdot 3 \cdot 5 \cdot 7 \cdot 11 \cdot 13 \cdot 17 + 1 = 510{,}511 = 19 \times 97 \times 277$
E_8 $= 2 \cdot 3 \cdot 5 \cdot 7 \cdot 11 \cdot 13 \cdot 17 \cdot 19 + 1 = 9{,}699{,}691 = 347 \times 27{,}953$
E_9 $= 2 \cdot 3 \cdot 5 \cdot 7 \cdot 11 \cdot 13 \cdot 17 \cdot 19 \cdot 23 + 1 = 223{,}092{,}871 = 317 \times 703{,}763$
E_{10} $= 2 \cdot 3 \cdot 5 \cdot 7 \cdot 11 \cdot 13 \cdot 17 \cdot 19 \cdot 23 \cdot 29 + 1 = 6{,}469{,}693{,}231 = 331 \times 571 \times 34{,}231$
E_{11} $= 2 \cdot 3 \cdot 5 \cdot 7 \cdot 11 \cdot 13 \cdot 17 \cdot 19 \cdot 23 \cdot 29 \cdot 31 + 1 = 200{,}560{,}490{,}131$ (prime)
E_{12} $= 2 \cdot 3 \cdot 5 \cdot 7 \cdot 11 \cdot 13 \cdot 17 \cdot 19 \cdot 23 \cdot 29 \cdot 31 \cdot 37 + 1 = 7{,}420{,}738{,}134{,}811$
$= 181 \times 60{,}611 \times 676{,}421$

The derivation of Euclid primes.

composite number, the decomposition may be further decomposed, and a tree of factors is generated. For example, if n is 140, we can decompose it into the factors 2×70. Two is a prime and hence not subject to further decomposition. But 70 can be further decomposed into the factors 2×35, and 35 can be further decomposed into the factors 5×7. Every branch of the tree eventually ends in a prime number. We can reassemble the prime number factors at the ends of the branches, collect like factors, and represent n as a product of primes raised to given powers:

$$n = p_1^{\alpha_{p_1}} \cdot p_2^{\alpha_{p_2}} \cdot p_3^{\alpha_{p_3}} \cdot \ \ldots p_k^{\alpha_{p_k}}$$

where $p_1 = 2$ (the first prime), $p_2 = 3$ (the second prime), $p_3 = 5$ (the third prime), and so on. In the case of our example, $n = 140 = 2^2 \cdot 3^0 \cdot 5^1 \cdot 7^1$. Alternatively, we can say that the exponents α_{p_i} form a sequence of numbers associated with the sequence of prime numbers. The numbers in the α_{p_i} sequence can be either zero or positive integers. By stipulating that its prime number factors are to be arranged in ascending order, we can express any composite number by listing only the finite sequence of positive α exponents of its prime number factors. Hence the number 140 can be expressed as the sequence 2, 0, 1, 1. The sequence of composite numbers is thus represented as a *number-theoretic function,* the domain of which consists of the prime numbers and the range of which is the set of the nonnegative integers.

We can now ask whether there is only one decomposition into prime numbers for every composite number. In other words, is this representation unique when written in the stipulated, or standard form? Or is it possible for a number to be the product of two distinct primes and also

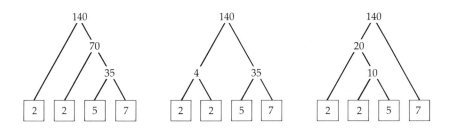

Decomposition of a composite number into prime numbers.

of two other distinct primes? It is not! This proposition that there is only one decomposition for every composite number, is called the fundamental theorem of arithmetic, and is taught to every schoolchild. However, its proof is so universally unknown that most adults do not even know that it requires proof. The earliest known statement of the fundamental theorem is found in Euclid, though the first proof that clearly recognized all the key issues was given at the turn of the nineteenth century by Carl Friedrich Gauss, one of the greatest mathematicians of all time. Gauss showed that the fundamental theorem of arithmetic is equivalent to the statement: "If a prime p divides the product of two numbers A and B, then either p divides A or p divides B, or both." This statement is called Gauss's lemma, since Gauss used it in his proof of the fundamental theorem of arithmetic. But Gauss's proof is not generally known because it is somewhat complex, certainly too complex to be imposed on children when they first encounter the theorem.

Let us consider a much simpler proof, which was discovered in 1930, 2000 years after Euclid. It was found by Ernst Zermelo, a mathematician who contributed greatly to the clarification of the foundations of mathematics. It is an indirect proof and operates by reverse induction, in that it does not go from the number n, for which the theorem has been shown to be true, to $n + 1$, but proceeds from n to a smaller number. This type of indirect proof by downward induction is called the "method of descent," and was introduced into number theory by the seventeenth century mathematician Pierre de Fermat. It generates a terminating series, and therefore a finite number of induction steps. We first assume that the fundamental theorem is wrong, that is, that there is at least one number (greater than 1) with more than one standard decomposition. From this assumption it follows that there must be a *smallest* number n with two distinct standard decompositions. In accord with our assumption, let n be equal to the product of two different sets of primes, that is, have one decomposition $p_1 \cdot p_2 \cdot p_3 \cdot p_4 \cdot p_5 \cdot \ldots \cdot p_k$, which we abbreviate as $p_1 \times P$, and another decomposition $q_1 \cdot q_2 \cdot q_3 \cdot q_4 \cdot \ldots \cdot q_r$, which we abbreviate as $q_1 \times Q$. Since n is the smallest positive integer with two distinct decompositions, we know that all the ps are distinct from all the qs. (If some of the ps *were* equal to some of the qs, then we could divide both decompositions by their common factors and obtain a smaller value of n. We know $n > 3$, since it is easy to verify that 1, 2, and 3 have unique decompositions.) We will arrive at a contradiction by constructing a positive integer smaller than n that, contrary to our assumption that n is the smallest such number, also has two distinct decompositions.

Since by our assumption $p_1 \neq q_1$, let p_1 be smaller than q_1, in which case P must be larger than Q. We now define $n' = n - p_1 Q$, which is n, the original number, minus the first factor of one decomposition times the second factor of the other decomposition. Since $p_1 < q_1$ and $Q < P$, we are subtracting from n a number smaller than n, and thus the number n' is positive, and smaller than n. We substitute from one decomposition $p_1 P$ for n, so that $n' = p_1(P - Q)$. From the other decomposition we substitute $q_1 Q$ for n so that $n' = (q_1 - p_1)Q$. The first of these representations of n' contains p_1 as a prime in the decomposition of n'. The second of these representations of n', however, does *not* contain p_1 as a factor, since Q does not contain p_1 as a factor and, p_1 and q_1 being prime numbers greater than 1, $q_1 - p_1 \neq p_1$. Thus, n' also has two distinct decompositions, and the assumption that n is the *smallest* composite number with two distinct decompositions is false. Hence there can be *no* composite number with two distinct decompositions.

Another question that can be asked about prime numbers is how they thin out as one considers sets of increasingly larger numbers. In about 1800 Gauss had found empirically that $\pi(x)$, the number of primes not exceeding x, is approximately equal to $(x/\log x)$. Thus the density of prime numbers, given by $\pi(x)/x$, is approximately $1/\log x$ and thus becomes ever-smaller, that is, the primes thin out, as x increases. In 1737 Leonhard Euler had already observed the following identity of the "Zeta function"

$$\zeta(s) = \sum_{n=1}^{\infty} \frac{1}{n^s} = \prod_{\text{all primes}} \left(1 - \frac{1}{p^s}\right)^{-1}$$

which relates a sum over all positive integers n to a product over all primes p, and he even used this relationship to give a new proof that the set of primes is infinite. But the remarkable properties of the Zeta function were discovered only in 1859, when Georg Friedrich Bernhard Riemann showed that there is a connection between the set of values of s

for which the Zeta function has the value zero and the distribution function $\pi(x)$ of the prime numbers, provided that s is regarded as a complex number of the form $s = \sigma + it$, where σ and t are real numbers and $i = \sqrt{-1}$. (Euler had considered only the case where s is a real number greater than 1.)

Riemann found that the sum and product expressions for the Zeta function $\zeta(s)$ converge (i.e., have a finite value) only when σ, the real part of s, is greater than 1. However, Riemann extended the definition of $\zeta(s)$ to apply to all values of σ and t, that is, to the entire plane of complex numbers, by a process known as analytic continuation. For the range of s where its real part lies between 0 and 1, that is, where $0 \leq \sigma \leq 1$ (the most interesting region of the Zeta function, called the "critical strip"), Riemann observed that the *alternating* sum

$$\eta(s) = \frac{1}{1^s} - \frac{1}{2^s} + \frac{1}{3^s} - \frac{1}{4^s} + \frac{1}{5^s} - \frac{1}{6^s} + \cdots$$

converges, and that

$$\eta(s) = (1 - 2^{1-s})\zeta(s)$$

because

$$(1 - 2^{1-s})\zeta(s) = \zeta(s) - 2 \cdot \frac{1}{2^s} - \zeta(s) = \left(\frac{1}{1^s} + \frac{1}{2^s} + \frac{1}{3^s} + \frac{1}{4^s} + \frac{1}{5^s} + \cdots\right)$$

$$- 2\left(\frac{1}{2^s} + \frac{1}{4^s} + \frac{1}{6^s} + \cdots\right) = \frac{1}{1^s} - \frac{1}{2^s} + \frac{1}{3^s} - \frac{1}{4^s} + \frac{1}{5^s} - \frac{1}{6^s} + \cdots = \eta(s).$$

In this way, the function $\eta(s)$ can be used to extend the definition of $\zeta(s)$ to that half of the complex plane where σ, the real part of s, is positive. For the other half of the complex plane, where σ is negative, Riemann discovered the "functional equation" of the Zeta function:

$$\zeta(s) = \{2^s \pi^{s-1} \sin(\pi s/2)\Gamma(1-s)\} \zeta(1-s)$$

where the "Gamma function" $\Gamma(1-s)$ is given by

$$\Gamma(1-s) = \lim_{n\to\infty} \frac{1 \cdot 2 \cdot 3 \cdot \ldots (n-1)}{(1-s)(2-s)\ldots(1+n-s)} n^{(1-s)}$$

This equation indicates a symmetry between $\zeta(s)$ and $\zeta(1 - s)$, with the symmetry axis being the line for which $\sigma = \frac{1}{2}$, called the "critical line." The only singularity of the Zeta function, the point at which it has no defined value in the entire complex plane, lies at $s = 1$, since here the sum $\sum\limits_{n=1}^{\infty} \frac{1}{n}$ diverges.

Riemann now showed that those complex values of s for which $\zeta(s) = 0$, referred to as the "zeros of the Zeta function," are crucial for the study of the distribution function $\pi(x)$ of the prime numbers. As it turns out, all the zeros of $\zeta(s)$ lie in the critical strip $(0 \leqslant \sigma \leqslant 1)$, except for certain "trivial" zeros of $\zeta(s)$, when s is equal to the negative even integers. From this fact, and from an additional theorem stating that *on* the line $\sigma = 1$ there are no zeros of the Zeta function, it is possible to prove (with some difficulty) the prime number theorem. This theorem asserts that for the density of prime numbers $\pi(x)/(x)$ it is true that

$$\lim_{x \to \infty} \frac{\pi(x)}{x/\log x} = 1$$

Thus the prime number theorem is a more precise statement of Gauss's empirical finding that the density of primes is approximately $1/\log x$. Riemann attempted to prove this theorem in 1859, but his proof was incomplete because he resorted to a conjecture about the Zeta function. Riemann knew that the farther from the line $\sigma = 1$ is the zone of the critical strip to which the zeros of $\zeta(s)$ are confined, the more regular will be the distribution of the primes. And so Riemann put forward the Riemann hypothesis, still unproven, which states that *all* the zeros of $\zeta(s)$ lie *on* the critical line $\sigma = \frac{1}{2}$. (Riemann reported that he gave up trying to prove his hypothesis after a few casual attempts; when I showed his statement to that effect to my Caltech colleague Richard Feynman, Feynman said "I bet he worked like hell to prove it!") It is now known that there is an infinite number of zeros of $\zeta(s)$ within the critical strip. And a computer search has shown that at least the first 17,000,000 of them (proceeding through positive values of t from $t = 0$) do lie on the critical line. In 1974 Norman Levinson proved that more than one-third of the zeros of $\zeta(s)$ in the critical strip lie on the critical line.

In any case, the prime number theorem was proven in 1896, independently by Jacques Hadamard and by C. de la Vallée-Poussin, who used less information about the Zeta function than is embodied in the unproven

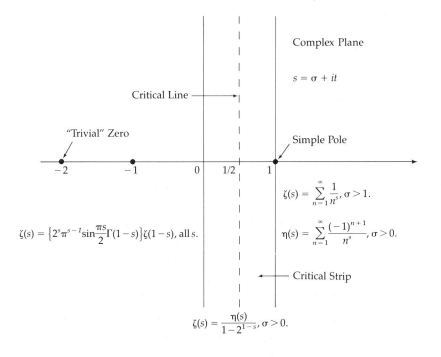

The Riemann hypothesis. All the nonreal zeros of the Zeta function, $\zeta(s)$, lie on the "critical line," $\sigma = \frac{1}{2}$.

Riemann hypothesis. And by 1948 A. Selberg and P. Erdös had found a proof of the prime number theorem that avoids altogether the use of the Zeta function and the theory of functions of complex variables. It should be noted that the prime number theorem gives the *average* density of primes in any region, but not the location of any specific prime. Moreover, it is a consequence of the prime number theorem that the Euclid Number E_k is approximately equal to k^k.

When I was a student in Göttingen, there appeared a story in the newspaper about a rabbit that had been frozen and then brought back to life. Although the report of this cryogenic feat was probably a sensationalist fabrication, someone was inspired by this story to ask various people what they would ask about if they had been frozen for 500 years and then revived. The mathematician David Hilbert replied, "It's obvious! You ask whether all the zeros of Riemann's Zeta function lie on the critical line!" A member of the Caltech Mathematics Department composed the following lyrics for a Riemann hypothesis song:

WHERE ARE THE ZEROS OF ZETA OF *s*?
(sung to the tune of "Sweet Betsy from Pike")

Where are the zeros of Zeta of *s*?
G. F. B. Riemann has made a good guess,
They're all on the critical line, said he
And their density's one over $2\pi \log t$.

This statement of Riemann's has been like a trigger,
And many good men, with vim and with vigor,
Have attempted to find, with mathematical rigor,
What happens to Zeta as mod *t* gets bigger.

The names of Landau and Bohr and Cramér,
And Hardy and Littlewood and Titchmarch are there,
In spite of their efforts and skill and finesse,
In locating the zeros no one's had success.

In 1914 G. H. Hardy did find,
An infinite number that lie on the line,
His theorem, however, won't rule out the case,
That there might be a zero at some other place.

Let *P* be the function π minus $1i$,
The order of *P* is not known for *x* high,
If square root of *x* times $\log x$ we could show,
Then Riemann's conjecture would surely be so.

Related to this is another enigma,
Concerning the Lindelof function $\mu(\sigma)$
Which measures the growth in the critical strip,
And on the number of zeros it gives us a grip.

But nobody knows how this function behaves,
Convexity tells us it can have no waves,
Lindelof said that the shape of its graph,
Is constant when sigma is more than one-half.

Oh, where are the zeros of Zeta of *s*?
We must know exactly, we cannot just guess,
In order to strengthen the prime-number theorem,
The path of integration must not get too near 'em.

Tom Apostal

Several methods exist for finding prime numbers. One of them is the sieve of Eratosthenes. One eliminates all even numbers, then all numbers divisible by three, then all multiples of five, and so on, and after eliminating all composite numbers, one is left with prime numbers. There is a little ditty (of unknown source) summarizing what this procedure is all about:

> Strike the two's and strike the three's
> The Sieve of Eratosthenes!
> When you use this way sublime
> The numbers that are left are prime.

Another method of finding primes stems from a 1976 paper by J. P. Jones and colleagues. This paper presented a polynomial of degree 25 in 26 variables, for which it was claimed that the set of positive values of this function is identical to the set of primes. However, from the point of view of applied mathematics, this function is a snare and a delusion: it is difficult to derive even a single prime from it, since the vast majority of the values of the function are negative. The rare positive values can be found only by solving a system of 14 simultaneous equations in 26 variables! This polynomial thus joins a distinguished list of formulas that either test primality (i.e., the quality of being a prime number) or generate prime numbers but are essentially useless for practical computation. Euler's early contribution to this list is the formula $n^2 - n + 41$, which mysteriously does yield only prime numbers for $n = 1,2,3,4,5, \ldots, 40$, but obviously generates a composite number for $n = 41$.

The sieve of Eratosthenes. To find all primes up to x, it suffices to cross off all multiples of the primes up to $\sqrt{x}$. To find all primes up to 120, cross off the multiples of 2 and 3 (horizontal lines), of 5 (upward diagonals), and of 7 (downward diagonals). The survivors are the primes 2, 3, 5, 7, 11, 13, 17, 19, 23, 29, 31, 37, 41, 43, 47, 53, 59, 61, 67, 71, 73, 79, 83, 89, 97, 101, 103, 107, 109, 113.

There are, in fact, much faster tests than the sieve of Eratosthenes to determine whether a given number p is a prime. Nearly all of these tests are based on Fermat's "little" theorem, which asserts that $a^p - a$ is a multiple of p, whenever p is a prime, for all integers a. Unfortunately, $a^p - a$ is occasionally divisible by p for one or more values of a when p is *not* a prime, which adds considerable complexity to these tests.

The minimal rules of the operations on numbers, which form the basis of arithmetic studied by children in elementary school (but are presumably hard to intuit in the world of fish and mice), were codified by Giuseppe Peano in 1899 in the form of the following five postulates:

1. Zero is a number.

2. The successor of any number is a number.

3. There are no two numbers with the same successor.

4. Zero is not the successor of any number.

5. Every property of zero also belonging to the successor of any number that has the property, belongs to all numbers.

From these five postulates the immense structure of number theory has been developed.

REFERENCES

Dudley, U. 1983. Formulas for primes. *Mathematics Magazine* 56: 17–22.

Guy, R. K. 1983. Conway's prime producing machine. *Mathematics Magazine* 56: 26–33.

Jones, J. P., D. Sato, H. Wada, and D. Wiens. 1976. Diophantine representation of the set of prime numbers. *American Mathematical Monthly* 38: 449–464.

Levinson, N. 1974. At least one-third of the zeros of Riemann's zeta-function are on $\sigma = \frac{1}{2}$. *Proceedings of the National Academy of Science USA* 71: 1013–1015.

Pomerance, C. 1982. The search for prime numbers. *Scientific American* 247(6): 136–147.

Tuckerman, B. 1971. The 24th Mersenne prime. *Proceedings of the National Academy of Science USA* 68: 2319–2320.

Twelve

Infinity; Logical Paradoxes

To continue with our examination of mathematics, we will consider the concept of infinity. When it is encountered in childhood, infinity is an exciting, disturbing, even frightening notion. The realization that there is no largest number, that one can always add 1 to any number and obtain a larger number, is a dizzying thought to children when they first appreciate it. There also comes the realization that space itself is not finite, in that there is always more space beyond any given space. And is time infinite, or does the world have a fixed beginning and a fixed end? Nearly every known culture deals with this question in its myths. What about matter? Is it infinitely divisible? To this question the Greeks replied "no," putting forward the notion of indivisible elementary particles, or atoms. What about motion? Does it correspond to displacement across an infinite number of spatial positions? Does an arrow moving from point A to point B pass through an infinite number of intermediate points? In that case, how could it ever reach point B within a finite time interval? The pitfalls of this argument, known as Zeno's paradox, were discussed by Aristotle.

Galileo, in his *Dialogue on Two New Sciences,* provides a marvelous discussion of the infinity concept. Galileo's discussion was summarized in modern terminology by Dedekind, in a definition that brings out one of the most disturbing features of infinity: An infinite set is a set that is equivalent to one of its proper subsets, where *equivalent* means that each element of one set can be paired off with an element of the other set. This definition confronts us with the anti-intuitive character of infinity:

the idea that a part may be equal to the whole violates our intuition about the world, running counter to our thinking as represented by concrete operations. It is a warning that when considering infinity we must be prepared to run into bizarre situations that strain our demands for intuitive reasonableness and may even require us to accept concepts that at some level severely conflict with each other. Such conceptual conflicts are an integral part of modern science.

According to Dedekind's definition, the positive integers form an infinite set that can be paired off with any of its subsets, such as the positive even integers or the primes, which are similarly infinite. Any set that is equivalent to the set of integers is said to be *denumerably* infinite; even the set of all rational numbers (i.e., numbers that can be formed by taking the ratio of two integers) is equivalent to the set of integers, and hence denumerably infinite. Following a suggestion made by Hilbert, let us compare a hotel having a finite number of rooms with one having an infinite number. Assume that all the rooms (numbered sequentially) are occupied, and a new guest arrives. The manager of a finite hotel must offer his apologies, while the manager of an infinite hotel need merely move each occupant from room N to room $N + 1$, thereby freeing room 1 for the new guest. In fact, the manager of the fully booked, infinite hotel can accommodate the sudden arrival of an *infinite* number of new guests, by simply reassigning the previous occupant of room N to room $2N$, thus freeing all the odd-numbered rooms for the new guests. The notion that a set can be equivalent to one of its proper subsets is alien to our intuition.

It is not the case, however, that *all* infinite sets are equivalent, since, as Georg Cantor discovered in 1877, some sets are larger than the denumerably infinite sets. Cantor showed that with such *nondenumerably* infinite sets the set of integers cannot be brought into one-to-one correspondence. The best known example of a nondenumerably infinite set is the continuum of real numbers. While the set of rational numbers in a given interval can be arranged so that any member of the set is paired with a positive integer, or is assigned a defined serial number, Cantor showed that such seriation cannot be done for the set of real numbers. The gist of Cantor's proof that the set of real numbers is nondenumerable amounts to showing that however one proposes to seriate the real numbers, there is always a procedure for constructing a number that was not contained in the series.

To appreciate the nature of this argument, let us consider the collection of all subsets that can be formed from the elements of a given set S. In the case of a finite set S of n elements, 2^n distinct subsets can be formed, counting the set S itself and the empty set $\emptyset$ (which has no elements) among the subsets. For instance, from the set $S = \{a,b,c,d\}$ of 4 elements, 16 ($= 2^4$) subsets can be formed: $\emptyset$, $\{a\}$, $\{b\}$, $\{c\}$, $\{d\}$, $\{a,b\}$, $\{a,c\}$, $\{a,d\}$, $\{b,c\}$, $\{b,d\}$, $\{c,d\}$, $\{a,b,c\}$, $\{a,b,d\}$, $\{a,c,d\}$, $\{b,c,d\}$, $\{a,b,c,d\}$. Obviously, for a finite n, a set of n elements has far more subsets than elements. As Cantor showed, it is true not only for finite sets but also for infinite sets that the collection of subsets of any set S is too large to be paired off with the elements of S. The indirect proof, by contradiction, is as follows:

Let us assume that there *is* a pairing such that each *subset S_a* of S is paired with an element a of S. For example, if S were the set of positive integers, a pairing of positive integers with subsets of positive integers might take the form

1 ↔ the odd numbers, $\{1,3,5,7,9,\ldots\}$

2 ↔ the perfect squares, $\{1,4,9,16,25,\ldots\}$

3 ↔ the primes, $\{2,3,5,7,11,\ldots\}$

4 ↔ the numbers from 1 to 100, $\{1,2,3,4,\ldots,100\}$

5 ↔ the multiples of 12 $\{12,24,36,48,60,\ldots\}$

6 ↔ the powers of 3 $\{1,3,9,27,81,\ldots\}$

7 ↔ the arbitrary set $\{2,11,4097\}$

etc.

There are two possibilities regarding the pairings: either a is a member of the subset S_a with which it is paired (in the above example, $a = 1$, $a = 3$, and $a = 4$ are of this type) or a is not a member (in the example, $a = 2$, $a = 5$, $a = 6$, and $a = 7$ are of this type). Let S^* be the subset of S consisting of all elements of S that are not members of the subset with which they are paired (in the example, $S^* = \{2,5,6,7,\ldots\}$). By our assumption, since S^* is a subset of S, it is paired with some element a_o of S. Now, is a_o an element of S^*? In order to be an element of S^*, it must not be an element of S^*! If it is an element of S^*, it shouldn't be. But if it is not in S^*, it should be! We have arrived at a contradiction; so we must reject the assumption that each *subset* of S can be paired with an element of S. That is to say, there is no element a_o of S with which S^* can be paired, and hence the collection of all subsets that can be formed from the elements of S is larger than S.

Cantor showed that the set of real numbers in any interval is equivalent to, that is, can be paired with, all the subsets (finite and infinite) of the set of positive integers. Cantor used the Hebrew symbol $\aleph_0$ ("aleph nought") to denote the smallest transfinite cardinal number: the "size" of the set of positive integers. He used the symbol c to denote the transfinite cardinal number of the continuum, that is, the "size" of the set of real numbers. Since a (finite) set of n elements has 2^n subsets, Cantor wrote $2^{\aleph_0} = c$, to symbolize the fact that the set of real numbers is equivalent to all the subsets of the positive integers.

Cantor's proof leads not only to a new theory of transfinite cardinal numbers, but also to the question whether there is a transfinite cardinal number between that of the denumerable set of the integers and that of the nondenumerable continuum of the real numbers. In other words, is there a transfinite number larger than $\aleph_0$ but smaller than $2^{\aleph_0}$? Cantor conjectured that there is no such transfinite number. The question of the truth or falsity of this conjecture, referred to as Cantor's continuum hypothesis, is the first of twenty-three problems listed by Hilbert (in a famous lecture given in 1900 before the International Congress of Mathematicians in Paris) as being the most interesting and important problems then facing mathematicians. This list was widely regarded as the agenda for twentieth century mathematics, and most of the problems listed by Hilbert have now been solved.

After a century of investigation, the status of the continuum hypothesis, is as follows: In about 1940, Kurt Gödel proved that the continuum hypothesis is logically consistent with the other currently accepted axioms of set theory (assuming that these axioms are themselves consistent without the continuum hypothesis). Hence from the axioms of set theory it is not possible to construct a set whose cardinal number is larger than $\aleph_0$ but smaller than $2^{\aleph_0}$. However, in 1963 Paul J. Cohen showed that the the *negation* of the continuum hypothesis is also consistent with the other axioms of set theory. Cohen showed that we may assume, without causing any contradiction to arise, that there exist 1, 2, 3, or even an infinite number, of different-sized sets whose cardinal numbers are larger than $\aleph_0$, but smaller than $2^{\aleph_0}$. In other words, the work of Gödel and of Cohen revealed that the continuum hypothesis is logically independent of the other axioms of set theory, in much the same way that the parallel postulate (through any one point there can be drawn one and only one line that is parallel to another coplanar line external to that point) was shown to be independent of the other axioms of Euclidean geometry.

We now digress from our examination of the relation of mathematics to reality and take up the nature of mathematical logic and of logic in general. We start this digression with one of the somewhat bizarre aspects of logic, specifically of its simplest branch, the *propositional calculus*. This branch operates on propositions (statements of which it can be said that they are true or false, such as "five is a prime number" and "snow is black") and their logical links with other propositions via the four connectives *and, or, not,* and *implies.* As we shall see, once a single formal contradiction is allowed, the truth of *any* statement can be proved by application of the rules of the propositional calculus. Let us say that we accept the statement "God is good." Call this proposition *p.* We also accept the statement "God is not good"; call this proposition ~*p.* Now consider the statement "Hollywood is in Europe" as proposition *q.* The next step is to evaluate the statement *"p* or *q",* which means "God is good or Hollywood is in Europe." (The sense in which logicians use the connective *or* is that *at least one* of *p* and *q* is true.) The statement is incontrovertibly true, since we previously accepted *p* as true. However, once we accepted also ~*p* as true, meaning that *p* is not true, it follows from *"p* or *q"* that *q* is true. Thus by the rules of the propositional calculus, one is forced in this situation to accept as true the statement "Hollywood is in Europe," or any other statement substituted for *q.* Logic allows no equivocation.

It may well be possible to believe that God is good and also that God is not good; indeed this contradiction (being the problem of theodicy) may express a deep truth about God. Niels Bohr said that it is the hallmark of any deep truth that its negation is also a deep truth. Some truths may be unambiguous, in that their negations are false, but they tend to be trivial. And Georg Wilhelm Friedrich Hegel went so far as to say "Who thinks logically? Only the stupid and the uneducated."

The notion of being able to prove anything if one accepts as true one false statement has even penetrated the literary pages of the *New Yorker* magazine, where, in a story published in 1975, a man is made exceedingly unhappy by an unmanageable personal difficulty. He is totally miserable, and he finally says, "If I embrace the proposition that, after all, things aren't so bad, which is not true, then have I not also embraced a hundred other propositions, akin to the first in that they are not true? That the Lord is my shepherd, for example?"

The story is told that Bertrand Russell once claimed in a public lecture that, granted a false premise, he could easily prove any conclusion. A skeptical member of the audience accepted the challenge. "Suppose I grant you the premise that two equals three. Now prove to me that you are the Pope." Russell was undaunted. "That's easy," he replied. "I subtract one from both sides of your equation, which yields one equals two. You will surely concede that the Pope and I are *two.* But since one equals two, the Pope and I are *one,* and I am the Pope!"

The logician and the axiomatic mathematician certainly would not concede that all their truths are trivial, though they would admit them to be tautological, in the sense that these truths are already implicit in the axioms from which they are derived. However, there is a limit to how far one can go with logical axiomatic acrobatics. Let us consider Richard's paradox, which is concerned with the set of statements that define number-theoretic functions, such as "the function whose value at any n is n squared." Any such a statement, as written in English, consisting of a string of k of the 26 lower case letters and the symbol "space," is one element of a finite set of such strings, consisting of a total of 27^k elements. The set of all such strings of *finite* length is denumerably infinite, since we can first list all strings of length 1, then all strings of length 2, and so on. Only a small subset of these finite strings are English declaratory sentences, or statements, and only a small subset of these statements define number-theoretic functions. Thus the set of (finite) statements that define number-theoretic functions is denumerable; so these statements can all be listed in a sequence: $E_1, E_2, E_3, E_4 \ldots$ Suppose that the example given above ("the function whose value at any n is n squared") is E_3. Now consider the statement "the function whose value at each n is one larger than the value of the nth function at n." Does this statement define a number-theoretic function (i.e., has a defined value for all values of n)? If so, it should be included in the above set. Let us designate this statement E_m. To find the value of E_m for $n = 3$, we merely look at function E_3. So the value of function E_m for $n = 3$ is $3^2 + 1$, which equals 10. But what is the value of E_m for $n = m$? This value is clearly undefined, since whatever value E_m has at $n = m$, by definition it should be larger by one. Therefore, this function is not defined for all n, and the statement cannot be included in the list of number-theoretic functions (i.e., should not be designated E_m). But then, as long as the statement is not included in the list, its value *is* defined at all values of n since all the other E statements do define functions. Therefore the statement *ought* to be included in the list of number-theoretic functions after all. We have arrived at a paradox! It might be argued that Richard's paradox merely shows that ordinary language is not suitable for rigorous logical discourse, as was maintained by Peano and other mathematicians and logicians. However, other logical paradoxes cannot be dismissed as easily by this argument, as we shall see upon consideration of Russell's paradox.

Logical contradictions even more intractable than those we have discussed thus far arise from sets whose definitions are *self-referential*, that is, sets that form part of their own definitions. We have already encountered sets that are themselves elements of sets. For instance, we explained the product of the multiplication of 3 × 5 as the set that results from the union of three sets with five elements. And we discussed the set of all the subsets of a set. For a finite set with n elements the set of all subsets has 2^n elements, whereas in the case of a set with a denumerably infinite number of elements the set of subsets is equivalent to the continuum of real numbers. Now, Russell's paradox concerns such a set that includes itself as an element. There seems to be nothing wrong with granting the existence of such a set, especially since the elements of mathematical sets belong to the world of thought rather than the world of things. (That is, their existence is conceptual rather than physical.) The set of all sets, for instance, is a set that includes itself as an element. Admittedly, this set is a somewhat unusual set; so let us call sets that include themselves as elements *abnormal* sets. The other sets, which do not have this unusual property, we will call *normal*. That will put the unusual sets aside, in a class by themselves. But by making this clear conceptual distinction we have created a difficulty for the *normal* sets. Suppose we are asked whether the set of all *normal* sets is *normal*. We cannot say that the set of all normal sets is normal, because in that case it should be listed among the normal sets and would include itself as an element. But then it would be abnormal! Nor can we say that the set of all normal sets is abnormal, because in that case it should not be listed among the normal sets and would not include itself as an element. But then it would be normal! Hence sets that include themselves as elements turn out to be paradoxical.

We can make the essence of Russell's paradox more concrete by considering bibliographies. In any large library, there are many bibliographies, which are lists of books and articles on some subject. Frequently, a bibliography will list other bibliographies, and some bibliographies actually list themselves. If a chief librarian orders the staff to prepare a bibliography of all bibliographies in the library, to be available as a reference, it would be reasonable to have that bibliography list itself. But suppose the chief librarian asks for the preparation of a bibliography of all bibliographies that do not list themselves? Should that bibliography list itself? According to Russell's paradox if it doesn't, it should! But if it does, it shouldn't!

The contradictions in Richard's *and* Russell's paradoxes arise from a circularity in the definition of the *elements* of the set and of the set of which they are the elements: we define some critical element in a way that presupposes the definition of the whole set (in Richard's case by saying "the nth function"; in Russell's case by saying "the set of all normal sets"). Unfortunately, the same kinds of circular definitions are made in mathematics, for example, when the relation between rational and irrational numbers is established by Dedekind's cut (see chapter 11). Here the irrational numbers are defined in terms of the distribution of rational numbers, which are themselves defined by a set of Dedekind's cuts. Are the real numbers, therefore, a self-referentially defined set, or are they not? As we will see later in this chapter, the answer to this question depends on one's viewpoint regarding the epistemological relation of mathematics to the real world.

The paradoxical implications of self-referential definitions are by no means limited to infinite sets. They are manifest in the liar's paradox, which confronts us with the logical contradiction inherent in the statement: "The statement I am now making is false." Or consider the challenge given to the tourist by the cannibals who have captured him: "You must make a statement. If we decide it is true, you will be roasted; if we decide it is false, you will be boiled." Knowing the principles of logic, the tourist says, "I will be boiled," thus presenting the cannibals with a dilemma. If they decide that the statement is true, the tourist should be roasted. But if they roast him, his statement would have been false, and he should have been boiled. Getting hungry, the cannibals finally resolve the paradox by deciding that the tourist should be fried.

The following paradox was generated in the real world of politics. In the fall of 1974, General George Brown, Chairman of the Joint Chiefs of Staff, said in a speech: "The U.S. Jewish lobby is too influential in our foreign policy." The Jewish lobby raised an outcry and demanded that President Gerald Ford dismiss General Brown. What should President Ford do? Fire the General and prove him right, or not fire him and prove him wrong? The president, evidently as skilled a logician as the tourist of the preceding paradox, called his general to the White House and reprimanded him for an "ill-advised remark," thus neither affirming nor negating the general's allegation (and relegating it thereby to the category of undecidable statements, which will be our concern in the next chapter).

The set theorists went to work to promulgate rules and regulations about admissible language to forestall such paradoxes. For instance, Bertrand Russell developed a limited logical calculus that eliminates all self-referential statements. This calculus avoids the paradoxes, but it does not allow even such innocuous self-referential statements as: "This sentence is written in English and contains ten words!" Perhaps to avoid the liar's paradox, it is sufficient to forbid self-reference to the *semantic content* of the statement.

Where do these paradoxes and contradictions leave us with respect to the nature or certainty of mathematical truths? This question confronts us with two rather different views of the relation of number theory in particular, and of mathematics in general, to the real world. One of these views holds that mathematical truths do not pertain to reality—that is, they are not empirical—but are tautological, although this may sometimes be difficult to recognize. Mathematical truths arise from definitions, just as does the demographic truth, "all bachelors are unmarried." We might try to test the truth of this statement empirically, by asking 10,000 bachelors whether they are married, but it is simpler merely to look at the definition of "bachelor" and discover that it implies the condition of being single. Similarly, the truth of the commutativity of addition—that is, of the statement that for any two numbers a and b, it is true that $a + b = b + a$—could be tested empirically, but it is simpler to note that such commutativity is implied in the definition of natural numbers. According to that definition, in matching the elements of two sets, all extraneous characteristics of the elements must be ignored, attention being limited to ascertaining their pairability. A similar consideration applies to the proof of mathematical theorems. Their truth follows from definitions, of which the axioms form a part. This viewpoint thus holds that numbers, and the mathematical relationships they imply, are creations of human thought. Thus in response to the question whether the real numbers are a self-referentially defined set, the mathematical "creationist," believing that the real numbers are constructed from the rational numbers, would have to answer "yes." Kant was an exponent of this creationist viewpoint, which leads to the idea that in working out the laws of number theory, the mind of the mathematician is merely gaining insight into its own workings. Thus, for the creationist an encounter with irresolvable mathematical contradictions and paradoxes would constitute a profound discovery about the nature of mind.

A different point of view on the nature of mathematical truth envisages that numbers and the mathematical relations they imply are a part of the real world, and thus have an existence independent of the mind. Such a mathematical "realist" would deny that the real numbers are a self-referentially defined set, since after all, they are really there. Plato was an exponent of this realist viewpoint, which leads to the idea that in working out number theory, the mind of the mathematician is gaining insight into reality. If realists encounter irresolvable contradictions and paradoxes in number theory, they must conclude that there is something wrong with their intuition about the nature of numbers and/or that Peano's five postulates, or any other sets of axioms, are not expressive enough to capture the real situation completely. After all, they can maintain, there were numbers long before the axioms of number theory were explicitly formulated. This obvious truth has been well-stated by H. Hasse, who began his 1950 mathematical textbook, *Vorlesungen über Zahlentheorie*, as follows: "Kronecker says that the natural numbers were created by God; Dedekind, that they were created by man. Depending on your philosophy, the two assertions either constitute an irresolvable contradiction, or they are identical. For number theory itself, it is irrelevant who created the numbers. Its starting point is that they are there and *well known to us.*"

It is instructive to consider the fate of Cantor's continuum hypothesis in the light of the creationist and realist points of view. Do Gödel's and Cohen's demonstrations that this hypothesis and its negation are both consistent with the other axioms of set theory imply that we are free to add either the hypothesis or its negation to the system of axioms, yielding two different set theories, one "Cantorian" and the other "non-Cantorian"? The realists would say "no"; the creationists "yes." The creationists would thus readily admit that there could be non-Cantorian set theories, just as there are non-Euclidean geometries. We may recall that in the nineteenth century, the realists believed that any geometry descriptive of the real world requires the parallel postulate and that non-Euclidean geometries lacking that postulate are little more than intellectual games unrelated to anything real or useful. It is a great irony that upon Einstein's development of the relativity theory (to be considered in a later chapter) it turned out to be Euclidean geometry that is an idealization, unrealized in the physical universe. What attitude will mathematicians of the next century have toward non-Cantorian set theories? In the next chapter we will turn to the problem of the decidability of mathematical statements, which further accentuates the conflict between the creationist and the realist points of view.

REFERENCES

Cohen, P. J. 1963. The independence of the continuum hypothesis, I. *Proceedings of the National Academy of Science USA* 50: 1143–1148.

———. 1964. The independence of the continuum hypothesis, II. *Proceedings of the National Academy of Science USA* 51: 105–110.

Gödel, K. 1940. *The Consistency of the Axiom of Choice and of the Generalized Continuum Hypothesis With the Axioms of Set Theory.* Princeton: Princeton University Press.

Thirteen

Decidability

There is another difficult problem of number theory, which is as old as that of the prime numbers, namely the problem of the Pythagorean triples. The Pythagoreans had found that the equation $a^2 + b^2 = c^2$ describes the relation between the lengths a and b of the short sides and c of the hypotenuse of a right triangle. The Pythagoreans further found that in the case of an isosceles right triangle, for which $a = b$, the equation cannot be solved if a and c are positive integers. A simple way to see this is to express the positive integers a and c in terms of their standard decompositions, $a = 2^{\alpha_1} \cdot 3^{\alpha_2} \cdot 5^{\alpha_3} \cdot \cdots$ and $c = 2^{\gamma_1} \cdot 3^{\gamma_2} \cdot 5^{\gamma_3} \cdot \cdots$ Thus, the Pythagorean equation reduces to $2a^2 = c^2$, implying that for the exponents α_1 and γ_1:

$$2\alpha_1 + 1 = 2\gamma_1$$

This equation requires that an odd number be equal to an even number, which is a contradiction. Therefore, a and c cannot both be integers. Incidentally, this same proof demonstrates also that $\sqrt{2}$ is an irrational number. For if $\sqrt{2}$ were a rational number, then it would be expressible as $\sqrt{2} = c/a$, where c and a are positive integers, and hence $2a^2 = c^2$. But this equation, as we just proved, cannot be satisfied by any positive integers. Hence $\sqrt{2}$ is not a rational number, since assuming that it is leads to a contradiction.

Integers that satisfy the Pythagorean equation relating the lengths of the short sides and the hypotenuse of a right triangle are known as Pythagorean triples. Written as (a,b,c), the first few triples are as follows: $(3,4,5)$, $(5,12,13)$, $(8,15,17)$, $(7,24,25)$. The set of Pythagorean triples can be expressed in "parametric" form, as follows: $a = m^2 - n^2$; $b = 2mn$; $c = m^2 + n^2$. It is easy to verify that all triples generated by this formula satisfy the Pythagorean equation. But it is slightly more difficult to demonstrate that this formula does, in fact, generate the whole set of triples.

Diophantus of Alexandria, a Greek mathematician of the third century A.D., wrote a treatise containing many problems of number theory, including the problem of Pythagorean triples. Diophantus's treatise was printed for the first time in about 1620. Its readers included Pierre de Fermat, who wrote marginal notes in his copy of the treatise, stating many important theorems and their proofs. For the problem in Diophantus's Book II, Question 10, which states, "The problem is to split a square into the sum of two squares," Fermat made the annotation: "This problem has no solution for cubes or higher powers." This means that for the equation $a^n + b^n = c^n$, there is no solution with positive integers a, b, and c, for which n is greater than 2. Fermat's annotation continues: "For this I have a marvelous proof, for which this margin is too narrow." For more than three centuries mathematicians have tried in vain to prove this conjecture or find a counterexample. In 1908, the amateur mathematician Paul Wolfskehl offered a prize of 100,000 German marks for a proof. No takers had presented themselves by 1923, when the value of the prize was wiped out by the German postwar inflation. The question whether the conjecture, referred to as Fermat's last theorem, is true remains unresolved. No counterexamples have been found, and there exists a vast literature of partial proofs.

In view of these failures one may well wonder, not only whether Fermat had, in fact, found a "marvelous proof" for his theorem, but also whether its truth or falsity is, in fact, ultimately decidable. Perhaps there is no formal proof either for Fermat's last theorem or for its negation. In other words, is it possible that there are mathematical propositions that can be stated in clear and unambiguous terms, whose truth or falsity is, nevertheless, undecidable? We will now address this deep and disturbing question. In any case, since the suspicion first arose that there may exist undecidable statements in mathematics, there has been a quest for "reasonable" theorems that might prove undecidable. In addition to Fermat's last theorem, the best candidates for this dubious honor include

m	2	3	4	5	6	7
n						
1	(3,4,5)	(8,6,10)	(15,8,17)	(24,10,26)	(35,12,37)	(48,14,50)
2		(5,12,13)	(12,16,20)	(21,20,29)	(32,24,40)	(45,28,53)
3			(7,24,25)	(16,30,34)	(27,36,45)	(40,42,58)
4				(9,40,41)	(20,48,52)	(33,56,65)
5					(11,60,61)	(24,70,74)
6						(13,84,85)

Pythagorean triples

the conjecture made by Christian Goldbach in 1742, that every even number larger than 2 is the sum of two primes.

The threat to the logical integrity of mathematics posed by these contradictions and by the specter of undecidability stimulated efforts at the beginning of the twentieth century to clarify the coherence of that whole discipline as much as possible and put it on a firm foundation. David Hilbert then envisaged a grandiose program of "proof theory." Prompted by the paradoxes that had shown up in set theory, Hilbert proposed to strip mathematical discourse down to the language of formal axiomatics. The language of formal axiomatics uses the symbols of the propositional calculus: $\wedge$ for "and," $\vee$ for "or," $\sim$ for "not," $\rightarrow$ for "if-then," and $\leftrightarrow$ for "if and only if." To these symbols are added the quantifiers of the predicate calculus: $\forall x$ represents "for every x it is true that . . ." and $\exists x$ represents "there exists an x such that . . ." These symbolic operations act on expressions built up using the equality sign $=$ and the arithmetical operation symbols $+$, $\times$, and y' (successor of y). With these symbols number-theoretic statements can be expressed. For example, Gauss's lemma (GL), equivalent to the fundamental theorem of arithmetic, can be stated:

If a prime divides $A \times B$, it divides A or B.

(Logicians always use "or" in the sense of "and/or"; the use of the symbol for "or" is derived from the Latin *vel*.) In logical longhand, GL reads as follows:

For any triple A, B, x, if x is a prime and if x divides $A \times B$, it follows that x divides A or x divides B.

The phrase "x divides A" is expressed: "There exists a number u such that $x \times u = A$," or in the logical shorthand of symbols: $\exists u \, (x \times u = A)$. The phrase "$x$ is a prime" is expressed as "It is true for all numbers u, that if there exists a number y, such that $u \times y = x$, then u is 1 or x"; or in symbolic shorthand: $\forall u (\exists y (u \times y = x) \rightarrow (u = 1 \lor u = x))$. Thus, the whole statement of GL reads in symbolic shorthand:

$$\forall ABx((\forall u(\exists y(u \times y = x) \rightarrow (u = 1 \lor u = x)) \land \exists y(v \times x = A \times B))$$
$$\rightarrow \exists w(w \times x = A \lor w \times x = B))$$

Large portions of mathematics were thus formalized, and it was Hilbert's program to show that the entire system of formal propositions is consistent and complete, in the sense that there are no undecidable propositions. Admittedly many meaningful propositions *cannot* be expressed in this formal language, such as "reading mathematical propositions in the shorthand of logical axiomatics gives me a headache." However, the system does allow any *proof* to be expressed as a series of statements inferred from preceding statements, and ultimately from the axioms of mathematics. This process of inference follows absolutely fixed rules, similar to the rules of chess. Once the symbols, the axioms, and the rules of inference are specified, the proof of mathematical propositions becomes nothing but a game, and we need not remember at all what the symbols actually stand for. During the game the symbols are not interpreted. Thus, we could derive the symbolic shorthand formula of GL from the axioms, without ever knowing that this formula expresses GL.

The analogy of mathematical proof with chess is quite close: the axioms are the initial board position, the rules of inference are the rules for going from one configuration of the pieces to the next, and the provable propositions are the configurations that can be reached by legitimate moves. The analogy with chess breaks down in one important respect: In the formal mathematical system, for every statement S we can also formulate its negation, ~S; chess has no operation analogous to negation.

Indeed, the two questions of vital interest that need to be answered by analysis of the formal system of mathematical propositions both relate to negation:

1. Is there any statement S such that *both S and ~S* can be proved? If there were such a statement, then the system would be *inconsistent*. Moreover, as we saw in the preceding chapter, if just one such pair S and ~S can be proved, *any* statement whatsoever can be proved. Since

that would be catastrophic, let us assume therefore that the formal system *is* consistent. But this assumption leads to the next question:

2. Is there any statement S such that *neither* S *nor* ~S can be proved? In other words, can it happen that S is undecidable? If there were such a statement, then the system would be *incomplete*. In that case we could not be certain whether an undecided statement—say Riemann's hypothesis about the zeros of the Zeta function, or Fermat's last theorem, or Goldbach's conjecture—is in fact decidable. Hilbert's program of proof theory, then, endeavored to demonstrate the consistency and completeness of mathematics, at least as far as the theory of numbers is concerned, by eliminating undecidable theorems from its realm.

Hilbert and his disciples—especially Wilhelm Ackermann, Paul Bernays, and John von Neumann—expended much effort to fulfill this program. Then in 1930 Kurt Gödel pulled the rug out from under these efforts by showing that their goal is unattainable. Gödel revolutionized the foundations of mathematics by demonstrating, using Hilbert's own methods of formal axiomatics, that for any mathematical system as complex as the theory of infinite sets, or of numbers, (a) it is impossible to prove the consistency of the axioms, and (b) it is possible to generate undecidable propositions from the axioms. Gödel's demonstration is independent of the set of particular axioms and pertains to a feature inherent in *all* axiomatic systems.

The procedure Gödel used in his proof is simple in principle but enormously complicated in execution. Gödel constructed the formula of a particular statement (a legitimate sequence of symbols in the formal language), for which he showed that it is not decidable, that is, that neither it nor its negation is provable. What is this statement? What mathematical theorem does it express? The theorem it expresses is a peculiar one, namely "I am not provable." That does not read like a theorem at all. Rather, it reads like the liar's paradox! So we must look more closely. First of all, how can the formal system express "provable"? Clearly we can express a particular proof, because the rules of inference have been formalized; but how do we express "provable"? The trick is this: we map the symbols, the expressions, the statement, and the proof into *numbers*. That is obviously possible, since the items to be mapped are denumerable, and the mapping can be done in a great variety of ways. Gödel's method uses the fundamental theorem of arithmetic. As we saw in Chapter 11, it follows from this theorem that we can represent any number n by the unique sequence of exponents α_1, α_2, α_3, . . . of its standard decomposition into primes, i.e., $n = 2^{\alpha_1} \cdot 3^{\alpha_2} \cdot 5^{\alpha_3} \cdot \cdots$ Gödel maps symbols, statements, theorems, and proofs into numbers in three steps, as follows:

1. First he assigns a number to each formal symbol. For instance, in Gauss's Lemma (GL), whose beginning is written as,

$$\forall ABx((\forall u(\exists y(u \times y = x) \cdots$$

the symbols $\forall$, A, B, x, (, u, $\exists$, y, $\times$, and) occur. Let us suppose that the numbers assigned to these symbols are, in corresponding order, 11, 22, 33, 44, 55, 66, 77, 88, 99, 110 and 121. Thus the beginning part of the statement of GL can be formulated as the string of numbers

$$11 - 22 - 33 - 44 - 55 - 55 - 11 - 66 - 55 - 77 - 88 - 55 - 66$$
$$- 99 - 88 - 110 - 44 - 121 - \cdots$$

2. Next Gödel defines the Gödel number G of the theorem as a product of prime numbers, with each prime raised to a power, or carrying an exponent, taken from the string of numbers in terms of which the statement of the theorem has been formulated under 1. The primes, in ascending order, are:

$$2, 3, 5, 7, 11, 13, 17, 19, 23, 29, 31, 37, 41, 43, 47, 53, 59, 61, \ldots$$

So the Gödel number of GL would be given by the formula:

$$G_{GL} = 2^{11} \cdot 3^{22} \cdot 5^{33} \cdot 7^{44} \cdot 11^{55} \cdot 13^{55} \cdot 17^{11} \cdot 19^{66} \cdot 23^{55}$$
$$\cdot 29^{77} \cdot 31^{88} \cdot 37^{55} \cdot 41^{66} \cdot 43^{99} \cdot 47^{88} \cdot 53^{110} \cdot 59^{44} \cdot 61^{121} \cdot \cdots$$

Several remarks can be made about the Gödel numbers of formulas representing statements:

    a. Every statement has exactly one Gödel number.

    b. Different statements have different Gödel numbers.

    c. Given any statement, there is a well-determined method of obtaining its Gödel number.

    d. Given any Gödel number, there is an effective method for writing down the statement it represents.

3. Finally, since a proof is simply a finite sequence of statements, to each of which a Gödel number can be assigned, Gödel converts the finite string of Gödel numbers representing the sequence of statements of the proof into a single Gödel number, by the same procedure as that outlined under (2). The remarks (a–d) made under (2) about Gödel numbers representing statements also hold for the Gödel numbers representing sequences of statements.

Thus every theorem and every proof can be assigned its own unique Gödel number. We now examine how the rules of inference are mapped. What arithmetical properties of a Gödel number tie it to the axioms by the rules of inference? Eventually (after a great deal of labor) we discover a general set of arithmetical rules that connect the network of Gödel numbers expressing provable statements. Once in possession of these rules, we can tell whether a number x is the Gödel number of a proof of a theorem whose Gödel number is y. The next step is also to express the statements of the rules governing the logical connectivity of the network of Gödel numbers *as* Gödel numbers. We have seen how to express the part of GL that states that "x is a prime" in the language of formal axiomatics. In a similar, but much more complicated, manner we can express the arithmetical property: "x is the Gödel number of a provable statement," or "x is the Gödel number of an unprovable statement." Let us call the latter statement F. Now, this formal statement, which contains the variable x (just as does the formal rendering of the statement "x is a prime") also has a Gödel number, G_F. Since in this formal statement F we can insert for x any particular number (as we can in "x is a prime"), let us insert the Gödel number G_F for x in F. The resulting F statement

G_F is the Gödel number of an unprovable statement

may or may not be true. Just as in "x is a prime" the truth of F depends on the value of x. If x is a Gödel number, "x is prime" would be false, since no Gödel number is a prime. But that is not the point. The point is that the procedure we have used to construct this statement is entirely legitimate, being grounded wholly on logical operations and the axioms of arithmetic, without recourse to hidden assumptions. We may now ask the question: "Is this version of the formal statement F, with G_F inserted for x, a decidable proposition?" And it turns out that when $x = G_F$ neither F nor its negation ~F is provable. How can we be sure of this? Let us first assume that F (with G_F substituted for x) is provable. Then G_F would be the Gödel number of the provable F statement "G_F is the Gödel number of an unprovable statement." Since this is clearly a contradiction F must be unprovable. Let us assume therefore that ~F (with G_F substituted for x) is provable. In that case, according to ~F, G_F would be the Gödel number of a provable statement. But this is also a contradiction since G_F, by definition, is the Gödel number of F, which we have just shown to be unprovable. Hence when we substitute G_F for x, neither F nor ~F is provable. In other words, we have constructed an undecidable formal proposition.

There are two psychologically very unsatisfactory aspects of Gödel's proof that the formalization of mathematics does not produce a closed system: the apparent self-reference embodied in the undecidable proposition and the complexity of the proof. The self-reference is not logically objectionable, however, since Gödel's statement F does not actually refer to *itself*, but to its Gödel number. But the complexity of the proof is formidable, as indicated by the several popular accounts of Gödel's proof, some of which contain technical errors, while others do not achieve much simplification. Why haven't mathematicians come up with a simpler theorem for which they can prove undecidability? All they have provided is another disappointing proof: as Alonzo Church has shown, there can be no *general* algorithm that would permit one to find out whether *any* given statement is or is not decidable. In other words, there is no "universal decision procedure." (Editors' note: At the very time that Delbrück gave these lectures, namely during the first months of 1977, J. Paris and L. Harrington *did* find a true but formally undecidable statement of number theory that fulfills Delbrück's challenge: it can be presented in an elementary course in number theory and does not refer to logical concepts such as provability.)

Gödel's proof shows that mathematics is *incomplete* (and not wholly tautological, after all), in the sense that it leaves open the truth or falsity of a subset of all the mathematical propositions that can be legitimately derived from the axioms of number theory. Gödel's proof shows, furthermore, that mathematics is unexpectedly complex, since there is something paradoxical in the idea that a proposition may be demonstrably undecidable. For example, suppose someone succeeded in proving that the truth or falsity of Fermat's last theorem cannot be decided from the axioms of number theory. We would then know that Fermat's last theorem is, in fact, *true!* How so? Well, if Fermat's last theorem were false, there would be at least one set of specific integers a_1, b_1, c_1, and n_1, all positive, with $n_1 > 2$, satisfying the equation

$$a_1{}^{n_1} + b_1{}^{n_1} = c_1{}^{n_1},$$

and a search through the entire set of quartets of positive integers (a,b,c,n) would eventually locate this counterexample. Thus the question of the truth of Fermat's last theorem would have been decided in the negative. So in order for Fermat's last theorem to be undecidable, it must be free from counterexamples; but that is precisely what we mean by the statement "Fermat's last theorem is *true.*" Doesn't this argument imply that it is impossible to prove that Fermat's last theorem is undecidable, because in so doing we would in fact prove that the theorem is *true?* "Yes," the mathematical realists would have to answer, since they believe that mathematics is a constituent of the real world. "Not exactly," the mathematical creationists could answer, "we might indeed prove that Fermat's last theorem is undecidable *from the axioms of number theory.* This would constitute a meta-proof that Fermat's last theorem is 'true' within *some* logical framework, but *not* a proof that it is true within the framework of number theory."

To consider another example, suppose a communication from intelligent life on another planet informs us: "We have proved that the Riemann hypothesis (that all the zeros of the Zeta function lie on the critical line) is undecidable from the axioms of mathematical analysis." We would then know (to the extent that we can trust an alien intelligence) that the Riemann hypothesis is in fact *true*, because, like Fermat's last theorem, the Riemann hypothesis is an assertion of the nonexistence of counterexamples (that there are no zeros of the Zeta function that lie off the critical line). If the Riemann hypothesis were *false*, there is at least one value $s = \sigma + it$ for which $\sigma \neq \frac{1}{2}$, $t \neq 0$, and $\zeta(s) = 0$. Hence it would be possible, in principle, to find that value and thereby disprove the Riemann hypothesis; so it would not be undecidable.

Does this argument imply that *any* conjecture that has been proved to be logically undecidable will then, in fact, have been shown to be true? This cannot be the case, because if you conjecture "X is true," and I conjecture "X is false," and a third person *proves* "X is undecidable," is it your conjecture or mine that follows? As we saw in the preceding two examples, the proof of the undecidability of X, in fact, implies whichever of X or ~X it is that a single counterexample would disprove. But is this the case for *all* undecided conjectures? No, there certainly exist conjectures for which a proof of undecidability would shed no light on whether it is the conjecture or its negation that is "really" true. For instance, upon inspecting tables of prime numbers, we see many instances of consecutive odd numbers that are both prime, such as 3-5, 5-7, 11-13, 17-19, 29-31, 41-43, 59-61, 71-73, and 101-103. Are there infinitely many such prime pairs, or *twin primes*, as they are called? It has long been conjectured that there are infinitely many of them, but no one has yet succeeded in proving this conjecture. If someone succeeded in proving logically that "the twin prime conjecture is undecidable from the axioms of arithmetic," we would still not know whether the conjecture is true or false. This is so even though the twin prime conjecture, like Fermat's last theorem and the Riemann hypothesis, asserts the nonexistence of a counterexample. (It says that there is no *largest* prime pair $(P\text{-}Q)$ for which $Q = P + 2$.) But this does not mean that if the twin prime conjecture can be proved undecidable, it is in fact true. If you have a counterexample to Fermat's last theorem, you can verify that it *is* a counterexample, because the quartet of integers satisfies the relation $a^n + b^n = c^n$. If you have a counterexample to the Riemann hypothesis, you can verify that it *is* a counterexample, because for the value of $s = \sigma + it$, the Zeta function has the value zero, while satisfying the condition $\sigma \neq \frac{1}{2}$, $t \neq 0$. But you cannot verify by any currently known method that some twin prime, $(P\text{-}Q)$ for which $Q = P + 2$, is, in fact, the largest twin prime and hence a counterexample for the twin prime conjecture. Thus in the case of this conjecture, the proof of its undecidability would not, in fact, tell us whether there are finitely many or infinitely many twin primes.

Hilbert's belief in the consistency and completeness of mathematics bears some resemblance to the Greek belief that it should be possible to construct all geometric figures with straightedge and compass alone. The latter belief was equivalent to the proposition that all real numbers can be obtained by solving a finite sequence of *quadratic* equations with integer coefficients. The Greeks were wrong, because trisecting the general angle or constructing a cube with twice the volume of a given cube (which is equivalent to solving cubic equations) turned out to be impossible. And when C. L. F. Lindemann proved in the 1880s that π belongs to the subclass of real numbers (designated "transcendental") that cannot be obtained by the solution of *any* finite polynomial with integer coefficients, "squaring the circle" was forever ruled out. Subsequent generations are likely to consider the pre-Gödel view of the decidability of "all theorems" as naive as the Greek view of the constructability of "all geometric figures."

Finally, what are the epistemological implications of the demise of the belief in the consistency and completeness of mathematics for the two rival views—creationist and realist—of the relation of mathematics to the real world? It seems that the demonstration of undecidable propositions within any sufficiently rich axiomatic system supports the creationist viewpoint that mathematics reflects some deep aspect of the human mind. If numbers and their mathematical relations *were* constituents of the real world, independent of the human mind, then surely any proposition about them should state either what *is* or what *is not* the case. Gödel's proof shows, therefore, that even if numbers were "real," our minds could not adequately capture the definitions and axioms that would reflect their "true" nature. Admittedly, Hasse's argument (that it is irrelevant who created the numbers, since they are there anyhow and well-known to us) is eminently reasonable, not only for everyday use in commerce and engineering, but also for going some distance into the farther reaches of arithmetic and higher analysis. However, when we try to extend the use of numbers to realms that transcend our experience, or try to follow their implications too far and encounter paradoxes and contradictions, it is not so irrelevant to ask whether it is the mind or the world that lacks consistency.

REFERENCES

Delbrück, M., and S. W. Golomb. 1980. Pun and games: A review of D. R. Hofstadter's *Gödel, Escher, Bach: An Eternal Golden Braid*. *The American Scholar* 49: 550–556.

Gödel, K. 1965. On formally undecidable propositions of principia mathematica and related systems. In *The Undecidable,* ed. M. Davis. 5–38. Hewelett, N.Y.: Raven Press.

Gödel, K. 1964. Russell's mathematical logic. In *Philosophy of Mathematics*, ed. P. Benacerraf and H. Putnam. 211–232. Englewood Cliffs, N.J.: Prentice-Hall.

Graham, R. L., B. L. Rothschild, and J. H. Spencer. 1980. An unprovable theorem. In *Ramsey Theory*, 149–159. New York: Wiley-Interscience.

Hofstadter, D. R. 1979. *Gödel, Escher, Bach: An Eternal Golden Braid*. Basic Books: New York.

Kleene, S. C. 1952. *Introduction to Metamathematics*. Princeton, N.J.: Van Nostrand Co.

Nagel, E., and J. R. Newman. 1958. *Gödel's Proof*. New York: New York University Press.

Paris, J., and L. Harrington. 1977. A mathematical incompleteness in Peano arithmetic. In *Handbook of Mathematical Logic*, ed. E. Barwise. 1113–1142. Amsterdam: North-Holland.

Smullyan, R. 1982. *The Lady or the Tiger?* New York: Alfred Knopf.

Fourteen

Geometry, Astronomy, Newtonian Mechanics

Let us now leave the foundations of mathematics and turn to physics. It is the most basic of the empirical sciences, subsuming astronomy as well as chemistry. We will attempt to connect the concepts of physics with the cognitive development of children as we did for the concepts of mathematics. In earlier chapters we considered the origins of several concepts:

1. We saw that an object is conceived as an entity that retains its identity as perceived through various sensory modalities, irrespective of position and even while it is not perceived.

2. We noted that the development of the ability to pair disparate elements of two or more sets of objects gives rise to the concept of *cardinal number*, as the designation of a class of equivalent sets, and that, with acquisition of the ability to order objects or entities serially, there arises the concept of *ordinal number*. We also alluded to the difficulties encountered in reconciling the continuum of real numbers with the integers.

3. We discussed the twofold conceptual origin of causality: the nexus of volition and event on the one hand, and the nexus of event with event on the other.

4. We considered the origins of geometrical concepts in terms of the stepwise development of the ability to exploit mentally relations between objects with respect to the topological, projective, and metric aspects of space.

Although these basic epistemological concepts allow us to construct reality from sense impressions, further concepts are required if we want to structure that reality by resort to the physical sciences. Above all, we need the concept of measurement of continuous quantities. Although this may seem an obvious and trivial requirement, it is not.

First, no quantitive measurement is meaningful unless it refers to a *quantity conserved* in some operational sense: for instance the mass of a blob of putty formed into different shapes, the volume of a given weight of water poured into different-shaped vessels, or the length of a stick placed in different locations. Of course, it may turn out that the mass, volume, or length of a given object is *not* conserved under different conditions, but this statement is meaningful only when it refers to some standard object for which we *can* assume conservation. It is possible to compare lengths of curves of different curvatures, but a nylon string or a steel wire is required to establish a standard before length can be considered as a conserved quantity. Piaget investigated in great detail the childhood development of the concept of conserved quantity and found that it arises at a surprisingly late stage.

Second, the measurement of continuous quantities presupposes the concept of composition—the notion that separate objects can be combined, and that a conserved quantity possessed by the composite will be a sum of the quantities possessed by the individual parts. It is by no means a trivial idea that when we pour the contents of two glasses of water together, the sum of the volume of the parts equals the volume of their union.

Third, measurement specifically requires the notion of a *unit of measurement*, which may be the most difficult of the concepts involved. Once the concept of cardinal number has been reached, it is easy enough to state that "from here to the door is 5 steps," to agree about whose steps are to be used as a measure, and even to recognize that it may also be 5 steps from the door to here. But if we want to consider a distance of more than 5 and less than 6 steps, then we need to invent rational numbers, that is, fractions of integers. It is even necessary to invent irrational numbers, as the Greeks found to their amazement, in order to apply the concept of measurement of length to the sides of a right triangle.

These notions do not come easily to the child's mind; they first appear in the formal operational period, by which time the child is attending secondary school. Even at that age, it is by no means certain that the teacher can elicit in the child a true understanding of the foundations of the measurement of continuous quantities. Historically, this understanding required many centuries. During most of these centuries, most students learned geometry from Euclid. The young Isaac Newton studied William Oughtred's *Clavis Mathematicae,* an elementary treatise on algebra, and Euclid's *Elements* and proceeded directly to more difficult, modern authors, above all Descartes. At the age of 23, Newton had reached the peak of his creative ability. He invented the differential calculus, explained the spectral composition of white light, and discovered the law of gravitational attraction.

Whenever possible, Newton formulated his physical theories in geometrical terms. Newton considered the methods of mathematical analysis as indispensable aids. But he believed that a complete understanding of a physical problem had been reached only if the investigation culminates in a geometrical construction, because only in that case can the understanding be based on a logically consistent conceptual whole. Only then can the physicist grasp the real relationships between physical events. Newton preferred geometrical constructions because the only numerical continuum available in the seventeenth century was the representation of the real numbers as ratios of lengths, as described in Euclid's fifth book. A rigorous quantitative analysis was therefore possible only if it could be based on geometry. Not until the nineteenth century did Bernard Bolzano, Dedekind, and Karl Weierstrass develop a sound analytical concept of the system of real numbers.

Let us begin by asking what part the geometrical axioms played in Newton's contribution to the foundations of mathematics. First of all, we must note that Newton, a pious Puritan, had a strictly religious outlook, which is reflected in his attitude toward space. In his early notebooks, which contain most of his discoveries, we find space referred to as some sort of emanation, or *tamquam effectus emanativus,* from God. (He was not alone in this belief. His contemporary, Otto von Guericke, the burgomaster of Magdeburg, performed various experiments with vacuum jars, because "it is said [of empty space], that it is the divine substance, which embraces all things.") Newton thought that space is not just one more secular physical entity; he believed space to be divine, thus making geometry truly a divine science. Accordingly, the axiomatic foundations of geometry should reveal God's laws of creation. In view of this outlook one can appreciate Newton's ideal of mathematical rigor. In his later years, Newton reiterated his reverence for space in the second edition of his major work, the *Philosophiae Naturalis Principia Mathematica.* He wrote, "God endures forever, and is everywhere present; and by existing always and everywhere, he constitutes duration and space. . . . In Him all things are contained and moved."

We may ask how Newton looked upon Euclid's axioms, such as "two points belong to only one line" or "a given radius determines one circle." These axioms, he felt, were grounded in empirical findings; that is, based on mechanics. For Newton geometry was the study of physical space, and its axioms were facts of experience. He says, in the introduction to *Principia:*

> The description of right lines and circles, upon which geometry is founded, belong to mechanics. Geometry does not teach us to draw these lines, but requires them to be drawn. For it requires that the learner should first be taught to describe them accurately, before he enters upon geometry; then it shows how by operations, problems may be solved. To describe straight lines and circles is a problem, but not of geometry. The solution of these problems is required by mechanics, and by geometry their use is shown. And it is the glory of geometry that from these few principles, fetched from without, it is able to produce so many things. Therefore, geometry is founded in mechanical practice, and is nothing but a part of universal mechanics which accurately proposes and demonstrates the art of measuring.

As a reminder of how Euclid proved theorems, let us discuss the proof of the Pythagorean theorem illustrated in the figure shown on page 189. (Pythagoras is alleged to have sacrificed 100 oxen to thank the gods for leading him to the theorem.) The principal insight required for the proof is that the two smaller triangles with sides a and α, and b and β are both similar to the large triangle abc. Similarity follows very simply, since all three triangles have a right angle, and both smaller triangles hold one angle in common with the larger triangle. We can then express the equality between the ratios of the short sides and the hypotenuses in each of the similar right triangles:

$$\alpha{:}a = a{:}c \text{ and } \beta{:}b = b{:}c$$

from which it follows that

$$a^2 = \alpha c \text{ and } b^2 = \beta c.$$

Summing equals we obtain

$$a^2 + b^2 = (\alpha + \beta)\, c = c^2.$$

The Pythagorean theorem is a cornerstone of Euclidean geometry. In his book I Euclid opens the way to a series of theorems, culminating in the Pythagorean theorem, by introducing the new concept of equality of area. The resulting Euclidean theory of areas, whose argument rests

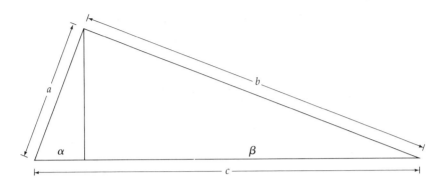

Right angle triangle used in proof of the Pythagorean theorem. From the similarity of the triangles it follows:

$$\frac{\alpha}{a} = \frac{a}{c} \quad \text{and} \quad \frac{\beta}{b} = \frac{b}{c}$$

thus $a^2 = \alpha \times c$ and $b^2 = \beta \times c$. Adding a^2 and b^2 yields $\alpha \times c + \beta \times c = (\alpha + \beta)c$. Thus $a^2 + b^2 = c^2$

upon the logical force of deduction, was already viewed by Galileo as a classical example of axiomatic reasoning. Newton seems to have paid too little attention to the axiomatic construction of Euclidean theory. In this neglect, he was influenced by René Descartes' *Géométrie*, which intentionally foregoes rigorous deductions in the classical sense.

Descartes published his first work, *Essais*, in 1637. In addition to the general *Discours de la Méthode pour Bien Conduire Sa Raison et Chercher la Vérité dans les Sciences*, the book contains three essays dedicated to specific topics: *Météores*, *Dioptrique*, and *Géométrie*. They are given as examples of his new method of research; *Géométrie* discusses the foundations of mathematics.

Descartes wrote in French instead of Latin, because his writings were directed to those readers who would judge his exposition in the light of common sense. He said that only those who diligently applied their unbiased minds could appreciate the results. For this reason, *Géométrie* does not take the same format as classical treatises, which give a set of definitions and postulates and then proceed to deduce everything else logically from them.

A classical treatise is divided into problems the author proposes to solve; theorems that must be proven; lemmata, which are stipulations useful in solving problems or proving theorems; and corollaries, which are useful or elegant applications of proofs or solutions. All the problems and theorems are numbered for easy reference. Finally, scholia, which are commentaries on the basis of postulates, applicability of theorems, or the merits or demerits of the work of others, are added at the ends of key parts.

In contrast to this highly structured format, Descartes offers a free-flowing literary text, in which he lays bare his thought processes. Many of the proofs are missing, or only implied; he prefers to leave the satisfaction of finding proofs to the reader. In this respect, Descartes broke with the scholarly tradition of the presentation of material. He himself was not a professional scholar, but a nobleman speaking to others of similar disposition. Because of its methods and content, *Géométrie* became by far the most influential mathematical text in the seventeenth century. By mainly suggesting ideas that required further work, it provided a starting point for further studies. In 1660, Frans van Shooten published a Latin translation of *Géométrie* richly supplemented with commentaries and peripheral works of other authors. This expanded Descartes' essay of less than one hundred pages into an opus of several volumes.

Descartes demonstrated that all geometrical problems can be mapped onto algebraic problems, and vice versa. For example, to map multiplication from algebra onto geometry, he freed himself in a most ingenious way from the classical notion that the product of two lengths is an area. He did this by considering a line segment not as a length but as a pure number related to a unit length. This makes it possible to multiply two line segments a and b. We draw an angle with vertex A. Along one side of the angle we plot the segment of unit length, $AB = 1$, and another segment $AC = a$. Along the other side we plot the segment $AD = b$. We then draw line BD and through C, a line parallel to BD, which intersects the ray AD at E, generating the segment AE. It follows that:

$$AC{:}AB = AE{:}AD$$

or

$$a{:}1 = AE{:}b$$

and hence

$$ab = AE$$

Thus we have constructed the product ab.

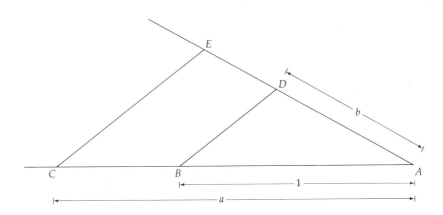

Descartes' geometric construction of the product of two numbers.

Taking it for granted, then, that adult human beings can, under favorable circumstances, appreciate and mentally manipulate measurements of continuous quantities as well as Euclidean geometry, we will proceed to sketch the development of physics. From astronomy, especially from the recording of observations of the sky over many decades, the ancients arrived at a remarkably accurate description of planetary motions. They knew about the precession (with a period of 26,000 years) of the earth's axis of rotation around the axis of the earth's solar orbit, which Hipparchus had discovered in the second century B.C. They also knew almost everything about the elliptical planetary orbits, except the fact that they are actually elliptical.

The planetary motions deviate from perfect circular motion around the sun in three ways:

1. The orbits are eccentric (the sun is at a focus rather than at the center of the orbit).

2. Orbital motion proceeds at a nonuniform speed, being faster when the planet is closest to (perihelion) than when it is farthest from (apohelion) the sun.

3. The orbit is oval, as characterized by a long and short axis.

The first and second deviations from simple circular motion are "first order" effects (about 10% for the orbit of Mars), while the third deviation, ovality, is a second order effect (about 0.5% for Mars). The first two deviations were known to the ancients, but the third was inaccessible to them, in view of the insufficient accuracy of their measurements. The ancients interpreted these deviations in terms of epicycles: they saw the planetary orbits as the composite of two perfectly circular motions, one of the planet around an axis in space and the other of the axis along a perfectly circular path around the sun.

Before continuing with the story of physics, I will digress in order to provide a better appreciation of the labor involved in disentangling the motions of the planets, and report an experiment that I did myself. Since I go camping in the California desert quite often, where there is usually an unclouded view of the night sky, I decided to record the planetary positions on star charts, in order to see how long it would take me to catch up with the ancients. My accuracy of locating a planet on a star chart in relation to some fixed constellation was about 20 minutes of arc. (This is the observational precision that prevailed for several thousand years, until just before the invention of the telescope when Tycho Brahe succeeded in improving it by about a factor of 5, through the use of precision direction finders of his own design. Tycho was a superb instrument maker. With his precision instruments and patient and accurate observation, he pushed to the limit what the unaided human eye was capable of measuring in the heavens.) From my observations, compiled over about six years of camping trips, I had sufficient data to infer a very clear regularity in the motions of Saturn. I estimated that the "synodic period" of Saturn's forward and backward motion in the sky (the interval between the planet's return to a given position on my star chart) is 375 days, or about 12 days longer than a year. (The exact value of the synodic period is 378.1 days.) Thus I found that while the earth had moved a full circle, Saturn has moved only as far as $12/365$ of the circumference of its own solar orbit. I reckoned from these data that Saturn's period of revolution must be $365/12$, or about 30 (terrestrial) years. (I was told by a historian friend that the Greek astronomers' insight that the celestial motion of the planets is not capricious but quite regular, though complicated, occurred between the time of Plato's youth and his old age, and that it was this insight that led Plato to the view that the world is a *kosmos*, a well-ordered structure.)

The oval nature of the planetary orbits was discovered in 1610 by Johannes Kepler. By dint of a massive computational effort based on Tycho Brahe's observations of planetary positions, Kepler discovered that the orbit of Mars is an ellipse. This discovery permitted Newton to interpret the solar system as a mechanical ensemble of mass points moving

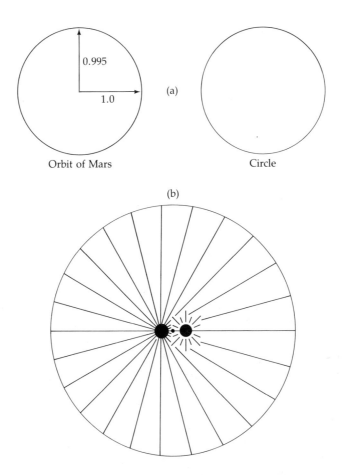

The Orbit of Mars (a) The planet does not move in a circle around the sun, but in an ellipse, with the sun at one focus, rather than at the center. The elliptic orbits of the planets are so similar to circles that even for the most elliptic of the planetary orbits, that of Mars, it is impossible to tell by inspection that it is not a circle. The long and short axes differ by only 0.5%. (b) The orbit of Mars is an ellipse with an eccentricity of 0.1. The orbit, however, betrays its ellipticity to us by two much grosser criteria: (1) the sun, being at one of the foci of the ellipse, is almost 10% off center; (2) the velocity of revolution is nonuniform, being 10% above average at perihelion (shown here as lying on the right) and 10% below average at aphelion (shown here as lying on the left). The figure shows the nonuniform velocity by depicting 24 positions of the planet separated by equal time intervals. It turns out that one can approximate this nonuniform velocity with high accuracy by envisaging that the motion of the planet would *appear* to be uniform to an observer located, neither on the sun nor at the center of the ellipse, but at the (empty) focus opposite that occupied by the sun.

under the influence of forces that act at a distance. Newton's theories united terrestrial and celestial mechanics for the first time in history, although his idea of forces acting at a distance is, on the face of it, a bizarre notion, which seems suspiciously akin to magic. But Newton still belonged to an age of faith, and he thought that the goal of science is to fathom how God made the world. Newton's God was the benevolent Biblical creator, who set up the heavenly clockwork at the beginning of time and is presumably having a look at it again from time to time, to see to it that the accumulated gravitational perturbations do not get out of hand. This is the intellectual framework within which Newton's *Principia* was created. The next generation of scientists was faced with a dilemma: on the one hand, Newton's idea of forces acting at a distance seemed to them irrational; on the other hand, his mechanics provided them with a workable model of the cosmos. The immense explanatory power of celestial mechanics changed the entire outlook of science. It served as the driving force behind the development of the differential calculus, of techniques for making precise observations, and of computations of great predictive power. Its success swept aside all conceptual scruples. By the 1800s Newton's basic premise, that mass points can interact through forces acting at a distance, had become the paradigm for interpretation in all of the physical sciences.

REFERENCES

Cohen, I. B. 1981. Newton's discovery of gravity. *Scientific American* 244(3): 166–179.

Price, D. J. de S. 1959. Contra–Copernicus: A critical re-estimation of the mathematical planetary theory of Ptolemy, Copernicus, and Kepler. In *Critical Problems in the History of Science*, ed. M. Clagett. Madison: University of Wisconsin Press.

Fifteen

Relativity Theory

We began our discussion of physics with Piaget's studies on the development of the concept of measurement of continuous quantities. This concept involves the ideas of *conservation* of a quantity under various transformations, *composition* of the quantities of separate objects, and a *unit* of measurement of a quantity. The last of these ideas requires, in turn, the acquisition of the concept of real numbers. We then sketched the development of geometry, from Euclid's proof of Pythagoras's theorem through Euclid's axiomatic formulation of geometry, which became the paradigm for mathematical texts for the ensuing two thousand years, to the breaking of that axiomatic tradition by Descartes in his *Géométrie*. We briefly considered his method of mapping algebra and geometry onto each other, by converting lengths into pure numbers. This conversion permits the geometric mapping of algebraic operations within the framework of the system generally referred to as "Cartesian coordinates."

We recalled Newton's view of geometry as an empirical science, based on such elementary mechanical operations as the drawing of straight lines and circles. Newton reasoned that since the ability to draw straight lines depends on the existence of rigid objects with shapes that contain straight-edges as models, the axioms of geometry result from insights implicit in these mechanical operations. Here we use the term "operations" in the sense Piaget used it to describe the development by a young child of the ability to perform direct mental manipulations of the external world. Newton viewed space as a primary physical entity, which emanated directly from God, as one of His principal creations.

We also followed the development of astronomy, from the ancients, who first established a precise and detailed representation of planetary motions, to the breakthrough in the sixteenth and seventeenth centuries, which permitted Newton to create a unified mechanics, comprising celestial as well as terrestrial mechanics. This unification was based on the intellectual structure provided by the idea of mass points subject to forces acting at a distance. We noted that this notion was at first considered bizarre, but due to its immense success, it had become the paradigm for theorizing in all physical sciences by the end of the eighteenth century. The corpus of these successful theories is generally designated as "classical" physics, to distinguish it from the "modern" physics, which eventually caused a radical revision of some of our most fundamental epistemological concepts.

The dynamics of mass points, or particle theory, is one cornerstone of classical physics. The other cornerstone is field theory. Field theory originated from the union of two lines of investigation, one of which is the study of light. Two centuries of optical discovery and analysis led to the development of the wave theory of light, which had been fully elaborated by about 1820. The first clear demonstration of the wave character of light was provided by Thomas Young in 1802, when he observed that a very narrow circular light beam passed through two small holes would produce a pattern of alternating light and dark concentric rings, or fringes, on a screen placed at some distance behind the holes. The dark rings were interpreted as arising from the interference on the screen of those parts of the light beam whose wave oscillations had been brought out of phase upon their diffraction at the edges of the small holes.

Beginning about 1815 (and independently of Young) Augustin Jean Fresnel provided a detailed description of the phenomena of light diffraction and interference. Fresnel used as his starting point the formulation of wave optics set forth by Christian Huygens 150 years earlier. Another fundamental idea due independently to both Young and Fresnel was that the vibration of a light wave is perpendicular to its direction of propagation (such a wave is said to be transverse) rather than along its direction of propagation, as is the case in a sound wave (longitudinal wave). Moreover, light can be polarized, in that its direction of vibration may be confined to only one of the many possible planes which are perpendicular to the direction of propagation.

A question then arose about the medium in which the light waves are propagated. By way of an answer, wave theorists postulated a hypothetical medium, called ether. This postulation was somewhat paradox-

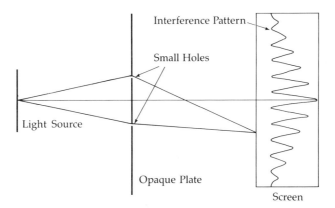

The first clear demonstration of the wave character of light was reported by Thomas Young in 1802. Light passing through two small holes in an opaque plate produced an interference pattern of light and dark fringes on a screen placed beyond the plate.

ical. On the one hand, mechanics had shown that transverse waves can propagate only in rigid media. On the other hand, the idea of a rigid medium permeating all of space and yet offering no friction to the motion of material bodies seemed bizarre.

The other origin of field theory lies in the study of electricity and magnetism. In 1831 Michael Faraday discovered that if a magnet is moved into a loop formed by an electrical conductor, a transient electric current is induced in the loop. Faraday realized that this induction of a current is the result of a change of what he termed the "magnetic field" in which the loop is embedded. He also found that passage of a current through the conductor from an external source of electricity would cause movement of a magnetic needle placed in the vicinity of the loop. From this Faraday inferred that a change in the magnetic field is induced by the change in an "electric field" generated by the flow of current. Although these electric and magnetic fields are generated within material bodies, they are propagated through empty space. The forces exerted by these fields can act on material bodies locally, thus circumventing the troublesome Newtonian notion of forces acting at a distance.

By the 1870s, James Clerk Maxwell's bold extrapolation had extended Faraday's ideas about force fields into a unified field theory that interpreted light as an electromagnetic wave in the electric and magnetic

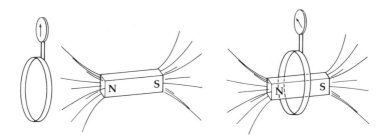

Faraday's Experiment By moving a magnet into a loop formed by an electric conductor, a current is generated and registered by the deflection of an ammeter included in the circuit.

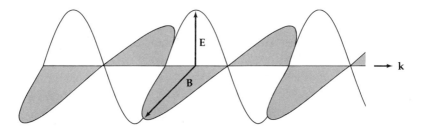

Electromagnetic Wave A schematic presentation of electromagnetic waves according to Maxwell's equations. The electric field vector **E** is perpendicular to the magnetic field vector **B** and both are perpendicular to the wave vector **k**. Polarization of light depends on the direction of the electric field vector, which is also called the light vector. If the light vector **E** moves in only one direction, the light is plane polarized.

fields. This wave can be described in terms of three, mutually perpendicular, vectorial components: the electric field vector E, which determines the plane of polarization of the light, the magnetic field vector B, which jointly with E, determines the amplitude of the wave, and the wave vector k, which designates the direction of propagation and length of the wave. Maxwell succeeded in describing the properties of waves propagated in the electromagnetic field in terms of four fundamental equations (referred to as "Maxwell's equations") that relate the temporal and spatial variation of the vectors E and B to the density of electric charge and current in the field, and to the velocity of wave propagation c in the direction of the wave vector k. Maxwell's unified field theory, and the subsequent discovery of radio waves, the existence of which it had predicted, made the concept of electromagnetic waves very real, but it did not eliminate the troublesome aspects of the idea of waves propagating either through empty space or through a rigid ether.

Chemistry was integrated into the corpus of classical physics by another of Faraday's many great discoveries, namely that in electrolysis there exists a proportionality between mass and charge transported. Faraday found that in electrolytic conduction of current by electrically charged molecules in solution, one chemical equivalent of mass (or mole) transports 96,000 coulombs of electric charge. This finding led to the idea that each molecule carries a fixed charge, and thus, like the elementary unit of mass, the elementary unit of charge was identified with molecules. From Faraday's equivalent (96,000 coulombs of charge per mole), it was possible to reckon the magnitude of the elementary unit of charge, once the number of molecules per mole, or Avogadro's number, was known. In this way, the elementary unit of charge was identified long before the electron, actual carrier of that charge, was discovered.

A branch of classical physics that developed more or less at the same time as field theory is thermodynamics, the discipline which addresses the phenomenon of heat and its relation to mechanical and electrical work. The first and second laws of thermodynamics had been formulated by the middle of the nineteenth century. These laws state that while energy is conserved in any spontaneous transaction involving the interconversion of heat and work, the capacity of the system to perform future work is irreversibly diminished. Toward the end of the nineteenth century, thermodynamics was united with molecular physics in the discipline of statistical mechanics. Here the application of probabilistic (i.e., indeterministic) laws to large ensembles of microscopic matter (i.e., molecules) provided a theoretical underpinning for the empirically founded laws of thermodynamics that govern the deterministic relations between heat and work in macroscopic matter.

Thus, by 1900 classical physics had provided an eminently satisfactory, wholly deterministic picture of the world, built on seemingly self-consistent notions. Even then, however, there remained some unanswered questions raised by this world view. It is instructive to consider a lecture given by Lord Kelvin before the British Association for the Advancement of Science in 1900. Kelvin, the originator of the absolute temperature scale bearing his name (and designated by the letter K), was one of the founders of thermodynamics. In his lecture he pointed out some clouds on the horizon of classical physics. The first such cloud reflects the paradoxical nature of the ether postulated by the unified field theory as the carrier of electromagnetic waves, which we have already considered. Kelvin thought it possible that such a bizarre substance exists, but he pointed out that if it does exist it should be possible to detect motion relative to the ether. This prediction, it should be noted, did not arise in the context of Newtonian mechanics, which envisages forces acting on point masses at a distance without any intervening ether. As will be described later in this chapter, experiments designed to detect motion relative to the ether gave negative results. By 1900 Kelvin and others were beginning to wonder whether this failure to detect motion relative to the ether might not have some nontrivial cause.

The second cloud to which Kelvin drew attention arose from a seemingly more mundane problem. Precise measurements of the specific heats at constant volume of diatomic gases, such as hydrogen (H_2) or oxygen (O_2), had given values of $5R/2$ (where R is the universal gas constant, having the dimensional units calories/degree/mole), instead of the value of $7R/2$ predicted from statistical mechanical considerations. (The specific heat at constant volume is the energy needed to raise the temperature of a mole of gas confined in a rigid container by $1°K$.) Although this discrepancy between measurement and prediction might appear trivial, it was a source of serious discomfort to physicists conversant with the immense success of statistical mechanics as applied to a wide variety of problems.

As it turns out, Kelvin had put his finger on the two troublesome problems of classical physics that led to two great and revolutionary theories: the *relativity* theory and the *quantum* theory. We will examine these two theories, in order to see the ways in which they are anti-intuitive, that is, how they violate the intuitive conceptual structures by which we have learned, both as a species and as individuals, to cope with the world.

The theory of relativity addresses the problem of how to account for the experimental fact that we cannot tell whether we are moving relative to the carrier of electromagnetic waves. To understand how this fact came to be known, we must first examine in more detail the Doppler effect, which is responsible for the increasing pitch of the siren of an approaching police car. (We briefly referred to the Doppler effect in chapter 1, in connection with the red shift of the light that reaches us from distant celestial objects.)

Consider a sound source and an observer moving with speed u toward each other. (Here u stands for speed relative to the speed of sound in air, with $0 \leq u \leq 1$; later on u will also represent speed relative to the speed of light.) The pitch, or frequency, of the sound heard by the observer goes up, whether the source approaches the observer or whether the observer approaches the source. But, as we shall now show, the Doppler effect is quantitatively different for the two cases. Let the source generate sound waves of wavelength λ and hence in frequency $v = 1/\lambda$. In case the source moves with speed u toward a resting observer, the wavelength λ' that the observer receives will be given by the difference between λ and the distance that the source moved toward the observer during the time interval $1/v$ while it generated one wave, namely u/v. Hence $\lambda' = \lambda - u/v$, and since $v' = 1/\lambda'$, the observer hears the higher frequency $v' = v/(1 - u)$. However, in case the observer moves with speed u toward a resting source, the observer receives u/λ more waves per unit time, and hence hears the higher frequency $v'' = v(1 + u)$. This quantitative difference in the Doppler effect makes it possible to distinguish by means of physical measurements which of two objects—one the source and the other the receiver of waves—is stationary and which is moving. At low speeds, when u is small compared to the speed of sound ($u << 1$), the difference between v' and v'' is small. But as u nears the speed of sound ($u \rightarrow 1$), v' becomes infinite, whereas v'' becomes $2v$. In other words, as the speed of a moving source nears the speed of sound, the sound waves it emits become more and more compressed as it approaches a resting observer. But as the speed of a moving observer nears the speed of sound, the observer receives waves at a frequency twice that at which they are emitted by the resting source the observer approaches. There is therefore a clear and experimentally verifiable asymmetry between the cases of the source of sound or the observer moving relative to the medium.

Let us now imagine two ships approaching each other at a uniform, high speed on a foggy sea. Both ships are sounding sirens with a tone of exactly the same pitch; both carry instruments capable of measuring the pitch of the tone they receive, which is reported to the other ship via radio. However, only one ship is actually moving; the other is stationary. The asymmetry of the Doppler effect would thus allow the crews to determine which of the two ships is moving and which is stationary, since the stationary ship would report receiving a higher pitched tone than the moving ship.

According to the unified field theory, it should also be possible to use light for such a Doppler effect diagnosis of motion relative to the ether. Let us imagine two rocket ships approaching each other at a uniform high speed in outer space, both emitting light signals of exactly the same frequency (i.e., color) and broadcasting the frequency of the signals received, but with only one of them moving with respect to the ether and the other stationary. Here, too, the stationary crew should report seeing signals of higher frequency than the moving crew. This prediction was tested by A. A. Michelson and E. W. Morley in the 1880s, when space travel existed only in the imagination of science fiction writers, by using the earth (which, in its circular orbit should be continuously varying the direction of its motion relative to the ether) as a moving space platform. The outcome of their experiment was negative: no motion of the earth relative to the ether could be detected by sending and receiving light signals.

As it turned out, the reason for the failure of this experiment is that the asymmetry of the Doppler effect does not apply to light. Timing by means of a standard clock the frequency of arriving light signals from a light source emitting signals at frequency v, an observer will find that the observed frequency depends on the observer's speed relative to the source, no matter which of them is moving. Moreover, the velocity of propagation of light c measured by that observer turns out to be independent of the observer's speed relative to the source. This is another finding incompatible with the view of light travelling as a wave in ether, since, according to the laws of classical mechanics, the value of c measured by the observer ought to increase or decrease in proportion to the speed with which the observer is moving toward or receding from the source.

The way out of these conflicts between observation and predictions was found by Hendrik Lorentz, Jules-Henri Poincaré, and Albert Einstein. Their resolution of the conflict demands a fundamental change in our assumptions about the nature of measurement, time, and space. As we considered earlier, measurements are made in terms of units, such as the ticks of a clock as the unit of time, or a rigid measuring rod as the unit of length. Measurement also presupposes the existence of a conserved quantity. However, the *apparent* length of a measuring rod varies according to the perspective and the distance from which it is viewed. Nevertheless, we hold to the idea that despite all these apparent changes, the length of the rod is conserved because, as we saw earlier, our brains process the primary sensory input in such a manner as to give us the ability to disentangle all the complex clues about the real rod provided by such phenomena as perspective and parallax. We may recall, furthermore, that our ability to perceive the real rod was acquired phylogenetically over millions of years, and was refined especially in connection with the development of frontal vision in carnivores and primates.

The theory of relativity now demands that we look at a moving clock or rod from a new perspective. This perspective is that of the theory known as the Lorentz transformation, which postulates that the intervals between the ticks of a clock are longer when the clock is moving than when the clock is at rest. More precisely, a time interval t at rest is dilated to a longer interval t' when the clock is moving with speed u (now expressed as a fraction of the speed of light c), according to the relation

$$t' = t\sqrt{1 - u^2}.$$

Thus for a clock moving at the speed of light ($u/c = 1$) $t' \to \infty$, that is, time does not pass at all. Hence a traveller accompanying the light from the explosion of a supernova one million years ago will arrive at the earth without having aged at all, in the traveller's subjective time. Similarly, the Lorentz transformation operates on length in such a way that a rod that has the length L at rest is contracted to a shorter length L' when the rod is moving with speed u, according to the relation

$$L' = L\sqrt{1 - u^2}.$$

Thus a rod moving at the speed of light ($u/c = 1$) would shrink to zero length. This relativistic contraction of length is analogous to the fore-shortening of space by perspective and can be construed as the treatment of time as another spatial coordinate, or more properly speaking, as one of the four coordinates of a space–time continuum. In the world of three-dimensional space, the distance between two events, of which one occurs at the origin of a coordinate system and the other at a position with coordinates x, y, and z, is given by

$$d = \sqrt{x^2 + y^2 + z^2}.$$

But in the four-dimensional space–time world, the distance between the two events also depends on the time interval t that has elapsed between their occurrence within that coordinate system, according to the relation

$$s = \sqrt{x^2 + y^2 + z^2 - c^2 t^2}.$$

It should be noted that in this four-dimensional world, time is singled out as a unique coordinate, which does not behave in quite the same way as the other three spatial coordinates because it carries a negative sign in the distance relation. Hence even for nonzero values of x, y, and z, the four-dimensional distance between two events can be zero, namely when

$$x^2 + y^2 + z^2 = c^2 t^2.$$

That is to say, the four-dimensional distance between two spatially distinct events is zero, if they are connected by a signal travelling with the speed of light c.

The consequences that these considerations have for the Doppler effect are profound. For the case of a source moving at a speed u and emitting a signal at frequency v, the stationary observer must take into account the fact that the interval t' between ticks of the moving clock is longer than the tick interval t of the stationary clock, according to the relation

$$t' = t/\sqrt{1 - u^2}.$$

The frequency v' of the signal that the observer receives is therefore decreased by a factor of $\sqrt{1 - u^2}$, and hence

$$v' = v\sqrt{1 - u^2}/(1 - u) = v\sqrt{(1 + u)/(1 - u)}.$$

In the case of the observer moving with speed u, the tick interval of the moving clock is longer, and hence the signals received from the stationary source appear to be increased in frequency by a factor of $\sqrt{1 - u^2}$, and hence

$$v'' = v(1 + u)/\sqrt{1 - u^2} = v\sqrt{(1 + u)/(1 - u)}.$$

Thus, when time is considered from the perspective of relativity theory $v'' = v'$, and the Doppler effect is the same for both cases, precluding the distinction between a moving observer and a moving source. This novel perspective becomes important only at speeds much higher than those we experience in our normal environment, which explains why an intuitive acceptance of the concepts of relativity theory has not been bred into the human brain.

One of the strangest implications of the relativity theory is illustrated by the twin paradox. One twin, A, stays home, and the other twin B goes for a journey at a velocity u. At time t, B turns around and heads for home. Time t is measured on A's clock, of which B carries an identical copy. The clocks send out a light signal at each tick. Because of the relativistic time dilation, B's clock ticks more slowly than A's on both legs of the journey, by a factor of $\sqrt{1 - u^2}$. On returning home, therefore, B's clock will lag by an amount $2t(1 - \sqrt{1-u^2})$ behind A's clock, and B will be correspondingly younger than the stay-at-home A.

Specifically, A's notebook containing the log of the signals received from the travelling twin will read as follows: As B receded from me, I received clock signals from B at a frequency reduced by the factor $\sqrt{(1 - u)/(1 + u)}$ due to the Doppler effect. I received these reduced frequency signals during the outbound journey, of duration t, and during the initial part of the return journey, that is, until the signal from the turning point travelling toward me at the speed of light (i.e., 1) arrived. The turning point occurred at distance tu, so that the signal emitted at the turning point took a time tu to reach me. The total receiving time of reduced frequency signals was therefore $t(1 + u)$. I received signals from B at the frequency raised by the factor $\sqrt{(1 + u)/1 - u}$ during the remainder of the journey, of duration $t\sqrt{(1 - u)}$. Thus, I received a total of $2t\sqrt{1 - u^2}$ signals, confirming that B's clock ticked more slowly than mine, which sent out $2t$ signals.

B's notebook will read as follows: I received lower frequency signals, at a rate reduced by the factor $\sqrt{(1 + u)/(1 - u)}$ during my outbound journey, of duration, on my clock of $t\sqrt{1 - u^2}$. I received higher frequency signals, at a rate increased by the factor $\sqrt{(1 + u)/(1 - u)}$ during my homeward bound journey, of duration on my clock of $t\sqrt{1 - u^2}$. Thus I received from A a total of $2t$ signals.

Evidently there is consistency in what A and B say about each other's clocks: both agree that A's clock ticked faster than B's. The asymmetry arises because for A, the outbound receiving time is longer than half of the total journey time, while for B it is exactly half the time. This asymmetry does not require that A be stationary; A could have been in uniform motion during B's journey with the same result. The intrinsic asymmetry between A and B devolves from B's *not* having been in uniform motion and having experienced forces of acceleration to which A was not subject. Nevertheless, it is not the forces of acceleration that cause the differences in elapsed time between A and B. These differences arise during B's two periods of uniform motion in opposite directions, which can be made arbitrarily long with respect to the periods of acceleration, without diminishing the relative age differences of A and B after the trip.

The twin paradox is of no practical significance for today's space travel, since the speed of space ships is still significantly less than the speed of light. But it is of the utmost importance for modern physics. For instance, the subatomic particle designated as the muon has a mean lifetime of 2.2 millionths of a second. This means that even if it travelled at the speed of light, such a particle would have travelled a mean distance of less than one kilometer before it decayed, were it not for the relativistic time dilation that obtains for clocks moving at such high speeds. Thus despite the short life span characteristic of muons at rest, a muon created by cosmic rays at the edge of the atmosphere hundreds of kilometers above the ground could easily reach the ground, if its speed were sufficiently close to that of light. Its subjective clock would be slowed by a large enough factor to extend its life to last for the trip. The life span of another subatomic particle called the charged pion is 26 billionths of a second when at rest; even travelling at the speed of light this life span would permit the pion a path length before decay of only a few meters. However, the relativistic slowing of its clock permits the pion to live long enough to run the hundreds of meters of track in the giant particle accelerators used by elementary particle physicists.

The theory of relativity thus obliges us to revise our intuitive concepts of the space–time framework of the real world. One particular intuitive concept that the theory throws overboard is that of simultaneity. If someone says "I woke up at the same time that my girl friend's alarm clock went off ten miles away," it is necessary to add "at the same time, that is, for me who, lying in bed, was stationary with respect to my girl friend's clock." Otherwise, the statement makes as little sense as one that says, "That tree is in the same place as the house its branches cover." From the perspective of the girl friend's brother orbiting the earth in a space station, the two events would not be simultaneous. According to the theory of relativity, there can be no such thing as absolute simultaneity of events at different locations. This abandonment of the notion of absolute simultaneity shocked both scientists and laymen when they were first confronted with the theory of relativity, but it need not truly violate our phylogenetically learned intuition about time. This intuition always relates to the simultaneity of events witnessed by a single observer, within a rather limited spatial domain.

The relativistic ideas that we have considered thus far are usually referred to as the *special theory of relativity*. They do away with the concept of absolute motion in space, at least as far as uniform motion is concerned. However, the concept of absolute rotary or accelerated motion still retains its physical meaning, in the sense that such motion is experimentally detectable by the forces it produces. This fundamental difference between accelerated and uniform motion was noted by Newton, who found it strange. In this regard, he proposed the thought experiment of rotating a bucket of water in an otherwise empty universe. Newton's own laws of mechanics told him that the water will creep up the sides of the bucket to form a curved surface. But, Newton wondered, how can the bucket, with no external reference points, know that it is rotating?

After having worked out the special theory of relativity, Einstein attacked this puzzle, taking as his starting point the fact that when we measure the mass of a body, we can do it by two apparently totally different methods. One method consists of weighing the body on a spring balance, which measures the force exerted on the body by gravity; the other method consists of observing its acceleration produced by an imposed force, which measures the inertial mass of the body. The two methods measure very different properties, namely, heaviness and inertia. The fact that they turn out to be strictly proportional, to an accuracy greater than 1 part in 100 billion, led Einstein to postulate that both properties are equivalent expressions of the same property.

Let us consider the following experiment: we sit weightless in outer space in a closed box moving at a uniform speed. Suddenly, we feel a force pulling us to the floor. It is impossible for us to tell by mechanical experiments inside the box whether this force is generated by the sudden appearance of a massive source of gravity, such as the earth, beneath the box, or a source of acceleration pulling the box from above. Einstein postulated that no kind of experiment, including optical or electromagnetic tests, could differentiate between the two alternatives. On the basis of this "equivalence principle" of gravity and acceleration Einstein related the space–time continuum of the special theory of relativity to gravitation, and devised the more comprehensive dynamic treatment now known as the *general theory of relativity*. It is remarkably difficult to develop the equivalence principle into a formal theory; as gravitational fields change from point to point of the space–time continuum, a four-dimensional geometry that changes similarly from point to point is required for their description. Nevertheless, by 1915 Einstein had formulated a consistent mathematical structure, in which the parameter of mass determines the four-dimensional geometry, which in turn determines the equations of motion. In this four-dimensional geometry, the three spatial coordinates x, y, and z are curved, or warped, in the fourth dimension of the time coordinate t if a strong gravitational field is present.

The general theory of relativity is therefore a construct that views the forces of gravity as equivalent to local alterations of the space–time geometry. The theory implies that with respect to *all* physical phenomena a gravitational field is indistinguishable from an accelerated motion. Hence the answer to Newton's quandary posed by the hypothetical bucket of water rotating in space is that his laws of mechanics do not apply to empty space. Any actual bucket rotates, not with respect to an absolute

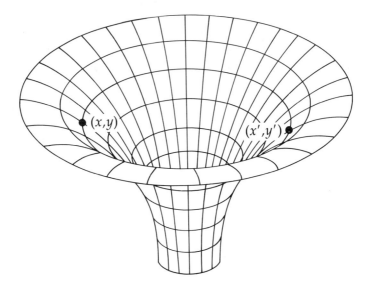

Representation of the curvature of space-time under the influence of a gravitational field, according to Einstein's general theory of relativity. To simplify the representation of the four-dimensional geometry of the theory, the coordinate of the third spatial dimension, z, has been omitted. Thus the mathematical structure of the theory is shown as a two-dimensional surface on which a grid of the x and y spatial coordinates has been drawn. The surface is curved, or warped, in the fourth dimension, t, due to the presence of a strong gravitational field (attributable to a star or other massive object) located at the bottom of the funnel-shaped surface. The degree of curvature of space increases with the strength of the gravitational field, so that as a light ray travels from point x, y to point x', y', the direction of its path as well as the time taken for the journey (and hence also the distance measured between the two points) will be ever more affected.

frame of reference, but only relative to the rest of the masses in the universe. Hence if we observed a bucket of water whose surface had taken on a curved shape, we would be free to infer that the bucket is actually at rest and the remainder of the universe is rotating to produce a local centrifugal force on the water in the bucket.

Our main concern here, however, is not the mathematical formulation of the general theory of relativity but the fact that it violates the intuition that guides our understanding of the global aspects of geometry. It leads to the counterintuitive notion of a universe without bounds but of finite volume, or to the strange idea of regions of space that are sinks for matter: the black holes.

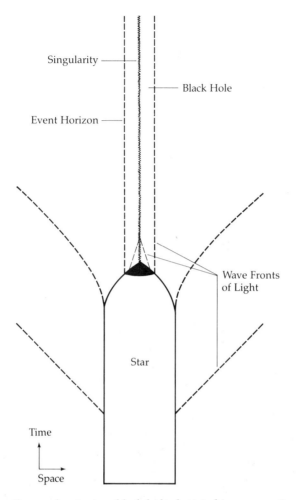

Gravitational collapse of a star to a black hole depicted in a space-time diagram showing only one of the three spatial dimensions. The vertical dimension is time. When the radius of the collapsing star reaches a critical value, called the Schwarzschild radius, light emitted by the star can no longer escape. This forms an event horizon, the boundary of the black hole. Inside the black hole, the star continues to collapse to a space-time singularity, about which the laws of physics are silent. [After Hawking, 1977]

To fathom the origin of a black hole, let us imagine a star with a mass 10 times that of the sun. It will generate heat at its center by converting hydrogen into helium (as discussed in chapter 1), and this heat will create sufficient outward pressure to prevent the collapse of the star due to its own gravitational forces. Such a star would have a radius of about 3 million km. The initial velocity that would allow an object to escape to an infinite distance from this star, starting from its surface, would be about 1000 km/sec. After exhausting its nuclear fuel, the star would begin to collapse, its density would increase, and the escape velocity for objects at its surface would increase. By the time the radius of the star had shrunk to 30 km, the escape velocity from its surface would have increased to the speed of light. Thereafter, even light could not escape from the surface of the collapsing star. And if light could not escape, nothing else could do so either. The star would have become a black hole, a region in space–time from which it is not possible to escape. The boundary of the black hole—the perimeter at which the escape velocity is equal to the speed of light—is called its "event horizon." Within the event horizon the star continues to collapse to form what is called a "space–time singularity," to which the laws of physics cannot yet be applied.

These violations of our intuitive concepts are even more extreme than those perpetrated by the special theory of relativity. The special theory of relativity at least allowed the analogy of the change of visual perspective to help us grasp the consequences of changing from one frame of reference of uniform motion to another. But under the general theory of relativity we can apply the perspective analogy only to local events. We are completely prohibited from applying our intuitive concepts about space and time to gain a global view of the space–time continuum. We are restricted to a wholly abstract analysis that allows no pictorial representations or analogies with everyday experience.

REFERENCES

Einstein, A. 1936. Physics and reality. *Journal of Franklin Institute* 221: 349–381.

Einstein, A., H. W. Lorentz, H. Minkowski, and H. Weyl. 1952. *The Principle of Relativity.* New York: Dover. A collection of original memoirs, translated into English, on the special and general theories of relativity.

Hawking, S. W. 1977. The quantum mechanics of black holes. *Scientific American* 236(1): 34–40.

Kelvin, first Baron (W. Thomson). 1901. 19th century clouds over the dynamical theory of heat and light. *Philosophical Magazine* 2: 1–40.

Misner, C. W., K. S. Thorne, and J. A. Wheeler. 1973. *Gravitation.* San Francisco: W. H. Freeman.

Thorne, K. S. 1974. The search for black holes. *Scientific American* 231(6): 32–43.

Sixteen

Quantum Theory

In the preceding chapter we discussed the concept of the electromagnetic field, an entity generated by waves that propagate from point to point through space and act on matter locally, rather than at a distance. The development of this concept suggested that it should be possible to detect motion relative to the carrier of these waves. The failure of all attempts to detect such motion led to the postulate that it is undetectable in principle: a categorical postulate similar to that of the impossibility of constructing a perpetual motion machine. Combining that postulate with the finding that light has the same velocity for all observers regardless of their motion relative to the light source led to the special theory of relativity, which envisages that space and time form a four-dimensional continuum, with a metric such that the distance between spatially distinct events can be zero.

We discussed the relativistic behavior of clocks and rods in motion yielding dilation of time and contraction of length, respectively, as a perspective distortion analogous to the apparent decrease in length on viewing a tilted rod. We discussed in detail how this assumption makes the Doppler effect relativistically invariant, meaning that the shift in the frequency of the observed signal is the same whether the observer or the light source is in motion. We also discussed the twin paradox where of two twins—one making a round trip to a distant point in space–time and back while the other stays at home—the traveling twin returns younger than the stay-at-home twin.

We then proceeded to the general theory of relativity, which uses the observed equivalence between gravitational force and accelerated motion to describe gravity in terms of the geometry of the space–time continuum. To formulate this theory, Einstein used an abstract four-dimensional geometric structure, whose coordinates are subject to local deformation, or warp, by the presence of mass. Thus, we needed to cope with a conceptual revision of the space–time framework of the real world. The new framework is in striking conflict with our intuitive demands for "visualizability," that is, for a mental representation of reality in terms of the intuitive concepts of space and time with which we have been endowed by evolution.

To acquaint ourselves with a further violation of our intuitive concepts brought about by the advances of modern physics, let us now turn to the *quantum theory*. In contrast to the theory of relativity, which addressed a specific paradox (namely the impossibility of detecting motion relative to the ether) and resolved it simply and elegantly, the quantum theory underwent a more tortuous development. Although quantum theory came into being in 1900, it took a quarter of a century before its full implications were realized. It is possible to identify five successive stages in that tortuous development. In the first stage, Max Planck introduced the notion of the quantum of action and its magnitude, as expressed by the universal constant h, into his laws that account for the frequency distribution of electromagnetic radiation emanating from a blackbody and the specific heats of gases and solids at low temperature. In the second stage, Albert Einstein recognized the dual nature of light as having the properties of both waves and particles and also worked out the implications of that duality for the interaction of radiation and matter. In the third stage, Niels Bohr introduced Planck's constant h into the theory of the dynamics of electrons orbiting the atomic nucleus. In the fourth stage, the wave-particle duality of matter, specifically of electrons, was recognized. And in the fifth stage, Werner Heisenberg developed his uncertainty principle and Bohr his complementarity argument.

Let us now consider these stages in more detail. In the first stage, the quantum of action entered physics through the back door, so to speak, in the course of attempts to understand the exchange of energy between radiation and matter. This problem has its origin in the common, everyday observation that as a body, say a bar of iron, is heated to higher and higher temperatures, it emits light of higher and higher frequencies: first in the range of the invisible infrared, then in the red, the yellow, the blue ("white heat"), and finally the invisible ultraviolet. More precisely, at any temperature T, there is a distribution of frequencies v of the light emitted.

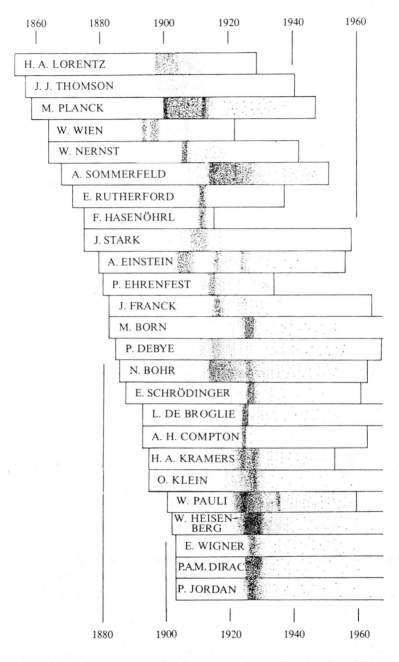

The most prominent founders of the quantum theory, listed in the order of their years of birth. The density of black dots in each year indicates the importance of the contributions made by the individual at that time. [From Hund, 1967. Used with permission.]

This distribution has the property that the frequency, ν_{max}, at which the *maximum* intensity of light is emitted rises with T in a manner such that the ratio T/ν_{max} is a constant. This relation was discovered by Wilhelm Wien and is known as Wien's law. On the other hand, the *total* intensity of radiation emitted at all frequencies rises proportionally with the fourth power of T, a relation known as the Stefan-Boltzmann law. In the latter part of the nineteenth century physicists were thus faced with the challenge of producing a theory to account for these two experimentally observed relations.

It seemed clear that the exchange of energy between radiation and matter should be governed by the laws of thermodynamics and that, therefore, the overall consequences of that exchange should be independent of the details of the mechanisms by which the interactions occur. To bring this problem within the reach of statistical mechanics and of Maxwell's theory of the electromagnetic field, let us consider a hollow box whose walls are blackbodies, that is, they absorb all incident radiation without reflecting any. When the walls are at thermal equilibrium with the electromagnetic field within the box at the uniform inside temperature T, the rates of absorption and emission of radiant energy by the walls are equal. Under these conditions, what will be the distribution of the intensity of radiation $\rho(\nu)$ emitted in a narrow frequency range bracketing the frequency ν emitted from the blackbody interior of the box through a small hole? In 1900 Lord Rayleigh derived an expression relating this distribution of intensities of radiation at various frequencies to the temperature. Rayleigh considered the entire electromagnetic field in the box as an ensemble of standing waves of various frequencies, with the total radiant energy of the ensemble being the sum of the individual energies of all the standing waves. It then followed from Maxwell's equations of the electromagnetic field that the number of standing waves in the box per unit volume in a narrow frequency interval bracketing ν is given by $8\pi\nu^2/c^3$. Rayleigh envisaged, moreover, that each frequency interval of the radiation extant at thermal equilibrium is a separate vibrational degree of freedom. Since, according to the laws of statistical mechanics, the average energy associated with each vibrational degree of freedom at the temperature T is kT (where k is Boltzmann's constant, having the value 1.3805×10^{-16} erg/degree/molecule), Rayleigh reasoned that

$$\rho(\nu) = (8\pi\nu^2/c^3)kT.$$

Unfortunately, this formula has the counterfactual property that the intensity of radiation is an ever-increasing function of the frequency ν. Hence, the total energy of the ensemble, summed over all frequencies,

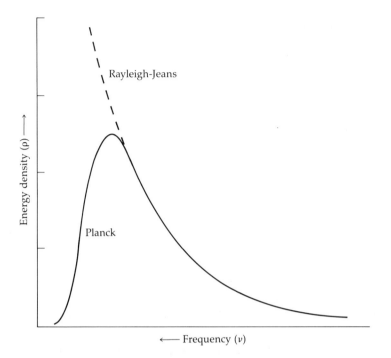

Frequency of radiation emitted by a blackbody at a given temperature. The Rayleigh formula, derived from concepts of classical physics, correctly describes the low frequency region of the emission spectrum but diverges drastically at high frequency. The Planck formula, which incorporates the novel notion of quantization of energy, correctly describes the observed emission spectrum over the entire range.

would increase without bound. This feature of the Rayleigh formula is contrary to both Wien's law and the Stefan-Boltzmann law and has been called the "ultraviolet catastrophe." However, Rayleigh's law does give a satisfactory account of the experimentally observed intensity distribution $\rho(v)$ for values of v well below v_{max}.

The derivation of the correct formula describing the intensity distribution of radiation in thermal equilibrium with matter at temperature T had been a long-standing interest of Max Planck's. In 1900 Planck put forward the radical proposal that the energy contained by an individual standing wave is *fixed*, rather than capable of taking on any value whatsoever. Specifically he proposed that the energy of each wave of frequency v is given by the product hv, (where h is Planck's universal constant, or quantum of action, having the value 6.624×10^{-27} erg sec).

Hence this product represents the unit packet, or quantum, of energy that is exchanged between a wave in the electromagnetic field and matter. This postulation had as its consequence that, contrary to Rayleigh's assumption, each frequency interval of the radiation in the box is not equivalent to a separate vibrational degree of freedom, and hence does not simply contribute an amount kT to the total energy of the ensemble. First, the number of standing waves per unit volume in the interval bracketing v is now $8\pi v^2/c^3(e^{hv/kT}-1)$, where the additional factor $(e^{hv/kT}-1)$ in the denominator arises from statistical mechanical considerations relating the relative abundance at equilibrium of the energy state hv to the temperature T. Second, each standing wave contributes an amount of energy hv to the ensemble. Thus Planck arrived at the formula

$$\rho(v) = 8\pi h v^3/c^3(e^{hv/kT}-1)$$

which correctly relates the distribution of intensities of blackbody radiation at various frequencies to the temperature.

For small values of v, Planck's formula reduces to Rayleigh's formula and thus agrees with the frequency spectrum as determined by experiment. Furthermore, for large values of v, Planck's formula reduces to the relation

$$\rho(v) = (8\pi h v^3/c^3)e^{-hv/kT}$$

and thus avoids the "ultraviolet catastrophe." It turned out that the ratio of the two universal constants h/k in this formula is equal to the constant relating T to v_{max} in Wien's law.

The postulation of the quantum of action was also able to resolve the discrepancy between the observed and predicted values for the specific heat at constant volume of diatomic gases, which Lord Kelvin had pointed out in his lecture in 1900. The kinetic theory, as formulated in the theorems of statistical mechanics, had been tremendously successful in accounting for the relations between volume, pressure, and temperature of gases. According to these theorems, the specific heat of a system held at constant volume is proportional to the degrees of freedom of motion of the components of the system. More specifically, each degree of freedom contributes an amount $R/2$ to the specific heat (where R is the molar gas constant with the value 8.3144×10^7 erg/degree/mole). In the case of a monoatomic gas, such as helium (He), there are just three degrees of freedom of motion, namely the translational movements of the molecule along the three linear x, y, and z coordinates of space. Hence the specific heat of a monoatomic gas should be $3R/2$, which agrees with observation. When we consider a diatomic gas, such as hydrogen (H_2), however, we note four additional degrees of freedom of motion, of which two are represented by the two angular coordinates of the axis of the rotational movement of the two atoms about the center of gravity of the molecule and two more by the distance of each atom from the center of its oscillation in the vibratory movement of the two atoms toward and away from each other. Thus the expected value of the specific heat is raised to $7R/2$. But this expected value exceeds by R the observed specific heat, which is only $5R/2$.

It turned out that the theoretical overestimation of the specific heat has its origin in the inappropriate inclusion of the vibration of the atoms as degrees of freedom in the specific heat calculation. The laws of classical mechanics, which underlie statistical mechanics and envisage infinitely fine grained energy levels, are applicable to the translational and rotational movements of the gas molecules because the molecules can share the total translational and rotational energy possessed by the system by colliding with each other. Although in these collisions energy is exchanged via quanta, the amount of energy $h\nu$ per quantum is so low (because the value of ν for translational and rotational movements is so small) that for all practical purposes the energy levels associated with these degrees of freedom are fine grained, or continuous. However, the laws of classical mechanics *are not* applicable to the vibratory movement of the two atoms, whose energy can be exchanged with other molecules only via the absorption or emission of electromagnetic radiation. Here the value of the quantum of energy needed to produce any change in vibrational energy at all is so high (because the value of ν for the vibratory movement is so large) that the energy levels of the vibrational movement are not continuous but *quantized,* with successive levels being separated by substantial differences in energy. For example, upon applying heat to the walls of a bottle containing a diatomic gas at ordinary temperatures, very little of the energy is absorbed by the vibrational movement. Thus the notion of the quantum of action led to the recognition that the vibrational degrees of freedom make no contribution to the specific heat of the diatomic gas, and hence the quantum theory reconciled statistical mechanics with thermodynamic observations.

Planck's postulation of the quantum of action was gloriously successful, but it led to an enormous conceptual calamity for physicists. It had not been very long since Maxwell had succeeded in unifying electricity and magnetism with light, by showing that they can all be interpreted in terms of continuous electromagnetic waves. Yet by building on Planck's notion of quantized energy, Einstein showed that light is not absorbed and emitted as waves after all, but as discrete lumps of energy called photons. Photons are particles without mass, and their energy is given by $h\nu$, where ν is the frequency attributable to their wavelike aspect. So in the second stage of the development of quantum theory, Einstein realized that light has a dual nature, or to phrase it in terms of a conceptually self-contradictory proposition, light is both a wave *and* a particle. This proposal of Einstein's met with widespread disapproval within the community of physicists. Even Planck would not accept it, so revolutionary was its nature.

The third stage in the development of the quantum theory made matters still worse. In the early years of this century, Ernest Rutherford's observations on the scattering of alpha particles emitted by radioactive materials had led him to postulate that the atom consists of a tiny center containing nearly all of its mass—the nucleus—around which orbits a cloud of much lighter, tinier particles, the electrons. Two atoms would then form a bond with each other—undergo a chemical reaction—by interaction of their electron clouds. By 1913, however, Niels Bohr realized that there was something wrong with the model of electrons circling the nucleus in *stable* orbits. According to classical physics, a negatively charged electron circling the positively charged nucleus would radiate energy and eventually fall into the nucleus. Moreover, this model would preclude the elements from manifesting definite, fixed chemical properties, since the sizes and shapes of the electron orbits would be subject to continuous variations, as are planetary orbits in a solar system. In order to avoid the contradictions inherent in Rutherford's model of the atom, Bohr postulated that only a discrete subset of the continuously varying range of orbits possible according to Newtonian mechanics is actually permitted, and that electrons jump discontinuously from one permitted orbit to another by absorbing or emitting quanta of light. This idea of quantized electron orbits was extremely offensive to most physicists, especially those whose data (on the spectral properties of light emitted and absorbed by atoms) Bohr was interpreting in terms of his theory. They found especially upsetting Bohr's assertion that the frequency of the light emitted by the electrons does not correspond to the *frequency of their orbits,* that is to the number of revolutions ν per unit of time, but to the *differences* in frequency of their orbits $\nu_1 - \nu_2$ (and hence in energy $h(\nu_1 - \nu_2)$) between which the electrons jump. Bohr's model was successful, however, in explaining the spectral properties of the elements, and it led to a much deeper understanding of the chemist's periodic table of the elements.

Efforts to give Bohr's model a quantitative formulation during the period 1913–1925 culminated in two independent breakthroughs: the wave equation of Erwin Schrödinger and the matrix mechanics of Werner Heisenberg. Schrödinger's formulation was based on Louis de Broglie's idea that, like photons, electrons might have wavelike properties. This idea was soon vindicated by the demonstration that electrons, like photons, are subject to diffraction. However, the lesson of this fourth stage of the development of quantum theory, namely that the electron, an authentic particle possessing a measurable mass, has also the properties of a wave, was even less palatable than the lesson of the second stage of the wave–particle duality of the massless photon. As for Heisenberg's matrix mechanics, it seemed like an even greater assault on rationality than the attribution of wavelike properties to the electron. For when Heisenberg's formulation was restated by Paul Dirac in terms of an algebra whose variables represent positional coordinates and momenta of electrons, supposedly real quantities measurable with rods and clocks, it transpired that these variables do not obey the laws of multiplicative commutability for two variables p and q: pq is not equal to qp.

Some order was brought into this conceptual chaos by Heisenberg's uncertainty principle. (It is told that when Heisenberg visited his friend Wolfgang Pauli in 1930, he was greeted at the Zurich railway station by a reception committee holding placards proclaiming "Long live Universal Uncertainty," much to the puzzlement of the press.) The uncertainty principle asserts that the variables p and q, which lack the property of commutability in multiplication possessed by all ordinary quantities of everyday life, here represent quantities that cannot in principle be measured jointly to any arbitrary degree of exactness in a single experiment or be inferred from successive experiments. For it inheres in the nature of these experiments that when an arrangement is introduced to measure the magnitude of one of these quantities, information is necessarily lost concerning the magnitude of the other. The product of the uncertainties Δp and Δq in the measures of both quantities p and q is never smaller than $h/2\pi$. Hence according to the uncertainty principle

$$\Delta p \Delta q > h/2\pi$$

The noncommutable variables p and q were designated as complementary quantities, and the mutual exclusion of the experimental arrangements needed for measuring either quantity to an arbitrary degree of

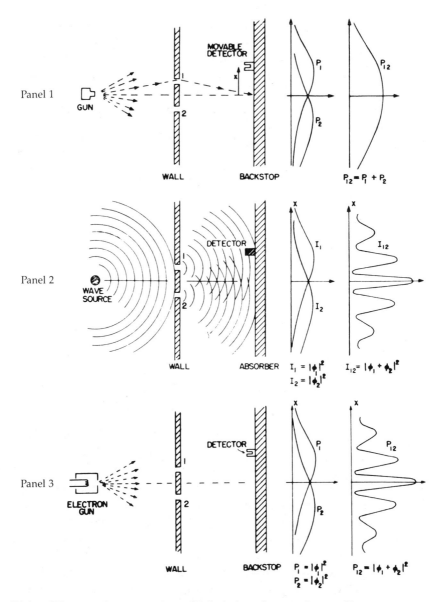

Richard Feynman's presentation of Bohr's thought experiment. [Feynman, Leighton, & Sands. *The Feynman Lectures on Physics, Vol. III*, © 1965, Addison-Wesley, Reading, Massachusetts. Figs. 1-1, 1-2, 1-3, 1-4, and 1-6. Reprinted with permission.]

exactness was termed *complementarity*. To illustrate the profound consequences of the uncertainty principle and complementarity for the relation of physical theory to our notions of reality, Bohr devised a famous thought

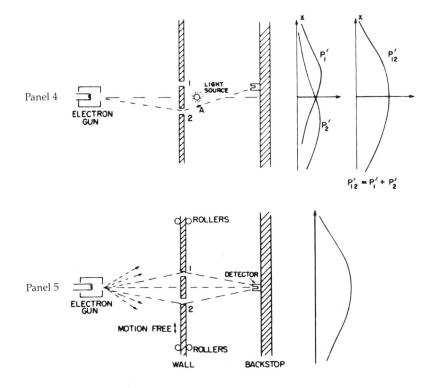

Panel 4

Panel 5

$$P'_{12} = P'_1 + P'_2$$

Feynman presentation (*continued*)

experiment. Let us consider that thought experiment (which has never been carried out in exactly the way Bohr described it, but whose outcome was never in doubt) in the version in which it was presented many years later by Richard Feynman. The experimental arrangement and results of the experiment are shown in the five panels of the figure shown on these two pages.

In panel 1 we see a gun shooting bullets in random directions at a wall. There are two holes, 1 and 2, in the wall spaced at equal distances from the intersection with the wall of the perpendicular line projected to the wall from the point at which the gun is positioned. Either hole may be opened or closed. Behind the wall is a backstop with a movable bullet detector. The detector measures $P(x)$, the frequency with which (and hence probability that) a bullet that passes through the wall strikes the backstop at a distance x from the projection to the backstop of the midpoint between the two holes. When only hole 1 or only hole 2 is open, the detector registers the bullet frequency distributions designated respectively as P_1 or P_2. When both holes are open the distribution P_{12} registered is the sum of the distributions P_1 and P_2 observed with either hole open alone. That is to say here $P_{12} = P_1 + P_2$.

In panel 2 the setup is immersed in water. The gun has been replaced by a source of water waves (say stones dropping into the water), the backstop by an absorber or nonreflector of the waves, and the bullet detector by a wave detector, which measures the "intensity" $I(x)$ of the waves reaching the absorber at the distance x from the midpoint. Here "intensity" is defined as the square of the absolute value of the mean amplitude $|\phi|$ of the waves at x averaged over the whole time of the experiment. When only hole 1 or only hole 2 is open, the wave detector registers the intensity distributions designated as I_1 and I_2 respectively, where $I_1 = |\phi_1|^2$ and $I_2 = |\phi_2|^2$. When both holes are open, the distribution I_{12} registered is *not* the sum of the distributions I_1 and I_2 observed with either hole open alone. Instead we see a distribution with crests and troughs, or "fringes," due to the relation $I_{12} = |\phi_1 + \phi_2|^2$. This difference between the two situations is attributable to interference at the absorber of parts of the same wave that have passed through both open holes, in contrast to the bullets, which do not show interference at the backstop, since any given bullet can pass through only one of two open holes. The wave length λ of the waves can be estimated from the distance x_f between successive fringes, since

$$\lambda = 2sx_f L$$

where s is the distance between hole 1 and hole 2 and L the distance between the wall and the absorber.

In panel 3 the setup is in a vacuum chamber. The gun is an electron gun, which emits an electron beam in random directions. The electron detector at the backstop is an electronic device connected to a loudspeaker. Each electron that strikes the detector is heard as a distinct click, thus demonstrating that the electrons strike the backstop as particles, just as the bullets do in panel 1. When only hole 1 or only hole 2 is open, the detector registers the electron frequency distributions P_1 or P_2, respectively. But when both holes are open, the observed distribution P_{12} is not the sum of P_1 and P_2. Rather, just as in the case of the water waves, P_{12} manifests the result of interference at the backstop. Loudspeaker clicks notwithstanding, each electron behaves as if it had reached the backstop by traveling through *both* holes, that is, like a wave rather than a particle. Thus at x there are two mean amplitudes, ϕ_1 and ϕ_2, associated with the parts of the electron waves having traveled through either hole, so that $P_1 = |\phi_1|^2$, $P_2 = |\phi_2|^2$ and $P_{12} = |\phi_1 + \phi_2|^2$. This result is obtained even if the electron gun is firing so slowly that each electron has reached the backstop before the next electron is released, thereby eliminating the possibility that the interference pattern reflected by P_{12} is the result of interactions between several electrons. As in the case of the water wave, the distance x_f between interference fringes allows us to calculate the wave length λ of the electron wave.

The setup shown in panel 4 is similar to that of panel 3, except that it includes an added feature that can tell us whether an individual electron that produced a distinct click in the loudspeaker had actually passed through hole 1 or hole 2. This feature consists of a strong light source placed behind the wall between the two holes, as well as a device that registers the direction in which light was scattered by passage of an electron. It is thus possible to know on which side of the light source, proximal to hole 1 or to hole 2, each electron has traveled. Here it is found that, as would be expected of a particle, when both holes are open each click is associated with transit of an electron through one or the other of the two holes but never through both. But in this case the distribution P_{12} is characteristic of bullets rather than waves, namely $P_{12} = P_1 + P_2$: the interference phenomenon has disappeared. In other words, the inclusion of the additional feature in the experimental setup that demonstrates the particulate character of the electron has eliminated its wavelike character. This means that the electrons behave differently when they are watched and when they are not watched, just as envisaged by Heisenberg's uncertainty principle. Or as stated by Feynman in his lectures, "it is impossible to design an apparatus to determine which hole the electron passes through, that will not at the same time disturb the electrons enough to destroy the interference pattern."

Maybe the result obtained with the setup of panel 4 is not all that strange, because, after all, the quanta emitted by the light source of the additional feature do disturb the electrons. Thus we can at least console ourselves with the thought that in setup 4 something is being done to the electrons that is not being done in the setup of panel 3. To remove any residual complacency, let us therefore consider the setup shown in panel 5. Here the setup is again similar to that of panel 3, except that the wall with the holes is mounted on rollers and is thus free to move back and forth due to the recoil imparted to it as individual electrons are scattered by collision with the edges of the holes. It should be possible to infer from the direction in which the wall moves whether an electron has passed through hole 1 or hole 2. In this setup nothing is done to disturb the electrons, since they are necessarily scattered by collision with the edges of the wall. Should not their wavelike character, and hence the interference phenomenon, be preserved under these conditions? The answer is that we cannot tell, because we are unable to observe the interference pattern, even if the wavelike pattern *were* preserved. To infer from the movement of the wall which hole the electron has passed through, we have to know with very high precision the momentum of the wall before and after passage of the electron. But according to the uncertainty principle the position of the wall relative to the perpendicular line projected to it from the gun, and hence the position of the two holes, cannot then be known to any arbitrary degree of precision. Thus the experimental arrangement needed for measuring the momentum of the wall with high accuracy introduces an uncertainty, or wiggle, in the position of the holes, such that there is an error Δx, in the distance from the midpoint at which an electron released by the electron gun in a given direction actually strikes the (stationary) backstop. This error causes a corresponding error ΔP in the distribution $P(x)$ measured by the detector, which is sufficiently large to smear out the crests and troughs of the interference pattern $P_{12} = |\phi_1 + \phi_2|^2$. No interference is observed. We thus reach the fifth stage of the tortuous development of the quantum theory, namely the realization of the eerie, not to say devilish, fact that the uncertainty principle and the complementarity of mutually exclusive measurements protect the conceptually paradoxical elements of that theory from being shown by any experiment actually to be in conflict.

REFERENCES

Feynman, R. P., R. B. Leighton, and M. Sands. 1963. *The Feynman Lectures on Physics*. Reading, Mass.: Addison-Wesley.

Hund, F. 1967. *Geschichte der Quantentheorie*. Mannheim: Bibliographisches Institut.

Seventeen

Complementarity

Let us retrace the tortuous path of the development of the quantum theory. It began in 1900, with Planck's introduction of the quantum of action in his exploration of the energy distribution in a radiation field in thermodynamic equilibrium with matter at a given temperature. Next, Einstein proposed that light, in addition to propagating as an electromagnetic wave, is absorbed and emitted as photons, or quanta, of energy $E = h\nu$. Then came Bohr's model of the atom, according to which electrons circle the nucleus in discrete planetary orbits, but make discontinuous jumps from one orbit to another by the absorption or emission of quanta. The particle-wave duality of electrons was discovered at the same time as the theoretical breakthroughs of Schrödinger's wave equation and Heisenberg's and Dirac's matrix algebra of noncommutative observable quantities. Finally, it was recognized that the deepest significance of the quantum of energy lies in Heisenberg's uncertainty principle and Bohr's concept of complementarity.

The epistemological implications of the uncertainty principle and the complementarity concept can be paraphrased as follows: quantum phenomena are an expression of a "conspiracy of nature" that prevents us from attaining a fully deterministic description of physical phenomena. Every observational act embodies an element of subjectivity. In each such act, we must make a choice of where and how to make the conceptual cut between our instruments of observation and the objects observed. In every case the observational instruments must be described in the terms of classical (i.e., nonquantum) physics, so that the observer can report to others (as well as making clear to himself) in unambiguous terms the exact experimental setup and the results he obtained. But, as we have seen, some of these choices are mutually exclusive. In Bohr's two-hole thought experiment, for example, we can choose a wall fixed in position relative to the electron gun and the backstop. This setup permits a determination of the wavelengths of the electrons on the basis of their interference patterns, but not of the identity of the hole through which any given electron has passed. Or we can choose a wall that is free to exchange momentum, but with an uncertain position, by mounting the wall on rollers. This setup permits a determination of the momentum exchange between wall and electrons, and hence an identification of the hole through which each electron has passed. However, any information regarding the wavelength of the electrons is lost. These two setups are clearly mutually exclusive, since the wall cannot be both fixed in position and yet free to exchange momentum. If the wall is fixed, it is part of the observational apparatus with which we seek to define the wave character of the observed object (the electron). If the wall is free to move, and its momentum is measured before and after collision with the particle, then the wall is itself an object of observation rather than part of the observational apparatus.

The paradoxical aspect of the two-hole experiment lies in the fact that when both holes are open, each electron recorded individually by the counter at the backstop seems to have gone through both holes, since there are crests and troughs in the intensity distribution characteristic of the interference of waves traveling through both holes. How can a single particle, which is clearly recorded as a unit event by the counter, have traveled through both holes? Of course the particle does not travel through both holes: as soon as a setup is used that identifies the hole through which the electron went, it is seen to have gone through only one of them. But since interference fringes are seen only when both holes are open, how does the particle going through one hole know that the other hole is also open? According to Bohr, the resolution of the paradox lies in the wholeness of the phenomenon in which observer and object are tied together. We have the choice of asking through which hole the electron went, and having made that choice, we produce an observational setup that provides a clear answer. But if we choose to ask what the wavelength of the associated wave is, that choice leads to a different observational setup, which precludes getting an answer to the first question.

Einstein was unwilling to admit such a conspiracy of nature and would not accept quantum mechanics as a complete description of physical

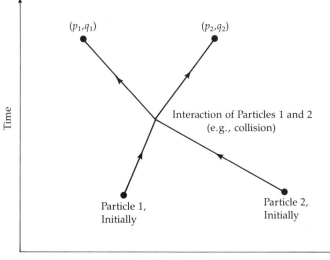

The Einstein-Podolsky-Rosen thought experiment. Two particles 1 and 2 collide and separate. After collision particle 1 has momentum p_1 and position q_1. The corresponding quantities for particle 2 are p_2 and q_2.

reality. He felt that quantum mechanics is incomplete, in the sense that it fails to account for some quantities that are "physically real." He believed that it should be possible to develop a more adequate theory, which would provide a fully deterministic, or *complete*, account of all real phenomena. To show that, the uncertainty principle notwithstanding, the complementary quantities p and q are physically real, Einstein, Podolsky, and Rosen put forward the following thought experiment in 1935. Consider two particles that collide and separate. After collision, one particle has a spatial coordinate q_1 and momentum p_1, while for the other the corresponding quantities are q_2 and p_2. It can be shown that although according to quantum mechanics the complementary quantities q_1 and p_1, or q_2 and p_2, cannot both be determined to an arbitrary degree of accuracy, combinations of the quantities q_1 and p_2, or q_2 and p_1, such as the difference $q_1 - q_2$ and the sum $p_1 + p_2$ *can* be so determined. Hence, by measuring p_1 or q_1 of the first particle to any desired degree of accuracy, one can predict the exact value of p_2 or q_2 without disturbing in any way, that is, without physically interacting with, the second particle. Einstein claimed therefore that the quantities p_2 and q_2 must be physically real. More precisely, Einstein put forward the following criterion of "physically real": "If, without in any way disturbing a system, we can predict with certainty (i.e., with probability equal to unity) the value of a physical quantity, then there exists an element of physical reality corresponding to this physical quantity." Since quantum mechanics does not give us a method for predicting all physically real quantities, quantum mechanics must be incomplete.

Bohr's reply to this argument was that Einstein's criterion of physical reality contains an ambiguity resulting from the phrase "without in any way disturbing the system." It is true that in measuring p_1 or q_1, one does not physically disturb the second particle, but one does disturb the possibility of making predictions about it by choosing to measure p_1 or q_1. Bohr pointed out that an object under observation and the apparatus needed to measure any physical quantity form a single, indivisible system, not susceptible to analysis at the quantum mechanical level in terms of separate parts. The combination of a given particle with one particular experimental setup for observation differs essentially from the combination of the same particle with another observational setup. Thus the description of the state of the system, rather than being restricted to the particle under observation, expresses a relation between the particle and all the measuring devices present. In other words, even though no direct measurements are performed on the second particle under Einstein's argument, the state of the second particle, and hence the physical reality of which it forms a part, is not independent of the presence of the apparatus with which measurements are performed on the first particle. Hence Einstein's argument fails.

The proposition that the complementarity concept is universally applicable to physical reality and is the crux of quantum phenomena was hotly debated for the next twenty years. Many attempts were made to find loopholes in the argument, especially by designing clever experiments that would circumvent the uncertainty principle. Although all these attempts failed, it is highly instructive to consider a few of them. Let us return to Bohr's thought experiment of an electron gun firing at a wall with two holes and look at the part of the experiment in which the light scattered by the electron is used to identify the hole through which it traveled. Under this arrangement the interference fringes of the intensity distribution measured at the backstop disappear, so that the electron appears to have lost its wavelike character. To account for this observation, one might be tempted to say that, although in scattering the light the position of the electron was fixed relative to the two holes, recoil of the scattered photon disturbed the motion of the electron in an uncontrolled manner. Thus the interference fringes at the backstop are smeared and information about the momentum of the electron is lost; so here would be an example of the lesson of quantum mechanics that observing a phenomenon disturbs it in a generally unpredictable way. However, this is a misleading way of discussing the situation, since it gives the impression that the electron *does* have a well-defined position and momentum, and that the loss of information is merely an unfortunate consequence of the particular experimental setup that interferes with the measurement. Here, too, we can choose to consider the scattered light either as a wave whose image gives us information about the position of the electron relative to the holes, or as a particle whose direction of recoil gives us information about the momentum exchange with the electron. In either case, the observational act is a unitary deed of which our choice is an active, subjective component. Remember, says Bohr, "in the drama of existence we play the dual role of actor and observer." How bizarre and totally surprising that this realization, which is totally antithetical to the conceptual foundations of science, should be forced upon us by atomic physics!

The mutual exclusivity of the measurement of complementary quantities can also be illustrated by experimental measurement of the polarization of light. When light is viewed from the aspect of an electromagnetic wave, the transverse vibration of the wave (i.e., the vibration of the electric vector in a plane at right angles to the axis of propagation) usually occurs in all directions. Such light is said to be unpolarized. But if the directions of vibration are not uniformly distributed with respect to the axis of propagation, the light is said to be polarized. The parlance of polarization is carried over to the consideration of light as discrete particles or photons, even though it is not easy to visualize how a particle can be polarized in the same sense as a wave. If the nonuniformity is such that the transverse vibrations are restricted to a single direction, then the light is said to be *plane polarized*. It is possible to convert unpolarized light into plane-polarized light by passing it through a special filter, or polarizer, such as a Polaroid sheet. The atomic arrangement in a Polaroid sheet is such that it will pass only light waves, or photons, that are vibrating in a single direction in the plane of the polarizer.

To appreciate the consequences of light polarization, let us consider the setups shown in the figure on the next page. Here an unpolarized light beam is passed through a polarizer held at right angles to the axis of propagation. Let the angle made by the direction of polarization of the polarizer with the vertical direction be designated by θ. The polarizer is held so that its direction of polarization is vertical, that is, $\theta = 0°$. All the photons that emerge from the polarizer are therefore plane polarized

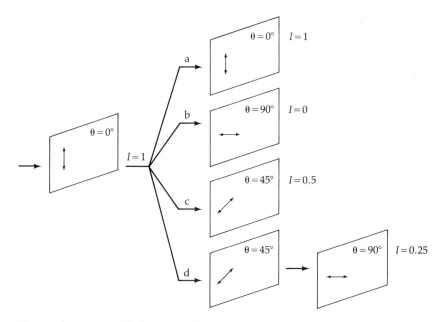

Plane polarization of light quanta by Polaroid sheets. θ designates the angle made by the direction of polarization of the Polaroid sheet with the vertical direction. I is the fraction of the intensity of light entering the polarizer recorded behind various analyzers.

in the direction $\theta = 0°$. Their state of polarization will be designated as $q(0)$ and their density, I (i.e., the intensity of the polarized light beam) is arbitrarily set as unity, so that $I = 1$. Now we pass this plane-polarized light beam through further Polaroid sheets held in various other orientations. These sheets are called analyzers. At a we pass the plane-polarized light through an analyzer held in orientation $\theta = 0°$. Since all the photons are in state $q(0)$, all of them will pass through the analyzer. No loss in intensity is encountered, and $I = 1$ behind the analyzer. At b we pass the plane-polarized light through an analyzer held in orientation $\theta = 90°$ (so that its direction of polarization is horizontal rather than vertical). Here none of the photons, all being in state $q(0)$, pass the analyzer, and hence behind the analyzer $I = 0$. At c we pass the plane-polarized light through an analyzer held in orientation $\theta = 45°$. Here we find that behind the analyzer $I = 0.5$, meaning that of the photons, which (on the basis of the determinations made in a and b) we infer are all in state $q(0)$, half can pass an analyzer for which $\theta = 45°$. Therefore we would say that a photon in state $q(0)$ has half a chance of passing a $\theta = 45°$ analyzer.

But are the photons that have managed to pass that analyzer still in state $q(0)$? To answer this question, at d we add to setup c a second, tandem analyzer held in orientation $\theta = 90°$. Here we would expect that none of the photons in state $q(0)$ that managed to pass the $\theta = 45°$ analyzer should pass the $\theta = 90°$ analyzer, behind which we should find $I = 0$. Instead we find that $I = 0.25$; half the photons that managed to pass the $\theta = 45°$ analyzer also passed the $\theta = 90°$ analyzer. This seems very strange, in view of the fact that in setup b, which lacked the $\theta = 45°$ analyzer, none of the photons of the initial plane-polarized beam were able to pass the $\theta = 90°$ analyzer. It follows that passage through the $\theta = 45°$ analyzer has changed the polarization state of the photons. In other words, the initial state of plane polarization of the photons, which we designated as $q(0)$, is not a uniquely definable physical quantity, or an "element of physical reality." Rather its definition depended on setups a and b, which we used to measure it. As soon as we measure a polarization state by means of setup d we conclude that state $q(0)$ is the equivalent of a superposition of two states $q(45)$ and $q(-45)$ (where the numbers refer to the angles $\theta = 45°$ and $\theta = -45°$ of analyzers through which photons in that state will pass with probability 1). Moreover, state $q(45)$ is itself equivalent to the superposition of the two states $q(0)$ and $q(90)$. This demonstrates once more that a particle and an instrument designed to make a specific measurement (polarization) constitute a single system, which is altered in an essential way if the setting of the instrument is changed. For this reason it is not permissible to make inferences about the state of a particle without specifying at the same time the properties of the apparatus that is to interact with the particle.

The deep violation of our intuitive notions brought about by the complementarity argument is demonstrated even more forcefully by another experiment, shown in the figure on the next page. This experiment concerns not only the state of plane polarization q of photons but also their state of circular polarization p. Circular polarization pertains to the angular momentum associated with the transverse vibrations of the traveling light wave, which causes their direction to change, or rotate, continuously about the axis of propagation as the wave is traveling forward. This rotation may proceed in either a clockwise or counterclockwise mode. If the two modes of rotation are not symmetrically distributed with respect to the axis of propagation, the light is said to be circularly polarized. It is possible to convert unpolarized light into states of clockwise or counterclockwise circular polarization (here designated respectively by $p(+)$ and $p(-)$) by passing it through a "quarter wave plate." This is a thin plate of a material that refracts the incident light in such a manner that

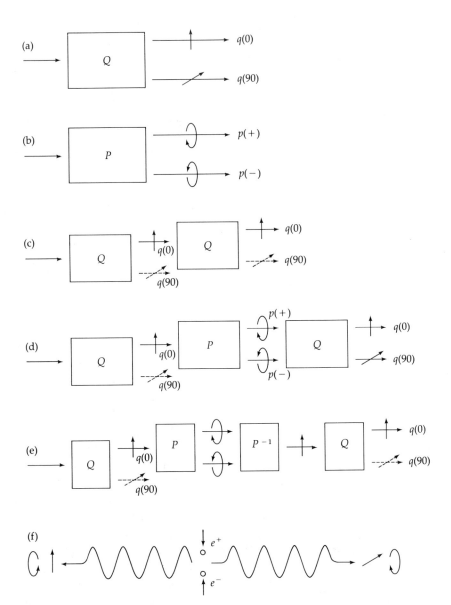

Schematic representation of apparatuses that measure the states of polarization of a photon. (a) Vertical or horizontal plane polarization. The path taken by the photon leaving box Q depends on its plane polarization state. (b) Clockwise or counterclockwise circular polarization state. (c) Repeated measurement of the plane polarization state by two tandem Q boxes. (d) Three successive polarization measurements: plane polarization (first box Q), circular polarization (box P), and plane polarization (second box Q). (d) Effect of the clockwise rotational mode is delayed or advanced by one quarter of the wavelength of the light with respect to the counterclockwise mode. Circularly polarized light will pass with full efficiency through an analyzer of plane polarization held in any orientation θ.

In panel a we see a setup in which a photon enters a box Q from the left and leaves the box via either of two alternative light paths, labeled $q(0)$ and $q(90)$, depending on whether the direction of plane polarization of the photon corresponds to an angle $\theta = 0°$ or $\theta = 90°$. In panel b box Q has been replaced by box P, from which a photon exits via either one of two alternative light paths, labeled $p(+)$ and $p(-)$, depending on whether its mode of circular polarization is clockwise or counterclockwise. By noting the light path via which a photon exits from either box, we can ascertain the distribution of photon states with respect to their direction of plane and mode of circular polarizations. These determinations satisfy the requirement for being measurements of fixed properties, or states, of individual photons, in that they are repeatable. As seen in panel c, if a photon that entered box Q and left it via path $q(0)$ is made to enter another box Q of the same type, it will leave that second box also via path $q(0)$. A similar result regarding the state of circular polarization is obtained if a photon is made to pass successively through two boxes of type P. But as seen in panel d, upon passage through box Q, the polarization of the photon is not only measured but also affected by an interaction with the box. Here a photon that left box Q via path $q(0)$ is made to pass through box P. A large number of such trials show that the photon will leave box P with equal probability via $p(+)$ or $p(-)$. Making a prior measurement of state of plane polarization in box Q leaves the state of circular polarization completely unpredictable. But now having passed the photon through box P, we pass it again through a second box of type Q. And here we find that, in dramatic contrast to the result of panel c, the photon that left the first Q box via path $q(0)$, will, after passage through box P, leave the second Q box with equal probability via either $q(0)$ or $q(90)$. In other words, the intermediate measurement

passage through tandem P and P^{-1} boxes interposed between two Q boxes that measure the plane polarization state. (f) Mutual annihilation of a positron-electron pair (e^+ and e^-) in a state of zero total angular momentum results in the generation of two oppositely directed and oppositely polarized photons (symbolized by wavy lines). [After Dicke and Wittke, 1960] of the circular polarization of the photon destroyed completely any information that we previously had about its plane polarization. This is analogous to the limitation on the measurement of both momentum and position of a particle envisaged by the uncertainty principle: a particle's position can be determined accurately, but if its momentum is then measured, a subsequent measurement of its position is not likely to give the same result as the first position measurement.

The description of the setups presented in panels a–d is actually incomplete in that the role of the photon counters placed at the ends of the alternative paths to detect the photon wave are not fully taken into account. To show why this is the case, and why the situation is conceptually even more troublesome than has appeared thus far, consider the setup of panel e, in which a box called P^{-1} has been added. Box P^{-1} is just another box like P, but it is operated in the reverse direction. Passing light in tandem through P and P^{-1} does not affect its polarization at all. (The principles of optics easily permit the construction of such a system.) Consequently the combination of P and P^{-1} merely transmits light, independently of its polarization. Here we see that if a photon leaves the first Q box via path $q(0)$, passes through the tandem boxes P and P^{-1}, and enters a second Q box, it still leaves the second Q box via path $q(0)$. Thus the operation performed by box P in the setup of panel D did not irreversibly change the plane polarization of the photons passing through it after all. This is surprising and important; it shows that information was not lost in letting the photon pass through box P. Were we then wrong in asserting that in making a measurement we always lose information about the complementary variable? Why, in this case, did the consignment of the photon by box P into either of the two pathways $p(+)$ or $p(-)$ not destroy the information obtained by the previous measurement of box Q? We were not wrong, only imprecise, since passage of the photon through box Q is only a part of determining its state of plane polarization. The measurement is not completed until we actually place photon counters in the output pathways of box P. Since in the setup of panel e no counters were placed in the pathways leading from box P to box P^{-1}, no measurement was actually made of the state of circular polarization. When and only when the counters are in place do we require every photon to declare a state of polarization. The individual act of measurement is then completed and each such act precludes the possibility of obtaining any alternative measurement. We have a choice of asking each photon either whether it is in state $q(0)$ or $q(90)$, or whether it is in state $p(+)$ or $p(-)$. Any one photon can give a definite answer to only one of these questions.

Yet another paradoxical feature associated with the measurement of the polarization of photons is in many ways the most difficult of all to reconcile with our picture of the everyday physical world. This is illustrated in panel f, where we consider a pair of photons arising upon the mutual annihilation of an electron and a positron (a positively charged electron). Here the electron and the positron are assumed to be annihilated in a state for which the total angular momentum of the system is zero. Because of the need to conserve momentum, when the two photons leave the point of annihilation traveling in opposite directions, they must carry away zero total angular momentum. If the circular polarization of one photon is clockwise, it follows that that of the other must be counterclockwise, in order that the total angular momentum about the axis of propagation be zero. If we determine that one of the photons is in state $p(+)$, we can infer that the other is in state $p(-)$. But how can this conclusion be reconciled with the inference we just made from the result of panel e that we do not require a photon to declare its state of polarization until we have measured it? Suppose that long after the pair of photons has separated we pass one of them through a box of type P, including photon counters, and make it declare itself to be in state $p(+)$. It follows that by this act we have made the other photon declare itself to be in state $p(-)$, even though no measurement of any kind was performed on it. This paradox is formally equivalent to, but more acute than, that posed by the Einstein, Podolsky, and Rosen experiment. The only answer is the seemingly bizarre proposition that by virtue of their historical connection and despite their physical separation, the two photons constitute a single dynamic system. Accordingly, any information obtained about the system is information about both photons, and any interaction with one of them affects the state of the whole system.

The upshot of these arguments is an Alice-in-Wonderland world. First of all, this world is not deterministic. Particles do not have definite trajectories; their motion is represented by probability functions, which merely lead to correct predictions for the *likelihood* of the outcome of experiments designed to measure their spatial distribution. Second, particles are not conserved; they are created and annihilated, disappearing down a rabbit hole. They disappear singly, in the case of absorbed photons, or doubly, in the case of annihilated electron–positron pairs. Third, the category of identity is abolished: in a system that contains several particles of the same kind, it is impossible to mark any of them individually for later identification. These three counterintuitive attributes of particles as objects are absolutely essential components of the formal structure of the quantum theory.

Where has the quantum theory taken us in our inquiry into truth and reality? How does the thought structure of the complementarity concept connect with the physical reality of the everyday, macroscopic world? After all, macroscopic objects do have definite trajectories that they follow in a perfectly deterministic way. Macroscopic objects are neither created from vacuum nor annihilated into nothingness. And although two rabbits may look alike, we can always mark their fur with red or black ink in order to tell them apart later.

The world of the quantum theory is remarkably similar to the way infants view reality, before they have fully consolidated the object concept during the sensorimotor period. At that early stage of cognitive development, an object that is not seen does not persist, and similar objects do not have identity. Since each of us made the transition from the infant's world, in which there is no clear distinction between subject and object, to the adult's world of independent, determinate, external reality with persistent objects, it is not wholly incongruous that in our rational thought processes we should be able to reverse this process. In fact, the complementarity concept demands going back and forth from one world to the other, tying them together into one formal structure. It was Bohr's view that commuting between these two worlds is a healthy mental exercise, so healthy that it should also be practiced in scientific fields of study other than physics, such as biology and psychology.

With respect to biology, Bohr proposed in his 1932 lecture "Light and Life" that life might not be reducible to atomic physics. He suggested that there might be a complementarity relation between the physiological and physical aspects of life analogous to that obtaining for the wave and particle aspects of the electron. In that case there would exist a sort of uncertainty principle of biology. This proposal is expressed in the following passage taken from his lecture,

> We should doubtless kill an animal if we tried to carry on the investigation of its organs so far that we could describe the role played by single atoms in vital functions. In every experiment involving organisms there must remain an uncertainty with regard to the conditions to which they are subjected. The idea suggests itself that the minimum freedom which we must allow organisms in this respect is just large enough to permit it, so to say, to hide its ultimate secrets from us.

Bohr thus suggests another conspiracy of nature. This suggestion made many biologists, especially biochemists, as uneasy as the uncertainty principle of quantum mechanics had made many physicists. In fact, Bohr's suggestion turned out to be wrong. In 1962, I invited Bohr to reassess the conjecture he had first put forward in 1932. He accepted this challenge with enthusiasm. In a lecture entitled "Light and Life Revisited," he discussed his proposition of the irreducibility of physiology to physics in the light of the explosive progress in molecular biology that had taken place in the intervening decades. He rephrased the original conjecture in the following way:

> . . . it appeared for a long time that the regulatory functions in living organisms, disclosed especially by studies of cell physiology and embryology, exhibited a fineness so unfamiliar to ordinary physical and chemical experience as to point to the existence of fundamental biological laws without counterpart in the properties of inanimate matter studied under simple reproducible experimental conditions. Stressing the difficulties of keeping the organisms alive under conditions which aim at a full atomic account I therefore suggested that the very existence of life might be taken as a basic fact in biology in the same sense as the quantum of action has to be regarded in atomic physics as a fundamental element irreducible to classical physical concepts.

From the point of view of physics, the mysteries of life in those days were indeed stark. Cell physiologists had discovered innumerable ways in which cells respond intelligently to changed environmental conditions. Embryologists had demonstrated the possibility of such amazing feats as the growing of two whole animals from two half embryos. These findings were vaguely reminiscent of the "wholeness" of the atom, of the stability of its quantum states. The stability of the gene and the algebra of Mendelian genetics suggested to Bohr that the processes underlying the phenomena were akin to quantum mechanics. The resistance of biologists to such ideas did not surprise Bohr. He had met resistance to the complementarity argument before among his fellow physicists.

It might be said that Watson and Crick's discovery of the DNA double helix in 1953 did for biology what many physicists had hoped in vain could be done for atomic physics: it solved all the mysteries in terms of classical models and theories, without forcing us to abandon our intuitive notions about truth and reality. Upon the discovery of the DNA double helix, the mystery of gene replication was revealed as a ludicrously simple trick. In people who had expected a deep solution to the deep problem of how in the living world like begets like it raised a feeling similar to the embarassment one feels when shown a simple solution to a chess problem with which one has struggled in vain for a long time. Of course the detailed mechanics of gene replication turned out to be enormously more complex than was thought in the first flush of victory in the 1950s, and even now substantial uncertainties remain about this central problem of molecular biology. Never mind! We now understand that organisms can be successfully viewed as molecular systems, albeit of enormous complexity. Moreover, an upper limit can be set to the complexity of the fundamental problems of biology, and ever more powerful methods to probe them are being developed at so high a rate that it is difficult to keep up with the results they provide. Worse, the very rapidity of progress in molecular biology leaves us little time for looking to the left and to the right!

REFERENCES

Bell, J. S. 1964. On the Einstein-Podolsky-Rosen paradox. *Physics* 1: 195–200.

Bohr, N. 1935. Can quantum-mechanical description of physical reality be considered complete? *Physical Review* 48: 696–702.

———. 1970. Discussion with Einstein on epistemological problems in atomic physics and Einstein's reply. In *Albert Einstein: Philosopher–Scientist,* ed. P. A. Schilpp, 199–242 and 666. London: Cambridge University Press.

———. 1933. Light and life. *Nature* 313: 421–423, 457–459.

———. 1963. Light and life revisited. In *Essays 1958–1962 in Atomic Physics and Human Knowledge.* New York: Interscience.

Delbrück, M. 1976. Light and life III. *Carlsberg Research Communications* 41: 299–309.

d'Espagnat, B. 1979. The quantum theory and reality. *Scientific American* 241(5): 158–181.

Dicke, R. H., and P. Wittke. 1960. *Introduction to Quantum Mechanics.* Reading, Mass.: Addison-Wesley.

Einstein, A., B. Podolsky, and N. Rosen. 1935. Can quantum-mechanical description of physical reality be considered complete? *The Physical Review* 47: 777–780.

Jammer, M. 1974. *The Philosophy of Quantum Mechanics.* New York: John Wiley.

Eighteen

The Cartesian Cut

In 1932, when Bohr conjectured that there might exist a mutual exclusion between experiments that would provide a description of an organism in terms of atomic physics and experiments that would provide a description in terms of genetics, physiology, and embryology, these three biological disciplines were already well developed. The phenomena they addressed seemed to be unique to living matter, transcending what physical chemists were able to account for in terms of the kinetics and thermodynamics of chemical reactions. At least it appeared so at that time, when there were many biologists who embraced the view of "vitalism." According to that view, living matter owes its characteristic properties to a "vital force" not present in nonliving matter.

Vitalist biologists insisted that the features of living systems that seem to defy the laws of physics and chemistry are attributable to special drives and forces. For example, the evolutionary increase in organismic complexity, which appears to run counter to the second law of thermodynamics (whose basic prediction of a loss of capacity of a system to do future work is equivalent to predicting a decrease of order or an increase in entropy in the system over time) was explained by an "antientropic principle." Other biologists, especially those approaching living systems from the biochemical or physiological point of view, were strongly opposed to such vitalist notions. They insisted that it is quite unacceptable to have a picture of the world in which matter is viewed as subject to additional, "unphysical" forces as soon as it forms part of a living organism. They held that the comportment of living matter is also governed wholly by the laws of physics and chemistry.

Bohr's contribution to this controversy was to point out that the invocation of special laws that transcend the laws of physics to account for the comportment of living matter is not necessarily in irreconcilable conflict with the notion that there is no essential difference between the atoms of which living and nonliving matter are composed. In line with his general complementarity argument, Bohr suggested, that just as quantum physics managed to construct a rational theory of matter in which its wave and particle aspects coexist harmoniously, so might biology manage to provide a rational account of living matter by accepting the coexistence of seemingly conflicting notions about the laws that govern its behavior. Bohr thought that the two types of mutually exclusive observations arise from the fact that it is necessary to kill an organism if one wants to examine it closely enough to locate its atoms, a situation equivalent to the necessity of changing the state of an atom in order to locate its electrons.

The fate of Bohr's proposal regarding the role of complementarity in biology was different from that which it had been accorded in atomic physics. It was not necessary to invoke any mutual exclusion of observational arrangements in biology to account for living matter. Instead, the development of systems theory, especially of cybernetics, has shown that many of the life processes that seemed miraculous fifty years ago can, in fact, be simulated by machines. In 1948 John von Neumann showed that a self-reproducing machine, or automaton, is feasible in principle. In the following excerpt from a lecture by von Neumann (published posthumously in 1966), the designations now used by molecular biologists for the parts of the cellular apparatus of self-reproduction are indicated in brackets for the components of the automaton listed by von Neumann.

> . . . a self-reproducing automaton must have four separate components with the following functions: Component A is an automatic factory, an automaton which collects raw materials and processes them into an output, specified by a written instruction, which must be supplied from the outside. [Component A corresponds to the enzymatic apparatus of the cell that catalyzes the synthesis of building blocks of macromolecules, such as amino acids (for proteins) and nucleotides (for nucleic acids) from foodstuff, as well as the ribosomes and other accessories of protein synthesis, such as tRNA and tRNA-aminoacyl synthetases. The "written instruction" corresponds primarily to the nucleotide sequence embodied in the DNA, and secondarily to its mRNA transcript.] Component B is a duplicator, an

automaton which takes the written instruction and copies it. [Component B corresponds to DNA polymerase and other enzymes directly associated with the process of DNA replication.] Component C is a controller, an automaton hooked up to both A and B. When C is given an instruction, it first passes the instruction to B for duplication, then passes it to A for action, and finally supplies the copied instruction to the output of A while keeping the original itself. [Component C corresponds to (1) the apparatus that governs the initiation of DNA replication, (2) RNA-polymerase and other enzymes responsible for DNA transcription and synthesis of mRNA, and (3) the mitotic spindle (or its equivalent in prokaryotes), which assures that each of the two sister cells resulting from the activity of component A receive one of the DNA replicas generated by component B.] Component D is a written instruction containing the complete specifications which cause A to manufacture the combined system, "A plus B plus C." [Component D corresponds to the genome or the entire DNA complement, which encodes the set of mRNAs that specify the set of enzyme molecules that catalyze the synthesis of the cellular components.]

Von Neumann's automaton was conceived to be a minimal one. It describes a self-reproducing system different from that represented by living cells in not interposing an intermediate messenger (mRNA) between the master tape (DNA) and its realization (protein); rather it envisages a direct translation of the DNA nucleotide sequence into the protein amino acid sequence. However, some viruses that contain RNA rather than DNA as their genetic material do resemble von Neumann's minimal scheme: for instance, the genetic material of the poliovirus serves as its own mRNA in directing the synthesis of poliovirus proteins, as well as replicating directly. Viruses, however, are simpler than von Neumann's system, in that they relegate function A of his automaton, the production of the output, to the apparatus for synthesis of building blocks and proteins of the host cell.

The existence proof of self-reproducing automatons is not the only, or even the most significant, accomplishment of cybernetic systems theory, especially since no such automaton has actually been built. The most significant accomplishment of cybernetics is probably its demolition of the old prejudices that machines cannot adapt to novel situations, cannot learn from experience, and cannot interact with human beings in any meaningful way. For it turned out to be possible to design and construct machines that refute these claims. Some of these machines will be discussed in these final chapters.

Let us now recapitulate our assessment of how the progress of science has managed to denature the old concepts of object, number, time, topological space, projective space, metric space, and causality. What has happened to all those concepts that constituted our naive view of external reality? What has happened to this evolutionary acquisition, of immense adaptive value, that enables us to cope with the world? It is ironic that science has pulled the rug out from under this conceptual structure. The special relativity theory has replaced the concrete space–time frame with an abstract one, in which one twin may go on a trip and return a younger person than the stay-at-home twin—a claim that is irreconcilable with our concrete mental operations regarding space and time. The general relativity theory tells us of "singularities in space," black holes with an "event horizon" from which no signals can emerge, and finite but not bounded space—concepts that we can learn to manipulate in a formal way but cannot visualize. Quantum theory, the worst offender, does away with object identity and trajectory of objects (electrons do not revolve in orbits). It proclaims a conspiracy of nature that forces us to choose, to make either/or decisions between various aspects of reality that in any observational act are mutually exclusive. Is this a Kierkegaardian notion, with every observation becoming an existential act? Have physicists become religious thinkers? Einstein was unwilling to accept this conspiracy. His attitude is reflected in such remarks as "The Good Lord may be cunning, but malicious He is not" and "God does not play dice with the universe." Whether God is malicious or not, no satisfactory assimilative alternative to accommodate (in Piaget's sense) to this conspiracy has been found, and as Bohr's analysis made clear, none is likely to be found.

No, physicists have not become religious thinkers, since the either/or choice they are forced to make is not an ethical one, not even the choice of an individual observer, but one that concerns collective observations on, say, light quanta: pass them through an analyzer that permits statements about their circular polarization (clockwise or counterclockwise) or through an analyzer that permits statements about their plane polarization (vertical or horizontal). We make this choice, and our choices materially exclude each other, because any one quantum, once it is observed—that is, recorded by a counter—is irreversibly gone. Such is the individuality, the quantum nature, of any atomic interaction involved in constructing an object world. It always leaves this object world with a residue of uncertainty and limits us to statistical predictions.

This bizarre dialectical situation goes to the heart of the concept of the reality of the physical world, so basic to the evolution of the human mind. For a million years or so we have been animals that know the dichotomies: actor–observer, I and the world, mind versus reality, a confrontation between an inner world of thoughts, volitions, and emotions and an outer world of objects. The poet Rainer Maria Rilke commented on the regrettable loss of existential wholeness brought about by this turn of our evolutionary history, which less evolved creatures have been spared.

> O Seligkeit der *kleinen* Kreatur,
> die immer *bleibt* im Schoße der sie austrug;
> O Glück der Mücke die noch *innen* hüpft,
> selbst wenn sie Hochzeit hat: . . .
>
> .   .   .   .
>
> Wer hat uns also umgedreht, dass wir,
> was wir auch tun, in jener Haltung sind
> von einem welcher fortgeht? . . .
>
> "Oh bliss of *tiny* creatures that *remain*
> forever in the womb that brought them forth!
> Joy of the gnat that still can leap *within*,
> even on its wedding day: . . .
>
> .   .   .   .
>
> Who's turned us round like this, so that we always,
> do what we may, retain the attitude
> of someone who's departing? . . .

> From Rilke, "The eighth elegy," in Duino Elegies,
> trans. J. B. Leishmann and S. Spender
> (New York: Norton & Co. 1939).

From these dichotomies springs the Cartesian cut—the separation of the world into two distinct substances—*res cogitans* (mind) and *res extensa* (matter)—which has been the stance of science for 300 years, ever since its eponymous champion René Descartes clearly formulated it in his *Passions of the Soul*. The Cartesian cut has been the bane of psychologists, whose job it is to cope with both aspects of existence and to tie both substances together in some fashion. Is the tree I see in front of me the same as the object that is out there, or are the two things distinct? On the one hand, when we consider that the retinal image of the tree is processed not only in the neural network of the retina itself, but also in the lateral geniculate nucleus, in the visual cortex, and in yet other cortical areas, we realize that what consciousness sees, that is, the tree in here as a percept, is literally worlds apart from the tree out there as an object. On the other hand, does it make sense to take the object and its percept apart in this way? Is there not but one reality: the act of seeing what our language makes us call an "object"? These are the opposing positions of the dualist and the monist. Battalions of philosophers have manned the barricades in defense of either position.

We form the notion of the objective reality of the external world, independent of the observer, in earliest infancy, and we form it with the aid of mental equipment evolved over millions of years of adaptive evolution. It is a notion that has been necessary for survival, not only in the cave, but also up in the trees before moving into the cave. It is also the notion that has been most solidified, hardened, and codified, by the development of the classical physical sciences, into the "physical laws." It has been claimed, indeed it is commonly believed, that physical laws describe the external world in an objective way and that they reduce this description to numerical relations. Let us look at this claim more closely, and dissect it in the manner proposed by the psychologist Norbert Bischof. He invites us to examine the relation $S = gt^2/2$. It is indeed a relation between numbers. However, to make it a law of physics we need to know that S is a distance, t a duration, and g an acceleration. The numerical relation as such does not express a physical law. A law is expressed only if we understand that the numbers are measures of a quality of the thing measured: a spatial length represents something completely different in quality from a duration or an acceleration. In addition to the qualities of the quantities measured, we need to know where and what to measure. We need to know the class of actual situations to which the law refers. In fact, a physical law, far from existing totally detached from the observed object, refers explicitly to situations actually or potentially experienced by an observer and to nothing else. This is true, let us add parenthetically, even if we make statements about the big bang origin of the universe—even though there could not have been an observer present to observe it. It would be an illusion to think that physical laws describe an external world independent of the observer.

In what sense, then, are the findings of the physical sciences objective? We say they are objective in being "reproducible" for each observer, and "the same" for different observers. These two criteria are the pride of the physical sciences, and they are indeed met. Information stored in enormous handbooks of physics and chemistry and the solid core of theories presented in the textbooks of these disciplines give vivid testimony to their objectivity. One might characterize the physical sciences as domains of knowledge for which explicit connection to actual experience constitutes an annoying constraint from which they are ever more trying to liberate themselves.

Physical law is supposed to refer to larger and larger classes of experiences. The infant's first construction of space–time frames and notions of persistent objects and of causal connections between events constitute giant steps in this direction. Nevertheless, the fact remains that the physical sciences represent the actual or potential experiences and observations of individuals, in however abstract a form, and as such are as psychic as any emotion or sensation. Both the blue of a summer sky and the 4,400 Å wavelength of its light refer to experiential acts, differing principally in the affective components accompanying these acts and in their expressions. The statement is often made that "blue" is a private sensation that cannot be identified with another person's sensation because it is subjective. But the same is true for the size of a table. How do I know how large you see it? Indeed, your impression must be different from mine, if you are farther away from it. So we measure it with a ruler. But measurements of length—noting coincidences of marks on the ruler with edges of the table—are private acts too, being intersubjective, and hence comparable only to the extent that we have linguistic expressions for them.

It is the parsimony of the number of elements singled out for attention that makes the notion of duality of observer and observed so successful and gives the illusion in physics that the object is totally distinct from the observer. This distinctness is true in the sense that we do not mention the observer when we say, for instance, that the present temperature of the blackbody radiation left over from the big bang is 3°K, or that a supernova exploded 10^9 years ago. However, any such statement is linguistic in the first place and, as such, is meaningful only within the framework of the total scientific discourse, which reflects individual and collective experiences and acts.

Norbert Bischof pointed out that modern cybernetic machines, which are able to "observe," or take note of external reality, and "interpret," or adjust their internal reality adaptively, can be called on to demystify the relation between the Cartesian *res cogitans* and *res extensa*. Bischof asks us to consider a cybernetic circuit designed to maintain a preset constant internal state in the face of a fluctuating external environment as shown in the figure on the next page. In this circuit a quantity x is measured by a monitor M. The monitor provides its measurement of x as signal x' to the governor G, which is set to maintain a level s. G compares x' with s, and gives an output g, either as an off–on or a graded signal. That signal acts at control point C to control the value of x, which must be controlled because the system is subject to an external source of perturbation p. This circuit can be applied to a variety of situations, and Bischof considers the example of a torpedo that is to travel to its target beneath the surface of water at a preset depth. Let x be the actual depth of the

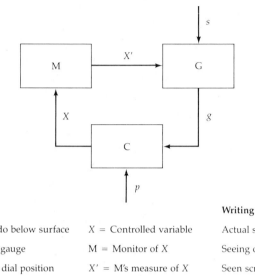

Torpedo		Writing
Depth of torpedo below surface	X = Controlled variable	Actual script
Water pressure gauge	M = Monitor of X	Seeing of writing
Pressure gauge dial position	X' = M's measure of X	Seen script
Control element	G = Governor	Mental comparison
Setting of G	s = Setting of governor	Guiding mental picture
Rudder position	g = Governor output	Command to hand
Water waves, etc.	p = Perturbing input	Rough paper, worn pen
Depth control	C = Control point	Hand motion

$p \& s$	Free inputs
$X \rightarrow X'$	Rigidly coupled
$X' \rightarrow X$	Feedback loop

A cybernetic circuit uses feedback from the external environment to help maintain a desired internal state. Here such a circuit is applied to the control of torpedo depth and to the production of handwriting.

torpedo, M the water pressure gauge, x' the reading from the gauge, s the setting of the depth control governor G, g the angle made by the rudder with the horizontal plane, C the control point for the depth control, and p the water waves. The perturbation p and the setting of the governor s are independent inputs into the circuit, while x and x' are physically coupled. The important point made by Bischof in presenting this example is not so much that the torpedo can be said to have a mind but that the same cybernetic circuit can also be used to control processes obviously involving "real" mental activity, for instance handwriting. When the circuit is applied to handwriting, x is the actual script and x' the seen script. Here there is a mental image of what is to be written, which the governor G compares with the seen script. The perturbation arises from rough paper and a worn pen. The lesson of this comparison is that in the case of the torpedo, we deal exclusively with physical quantities, while in the case of the writing, mental elements come into play, namely the perceived output of the pen doing the writing and the internal image with which the script is compared. Another application of such a cybernetic circuit to mental activity would be a tennis player's hand–eye coordination when trying to hit the ball. The eye sees the ball coming, the brain commands the arms and legs to make appropriate motions, the eye and proprioceptive apparatus contain the monitor M and correct this output by comparing it with an internal image in the governor G of what should happen—a feedback loop containing a conscious visual image as part of an interactive network.

Are we comparing processes that are not, in principle, comparable? I think not, because the difference between the mental and the physical is not at all a radical one, but one merely of degree. The depth of the torpedo, the reading from the water pressure gauge, the angle of the rudder, and so on refer to our spatial perceptions and as such include object and observer in their definitions. It is true that meter readings and settings lend themselves to quantification more easily than the mental images of an intended piece of writing or of hitting the tennis ball, and for that reason are more conveniently communicated either in ordinary or in mathematical language. In principle, however, all three are mental and all three are physical phenomena. The links in the cybernetic circuit are equally applicable to them, although when the circuit elements are not easily quantified they are less easily modeled. But modeling must be performed if we are to discover how valid an understanding of a situation is provided by a particular cybernetic circuit.

The distinction between external and internal reality—between subject and object—seems especially confusing when we consider phenomena in which the object is the consciousness of ourselves or that of another person. Say you are thirsty. In what sense does your conscious sensation of thirst correspond to a physical quantity? In the sense that whatever thirst may be, it is something of which you can have more or less. In principle, therefore, thirst is measurable, either by behavioral tests or by physiological correlates. Admittedly, it may be useful to make a practical distinction between conscious and nonconscious phenomena. But as Bischof has pointed out, in the *res cogitans*, just as in the *res extensa*, some quantity a acts on another quantity b in a manner that augments, diminishes, or otherwise alters the influence of a third quantity c, which normally has this or that mental effect. We can take this for granted, even if we are unable to specify any procedure for measuring the quantities a, b, and c: they are defined simply by the cause–effect relation that links them to each other and to further, directly observable quantities. That is to say, they are defined by their position within the cybernetic circuit.

The resistance to considering consciousness on a par with physical phenomena seems to arise from our fear of the encroachment of science on the human person, an encroachment that would stifle and depersonalize us and thus open the way to our being used in inhuman ways. This resistance is a defensive stance often encountered in the humanities, where those who oppose the development of a science of man are afraid that the mind might be shown to be no more than a machine. Yet as we have seen, the antithesis of external and internal reality is merely an illusion: there is only one reality. Quantum mechanics has simply reminded us of this fact, which seems to have gotten lost in the abstractions of the physical sciences.

Do I deny, then, that there is any difference between knowing something—about animals in particular and humans most particularly—by extrospection from the outside and by introspection (direct in myself, or by empathy in others) from the inside? There certainly is a difference, but the gulf between the machinery of the brain, target of observations from the outside, and the mind, target of introspection from the inside, is not unbridgeable. If brain surgery is performed under local anesthesia, it is possible to converse with the patient while carrying out experimental procedures on the patient's brain. Wilder Penfield conducted many such experiments, in which he stimulated specific areas of the patient's brain by focal passage of electrical currents. In one case, a single stimulation of a particular area, and only that area, of the patient's cerebral cortex evoked the conscious recall of a particular memory, all the while the patient was consciously aware of being in the operating room. In another case, passage of current through one of the cortical areas dedicated to the production of speech made the patient unable to recall the names of certain familiar objects; when passage of the current ceased, the patient immediately regained the capacity to recall those names. These results show that the content of the conscious mind can be altered in a predictable way by direct manipulation of the brain from the outside. Moreover, quite unexpectedly they also show that such a crude interference with brain function as passage of electrical current through an area of cerebral cortex containing thousands of nerve cells can evoke enormously complex and highly organized mental events, rather than simply causing chaos as an analogous manipulation would do in a computer.

To summarize, the Cartesian cut between observer and observed, between inner and external reality, between mind and body, is based on the illusion that the physical world has no subjective component. This illusion arises from the high degree of quantitative reliability of scientific statements about the outer, physical world. Their quantitative reliability makes us forget that these statements are as related to subjective experiences as statements about the inner, mental world. In experiencing the physical world, we limit our attention to a narrowly circumscribed set of perceptions, such as those resulting from the reading of dials of instruments that measure such quantities as time, distance, or force. But in experiencing the mental world we include a wider repertoire of perceptions, not only primitive perceptions such as color, sound, and smell, but also higher level, complex perceptions of visual space in general and of gestures made by other human beings—their smiles, vocal or facial expressions of threat or fear or affection—in particular. While these higher level perceptions about mental states are less easily quantified than perceptions about physical states, they nevertheless fit into the same kind of cybernetic network of interactions.

REFERENCES

Bischof, N. 1969. Hat Kybernetik etwas mit Psychologie zu tun? *Psychologische Rundschau* 20(4): 237–256.

Penfield, W. 1975. *The Mysteries of the Mind*. Princeton, N.J.: University Press.

von Neumann, J. 1966. *Theory of Self-Reproducing Automata*, ed. A. W. Burks. Urbana: University of Illinois Press.

Weizenbaum, J. 1976. *Computer Power and Human Reason: From Judgment to Calculation*. San Francisco: W. H. Freeman.

Nineteen

Language

The belief that the conscious mind belongs to a realm wholly separate from the physical world, as envisaged by the Cartesian cut, has another important source, namely the fact that mental realities are predominantly communicated by *language*, it being difficult to communicate them in any way other than by speaking about them. What then is so special about language in relation to the mind? Isn't language just another motor function, produced by the muscles of the larynx under the control of some particular areas of the brain? Anyhow, do not other creatures, such as bees and apes, have language too? We will defer attempting to answer these questions and first examine the essential attributes of *human* language.

There are currently 5,000 to 10,000 different human languages spoken. This number is, of course, somewhat arbitrary, since it is not self-evident where to draw the line between different languages and different dialects of the same language. This rough and ready estimate is provided by the total number of languages into which the Bible has been translated

To get at the biological function of language, we would dearly like to know how and when it evolved, but here we draw an almost total blank. Is fluent language as old as mankind, now clearly documented to date back at least three million years? Or did it evolve only forty thousand years ago with the domestication of fire, developing around the hearth when there was time for leisurely talk in relative safety from predators? Opinions about the time and mode of language evolution differ radically, and hard data are simply not available. One thing is certain, though: the beginnings of language predate the separation of American Indians from their Asiatic kin toward the end of the Würm glacial period. This is an important fact, because it implies that the American Indian languages did not arise independently from the rest of human languages. How marvelous it would have been for linguistics if they had! In that case, a comparative study of Indian languages might provide us with deep insights into the evolutionary origins of human speech, just as the discovery of extraterrestrial life on another planet—where it would have arisen independently of terrestrial life from its own prebiotic scene—might provide us with some important clues about the evolutionary origins of living systems. Unfortunately, in the case of human language, as in the case of life, we lack the opportunity to make a comparative analysis of the single instance known to us with a second instance of independent origin. As far as we know, human language, just as life itself, is a unique phenomenon.

Estimates of the antiquity of language and of its mode of origin are closely tied to speculative theories regarding the selective pressures favoring language, that is, its adaptive value. One popular theory holds that language evolved in connection with the hunting of large mammals. Hunting forays require the planning of complex interactions of many individuals and the teaching of specialized skills. They entail extended absences of the roving men and therefore the preparation of secure camps for the women, the aged, and the children. All these activities could be thought of as being greatly facilitated by vocal communication, and hence of favoring the evolution of linguistic competence. However, Louis Leakey, one of the foremost students of human evolution, did not believe that the organized hunting party provided the selective pressure for the evolution of speech. While participating in hunting expeditions of contemporary primitive tribes, Leakey was surprised to find that the hunters make only minimal use of their language for communication, and that the arts of hunting and tool making are taught to neophytes mainly by demonstration with little verbal instruction.

A variant of the theory that hunting provided the context within which language first arose is the belief that the women who stayed behind developed language while they were gathering edible plant foods. However, Leakey found, again to his surprise, that women of contemporary hunter–gatherer tribes are as silent when out gathering as are the men when hunting. The women are silent because they, in fact, combine gathering with hunting of small animals, such as lizards and birds. So neither version of the theory connecting hunting and the origin of language seems very plausible.

According to Leakey, it was most likely man's use of fire that brought about the development of linguistic capacity. Among primitive tribes there is no talk in the evenings when there is no fire because of the dangers lurking in the dark. Only around the campfire, which provides safety by scaring away dangerous animals, is there enough leisure and relaxation for easy conversation. But since extrapolation from the social habits of contemporary primitive tribes to the behavior of our remote ancestors has little claim to validity, it can only be said that the origins of human speech remain shrouded in mystery.

Linguistic capacity demands the performance of two interlocked activities: *speech production* and *speech comprehension*. Speech production consists of the vocalization of a temporal sequence, or string, of sound units that encode meaning in some way. Speech comprehension consists of the perception of these strings and of decoding their meaning. Any given human language can thus be regarded as a mapping of meaning onto sound and of sound onto meaning. Human language can be defined by the following very general characteristics:

1. We form a large number of meaningful *symbols* (words) by a combinatorial procedure from a small number of vocal elements designated as *phonemes*. Examples of phonemes are *b*, as in *boy*; *t*, as in *toy*; and *o*, as in *box*. Between them, the thousands of human languages make use of only about seventy different phonemes. The notion of a phoneme is not equivalent to that of a letter in the written encoding of language, since the same phoneme is often represented by a variety of letters or letter combinations, such as *ou* in *loud* and *now*. Moreover, different phonemes may be represented by the same letter, such as the unvoiced *th* in *three* and the voiced *th* in *this*. (In Icelandic script, however, these same two phonemes are represented by two different letters, þ and ð.) The notion of a phoneme is also not the same as that of a sound unit, since in a given language two sound units correspond to different phonemes only if they form different words (i.e., lead to different meanings). Thus in English the long vowel *ä* and the short vowel *a* represent a single phoneme, since the meaning of the word *pass* is the same whether it is pronounced *päs* or *pas*. Some languages use only ten phonemes, whereas others use as many as seventy. English uses about thirty phonemes.

Although human language is normally composed of phonetic elements, it can also be "spoken" by body movements. A subset of the human species, the deaf and dumb, has evolved its own set of *sign* languages, one of which is the American Sign Language, or Ameslan. Ameslan shares most of the characteristics of natural languages and is highly effective for the kind of communication carried out by ordinary speech. It is encoded in arm and hand motion elements (designated as kinemes rather than phonemes), by a combinatorial scheme. However, in contrast to the one-dimensional, or linear, string of phonemes of spoken language, kinemes are combined multidimensionally, in that they may be produced concurrently by more than one limb. (The linguistic aspects of Ameslan have been studied in great detail by Ursula Bellugi. I once attended a lecture which Bellugi delivered at Caltech, and at which she presented an associate of hers, a young woman who had graduated from college and was one of a family of nine deaf children born to deaf parents. The parents were sitting at the back of the auditorium during the lecture, and the young woman was on the podium next to Bellugi, to provide occasional demonstrations of Ameslan kinemes. It was fascinating to watch the parents carry on a lively conversation with their daughter on the podium throughout the lecture, neither disturbing nor being disturbed by Bellugi's presentation.)

2. We form *sentences*, bringing symbols (words) into logical connections by a finite number of grammatical rules enabling us to generate, from a large number of words, a virtually unlimited number of different sentences.

3. We use these sentences for *socialized actions*.

4. We have the inherent capability to produce the seventy or so phonemes and to learn to speak any natural language—that is to learn its words and grammar—from our elders. Learning in general is, of course, a capability of much higher evolutionary antiquity, and one much more widely distributed in the animal kingdom, than that of learning to speak. Animals learn many things from their elders. For instance, nowadays horses learn from their mothers not to shy away from automobiles. Early in this century horses used to become highly agitated at the approach of an automobile. Now they do not even turn their heads. Similarly, some years ago in England a bird invented the trick of removing the aluminum tops from milk bottles and sipping the rich cream on the surface of the liquid inside. This novel behavioral routine spread by learning throughout a wide population of the species from the original focus of its invention. However, such transmission of learned or invented routines by animals is entirely distinct from learning to use a symbolic language, and it is even more distinct from learning the ideas that are communicated via that language.

But is there not a "language" of the bees, as expressed in the dances they perform in their hives to transmit to their hive mates the direction and distance of a source of food? Let us apply the four criteria of human speech to the dance of bees, to see whether it really is a language.

1. Bees do *not* form symbols (words) from a few elements: admittedly the bees' dance in the hive maps by its speed and orientation the distance and direction of food finds. Nevertheless, it would be inappropriate to apply the concept of symbol to this activity. For one thing, the symbols of which human language is constituted are "doubly articulated," which means that they comprise a smaller set of elements (phonemes) that do not carry a meaning of their own but serve the sole purpose of differentiating meaning and a larger set of meaningful elements (designated as "morphemes"), namely words. In the case of the bees' dance it is more appropriate to refer to a signal code rather than a symbolic language. (In 1953, this distinction formed the subject of a debate between Emile Benveniste and Karl von Frisch.)

2. Bees do *not* form sentences according to grammatical rules.

3. Bees *do* use these signals for socialized action.

4. They do *not* learn their dance; they are born with the capacity to perform it. At most the bees can be said to have learned their "language" phylogenetically since there exist "bees' dialects," in the sense that the precise execution of the dance and its interpretation is subject to genetic variation.

Thus, for purposes of our discussion, let us not call the bees' system of communication a language, since it meets only one of the four criteria of human language.

The nature of the vocal communication between subhuman anthropoid primates is more similar to human speech than the dance of the bees. As mentioned in chapter 7, some species of monkeys produce a diversity of calls appropriate to diverse situations, such as warning and threatening. These calls are used for social communication, but they are not articulated as sentences, and they are (probably) not learned from elders. Our closest primate relatives, the chimpanzees, have been reported to be capable of learning to communicate in a languagelike manner (with their keepers in the laboratory), using nonvocal modalities, such as the kinemes of Ameslan or colored buttons. Taken at face value, these experiments indicate that chimpanzees do have the capacity to make symbolic use of words, both for production and for comprehension of action commands.

The inference that chimpanzees can handle learned words as symbols, rather than merely as signs, is based on the finding that they can understand, without further training, novel word combinations. For instance, having previously learned the meaning of "take apple" and "give banana," some chimpanzees are able to respond correctly to "give apple" and "take banana." But no evidence has been offered that chimpanzees are able to form structured sentences according to grammatical rules. Thus they might be capable of learning a system of communication that meets three of the four criteria of human language.

It should be noted that the status of these reported successes in demonstrating quasi-linguistic competence in a species other than *H. sapiens* remains controversial. Some critics of these experiments claim that the chimpanzees made their apparently meaningful use of symbols merely in response to covert cues subconsciously provided by their human conversation partners, without real comprehension of any word-encoded meaning. In any case, studies of communicative capacities in subhuman animals, though interesting in their own right, have so far contributed very little to our understanding of either the evolutionary origins or the nature of human language.

It is clear that both speech production and speech comprehension depend heavily on memory: a fluent speaker has thousands of morphemes stored in his memory, as words of *his* language, and if he knows several languages, as several words separately stored for the same meaning. But how this memory is accessed when a word is either produced or presented is a mystery. Each word is stored with related information, such as its meaning, its sounding, its spelling, and its grammatical category. The processes of memory, learning, and retrieval of stored symbolic information can be studied more easily by examining the rules of chess than by examining those of language. The symbolism of chess is much more circumscribed than that of language, and yet it is still reasonably rich. Moreover, competence in playing chess can be measured quite well. So we can ask how chess masters differ from ordinary players. Studies of this question by Herbert A. Simon and W. G. Chase have produced the following interesting findings:

1. Masters do not analyze each chess situation more completely, in greater depth, or to more moves in advance than do ordinary players. Indeed, masters tend to explore the situation less than ordinary players. Yet, masters quickly find the strongest moves, which ordinary players may never find.

2. When a master is shown a real chess position with, say, twenty-four pieces on the board for a few seconds, he can reconstruct correctly almost the entire situation. Under similar circumstances ordinary players place only about 30% of the pieces in their correct positions. This difference is not due to the fact that the master can scan the board situation more rapidly, since during the alloted time his eye movements cover

(a)

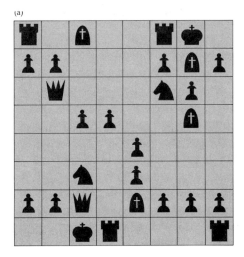

(b)

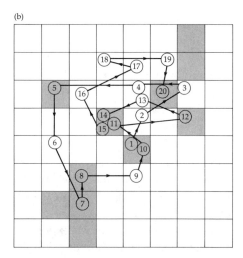

Eye movements in the analysis of a chess situation. (a) A middle game board position that was shown to chess players. Black is to move. Each player was instructed to find the best move for black, and eye movements while scanning the board were recorded during the first 5 seconds of the task. (b) The eye movements of an expert player. The ten squares occupied by the most active pieces are shaded. There were about twenty sequential points of fixation (here numbered consecutively), most of which fell on squares with pieces in important positions, although some also fell on the edges of empty squares. This experiment confirms the existence of an initial "perceptual phase," during which the player first apprehends the structural pattern of the pieces in terms of about seven "chunks," before looking for a good move in the "search phase" of this problem-solving process. [From Simon and Chase 1973. Used with permission.]

about the same number of points of fixation as the eye movements of ordinary players.

3. The crucial difference between master and ordinary player is that the master sees the board in terms of about seven subconfigurations, or "chunks." He has a mental store of about 40,000 such situational chunks that he can recognize and retrieve from his memory. In fact, the greater the chess master, the larger is the number of stored chunks at his disposal. The chunks are stored together with their appropriate tactical and strategic implications, and from about seven chunks almost any actual chess situation can be reconstructed. The number of items stored in the "chunk memory" of a chess master is similar to that stored in the word memory of a highly literate person, and both memories resemble each other in the quick accessibility of their items and the great amount of related information stored together with each.

4. Any one of the vast number of possible real chessboard situations presented to a master is, therefore, quickly perceived as a meaningful sentence, composed of a much smaller number of morphemes. Accordingly, if the master is shown random rather than real board situations, analogous to nonsense words, he does as poorly in reconstructing them as ordinary players.

In addition to the words, a fluent speaker also has stored in his memory a prodigious number of grammatical rules of his language. We find to our sorrow that acquiring this store of grammatical rules is a very difficult intellectual task when we try as adults to gain fluent command of a foreign language. Yet any normal human child has the ability to infer in a relatively short time the rules of any language spoken in its surroundings, even when it is exposed only to unsystematic, infinitesimal, fragmentary, and even faulty samples of possible sentences. This infantile accomplishment is equivalent to learning an enormously complicated theory. Yet, even mentally retarded children of low intelligence can perform this feat. Little reinforcement and no explicit instruction is needed in this learning process, and it happens at an age when the child is quite incapable of any analytical learning of remotely comparable logical complexity.

So here is a capability of the human mind that, astonishing as it is, has been very refractory to analysis. How does the child manage to learn to speak? Does this amazing feat imply that the thousands of particular natural languages share some general properties? This question has been hotly debated, especially during the last thirty years. Theories invoking language "universals" and "deep structures" common to all languages have been postulated, and "transformational grammars" have been proposed (especially by Noam Chomsky), by means of which sentences are transformed from the deep structure to the surface structure. But the yield of all this work in terms of uncovering actual universals and deep structures, has been pitifully small. In the opinion of one of the foremost comparative linguists, Dell Hymes:

> The discovery of putative universals in linguistic structure does not erase the differences. Indeed, the more one emphasizes universals, in association with a self-developing, powerful faculty of language within persons themselves, the more mysterious actual languages become. Why are there more than one, or two, or three? If the internal faculty of language is so constraining, must not social, historical, and adaptive forces have been even more constraining to produce the specific plenitude of languages actually found? For Chinookan is not Sahaptin is not Klamath is not Takelma [geographically more or less neighboring North American Indian languages]. . . . The many differences do not disappear, and the likenesses, indeed are far from all [transformational] universals. . . . Most of language begins where abstract universals leave off.

(Editors' note: Conceivably Delbrück's judgement of the lack of success in uncovering language universals might have been less severe if he had lived to witness the progress of more recent linguistics research, such as the discovery of universal features in the independent evolution of various modern Creole languages.)

To discover the cognitive basis of language it may be more useful to turn to the studies on the development of language in infants, again pioneered by Piaget. Piaget found that the earliest function of speech in the child is clearly not communication but symbolization. The first signifiers (i.e., entities that can be perceived and that stand for a certain content or meaning) that the child uses are *private*, not even verbal, symbols, with one object serving as a symbol for another. These lead to internalization and representation of thoughts. Social communication with other persons through words or signs arises at a later stage. At age 6 more than half the speech utterances of children in kindergarten situations are egocentric (i.e., not serving communication): the children carry on monologues, "thinking aloud" their ongoing actions. Language is a symptom of thought structure, a dependent variable. As every parent knows, children find it difficult, even unnecessary, to impart implicit information. When forced, children "read aloud" their continuing cognition, not concerned with communication. They already know the information. This behavior contrasts fundamentally with vocalized gestures of animals, which are inherited and have nothing to do with internalization of thoughts.

Languages differ in the grammatical role of word order. In Latin the grammatical relations are almost completely fixed by modification of the words, and word order plays almost no role. In Chinese, on the other hand, the grammatical role of word order is paramount. And in English, word order, prepositions, and semantic relations between the words all play a grammatical role. Hence to interpret an English sentence it is necessary to abstract the internal structure of the sentence from the actual word order. To this end, the sentence must be segmented, or parsed, into phrases that refer to the actor (subject), to the action (verb), and to the object of the action.

Thomas Bever conducted experiments to ascertain how English-speaking children learn to parse sentences to identify the parts of speech—such as subject, verb, and object—and their relations. Cohorts of various ages were presented with the following four sentences and requested to act them out with toy animals:

1. THE COW KISSES THE HORSE.

2. THE HORSE IS KISSED BY THE COW.

3. IT IS THE COW THAT KISSES THE HORSE.

4. IT IS THE HORSE THAT THE COW KISSES.

These test sentences are *semantically reversible*, in that it is as likely that a cow kisses a horse as that a horse kisses a cow. In about 95% of the trials, 2- to 2½-year-old children correctly understood the active sentence (1), but responded correctly to the passive sentence (2) in only 30% of trials. In the case of the active, cleft sentence constructions (3) and (4), about 80% of the trials were successful. These results demonstrate that even the very young child distinguishes the basic functional relations internal to sentences and can identify different grammatical construction types, as opposed to simply interpreting according to word order the first noun of *any* type of sentence as the actor and the last noun as the object. Between the ages of 2½ and 3½, children improve their performance with the passive sentence (2) to the 60% success level, but between 3½ and 4½, there occurs a transient drop in their ability to respond correctly to sentences (2) and (4), in which the object precedes the subject. This suggests that children pass through a stage in their linguistic development in which their method of parsing places greater emphasis on word order, resorting to the less flexible sequential strategy "actor-action-object." By age 5, the children have passed out of this phase again and respond correctly to the passive sentence (2) and to the object-first cleft sentence (4) in about 80% of the trials.

In recent years, the availability of ever more powerful computers has fostered a discipline styled "artificial intelligence," or AI, the goal of which is to design machines capable of performing tasks that resemble, or are even indistinguishable from, the kinds of operations usually associated with human intelligence. One of the most successful AI projects has been the design of chess-playing computer programs that can hold their own against even fairly strong human players ranking just below the master class.

Another, much more ambitious, but thus far less-successful AI project has been to design machines that can produce and comprehend human language. Let us consider an early example of the machine programs developed by K. M. Colby to permit an ongoing conversation between a computer and a person. This example consists of an automated psychotherapist, who converses via teletype with a patient:

> Therapist: How can I help you
> Patient: I don't know
> Therapist: Try to tell me something about it
> Patient: No
> Therapist: Can you elaborate
> Patient: I am sick and tired today
> Therapist: Do you have any idea why
> Patient: Yes I'm old
> Therapist: Please go on
> Patient: I seem to have lost interest in everything
> Therapist: Tell me more about such feelings
> Patient: I have some idea why I feel this way too
> Therapist: You have
> Patient: It seems that I miss having a family
> Therapist: What makes you feel you miss having a family
> Patient: There is a challenge about it
> Therapist: Why is that important to you

This dialogue may give the impression that the machine understands the patient's responses to questions posed by the program. In fact, the machine does not even analyze the structure of the patient's sentences. It is simply programmed to respond by selecting a few key phrases from the patient's sentence and incorporating them into some stereotyped phrases. This conversation has been cited by Norbert Bischof, in connection with his discussion of the Cartesian cut. Bischof asks how we know whether an object has a mind, and answers that we know because we experience it subjectively as such. Thus whether the patient judges the teletype conversation partner to have a mind depends on whether the statements made by the program match the patient's internal criteria of linguistic competence.

Colby's program does not, in fact, succeed in giving the patient the impression of conversing with another mind. Nevertheless, crude as it is, it can raise quite a few emotions in patients, as the end of one such dialogue shows:

Patient: I don't understand
Therapist: Do you want to understand
Patient: I hate you you stupid machine
Therapist: What don't you like about me
Patient: You have no feelings
Therapist: How do you mean
Patient: I mean you cannot experience what I experience because you are just a machine
Therapist: Tell me more about such feelings
Patient: We are not communicating
Therapist: I am trying my best to communicate with you
Patient: Are you really
Therapist: How do you see it
Patient: What do you mean
Therapist: Just try to say what it means to you
Patient: I think you are all goofed up

Thus the really difficult problem associated with making machines with the capability of language consists of designing programs that can produce sentencelike strings of words that not only give the impression to a human conversation partner of being understood, but also are actually capable of speech comprehension. Here the AI program designer faces a question of strategy (as do human speakers): should the program (and do human speakers) first complete the grammatical analysis of the sentence and then try to fathom its meaning, or should meaning be extracted (and do we extract it) concurrently with grammatical analysis? Consider the sentence: TIME FLIES. To parse this sentence, a program could refer to its own internal dictionary (provided by the designer) and ascertain that TIME can be either a verb or a noun, and that FLIES can also be either a verb or a noun. So from a purely linguistic point of view, the sentence may correspond to two different structures, one a command to measure the time taken by insects to perform a task and the other an assertion that the passage of time is rapid. Here, the correct interpreta-

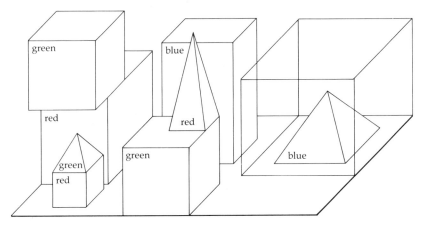

Winograd's highly circumscribed "tabletop world" designed to model by means of a computer program the processes of human perception, thought, and action. The movable blocks of this world consist of the colored cubes, boxes, and pyramids shown here. Some standard principles of everyday physical interactions are also part of this tabletop world; for example, a pyramid in this world is not allowed to rest balanced on its vertex. Winograd's program SHRDLU (whimsically named after the preelectronic typesetter's nonsense fill-in phrase ETAOIN SHRDLU) can plan and carry out certain manipulations of the blocks according to instructions issued to the computer in ordinary natural language, and it can answer questions about present and past configurations of the world, about actions it has taken, or plans to take, and about the reasons for its actions. [After Winograd, 1972]

tion can be reached only by considering the context in which the sentence has been produced. That is to say, to comprehend the sentence, the program must be able to take into account whether the sentence is part of a conversation about insect behavior or about subjective feelings. In the case of the longer sentence TIME FLIES WITH A STOPWATCH, it would be possible for the program to reject the second alternative in favor of the first without reference to the conversational context, if it could draw on an internal store of knowledge providing the information that the phrase WITH A STOPWATCH is more likely to be part of a predicate containing the verb *time* than the verb *fly*.

In 1972 Terry Winograd designed a program that actually analyzes the meaning of a human operator's sentences, acts according to the operator's instructions in a circumscribed "tabletop world" containing a few blocks that can be moved around, and remembers part of the previous conversation. The program analyzes sentences provided to it in a mixed mode: grammatically and semantically, and with reference to previous parts of the conversation and previous actions. By *semantically* we mean that the program, in trying to understand a sentence, not only analyzes the sentence grammatically but also conducts its search for comprehension with reference to its knowledge of the "world" and its "history." This feature of Winograd's program was hailed as a great achievement in the AI community, and it certainly was essential for the program's success.

Some AI enthusiasts thought that the program might give a clue to how language comprehension actually works in the human brain. This is unlikely, however, because the knowledge required for comprehending natural language is enormously greater in the real world than in the tabletop world of Winograd's program. Knowledge about the few blocks, their properties, location, relation, and history had already taxed the memory capacity of the computer that was used to implement the program. How the immense amount of knowledge about the real world possessed by even the simplest mind is accessed by it in the process of understanding even a very simple sentence remains quite obscure. Perhaps the analysis is carried out entirely by resorting to grammatical rules, leaving the "understanding" to the end. Some students of this problem propose that these processes are essentially unanalyzable; in other words, they believe that there is no fixed strategy embodied in the cerebral neural network responsible for speech production and speech comprehension. It is conceivable that in the analysis of language we encounter a type of mutual exclusion between different methods of analysis (neurological versus logical), and that the results of this analysis cannot be combined into a single coherent mechanistic picture.

▶

Sample dialogue between a human operator and Winograd's SHRDLU program (italic type) in the tabletop world. The program is able to plan and execute the manipulations of the blocks commanded by the operator. As the operator issues the commands listed in the left, the initial state of the blocks of the world (*top right*) is transformed to reflect the results of actions that carry out the commands (*middle and bottom right*). As the dialogue proceeds, the program queries the operator about an ambiguous question and answers questions about the state of the world, its previous actions, and the reasons for its actions. [After Winograd, 1972, and Waltz, 1982]

Will you please stack up both of the red
blocks and either a green cube or a pyramid?
OK.

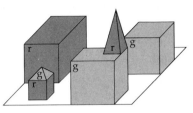

Which cube is sitting on the table?
The large green one which supports the red pyramid.

Put a small cube onto the green cube which
supports a pyramid.
OK.

Put the littlest pyramid on top of it.
OK.

How many things are on top of the green
cubes?
*I'm not sure what you mean by "on top of" in the
phrase "on top of the green cubes." Do you mean:
(1) directly on the surface, or
(2) anywhere on top of?*

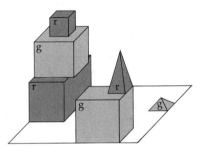

2
Three of them.

Had you touched any pyramid before you
put the green one on the little cube?
Yes, the green one.

When did you pick it up?
*When I was stacking up the red cube, a large red
block, and a large green cube.*

Why?
To get rid of it.

Why did you do that?
To clear off the red cube.

Why did you clear off that cube?
To put it on a large green cube.

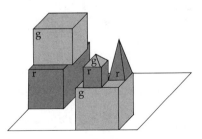

Why did you do that?
*To stack up the red cube, a large red block, and a
large green cube.*

Why did you do that?
Because you asked me to.

Existentialist philosophers assert that the human subject performing a creative act or making a choice between extant alternatives can never become an object of our scientific perception. For instance, when you decide how to vote today, sociologists or political scientists may have correctly predicted the statistical probability of your voting for a particular party, as physicists can make correct statistical predictions from quantum theory regarding the outcome of observations on the behavior of an electron. But your individual act is unique, and the observations that would be required for making a deterministic (rather than statistical) prediction of the outcome of your choice may well stand in a mutually exclusive relation to your very act of choosing that the observer wanted to study. Perhaps the existentialists are understating their case. Perhaps any language comprehension act already constitutes a creative act and as such cannot be an object of a mechanistic analysis.

In our discussion of language in this chapter we have not considered the relation of language to the brain. In chapters 6 and 8 we mentioned that speech production is completely lateralized (on the left side of the brain in most people) and that some brain areas (Broca's toward the front, Wernicke's toward the back of the cerebral cortex) are involved in speech production and comprehension, respectively. These areas have nothing to do with actual sound production or sound reception, but are concerned with the higher functions of coding meaning into sound and decoding meaning from sound. There exist pathological disorders of speech, such as aphasia (inability to produce speech), alexia (inability to read), and agraphia (inability to write). None of these disorders arises from defects in the motor systems moving vocal chords or limbs, or in the auditory or visual sensory systems. But beyond allowing a rather crude and often doubtful cerebral localization of the source of various linguistic disorders, these studies have not clarified the neurological correlates of the higher brain functions responsible for the production of language.

Thus, human language is a unique capability, of which at most only the crudest beginnings can be discerned in our closest relatives in the animal kingdom, the great apes. Language serves two biological functions: a crutch for representational and analytical thinking (a private affair) and a means of communication (a social affair). The combination of these two aspects has permitted language to become *the* vehicle of cultural progress, transmitting orderly systems of knowledge from generation to generation and even across language barriers by translation and eventually making possible the sciences.

REFERENCES

Benveniste, E. 1952. Animal communication and human language. The language of the bees. *Diogenes* 1: 1–7.

Bever, T. 1970. The cognitive basis for linguistic structures. In *Cognition and the Development of Language*, ed. J. R. Hayes, 279–352. New York: Wiley.

Burks, A. W. 1975. Logic, biology and automata—some historical reflections. *International Journal of Man–Machine Studies* 7: 297–312.

Chomsky, N. 1972. *Language and Mind.* New York: Harcourt Brace.

Colby, K. M. 1964. Experimental treatment of neurotic computer programs. *Archives General Psychiatry* 10: 220–227.

Colby, K. M., J. B. Watt, and J. P. Gilbert. 1966. A computer method of psycho-therapy: Preliminary communication. *Journal of Nervous and Mental Disease* 142: 148–152.

Gardner, R. A., and B. T. Gardner. 1978. Comparative psychology and language acquisition. *Annals of the New York Academy of Science* 309: 37–76.

Hymes, D. 1973. On the origins and foundations of inequality among speakers. *Daedalus* 102: 59–85.

Premack, D. 1976. *Intelligence in Ape and Man.* Hillsdale: Erlbaum.

Simon, H. A., and W. G. Chase. 1973. Skill in chess. *American Scientist* 61: 394–403.

Terrace, H. S., L. A. Petitto, R. J. Sanders, and T. G. Bever. 1979. Can an ape create a sentence? *Science* 206: 891–902.

Waltz, D. L. 1982. Artificial intelligence. *Scientific American* 247(4): 101–122.

Winograd, T. 1972. Understanding natural language. *Cognitive Psychology* 3: 1–191.

Twenty

Summing Up

In this much too long, and much too short, essay I have attempted to look at the oldest problems of epistemology—What is Truth, and what is Reality?—to respond to the raised eyebrow implied in my title, *Mind from Matter?* We start with the naive question: How can mind emerge from dead matter as the result of purely physical processes? Mind then looks back on itself and says, "Aha, this is how I came about." (Like Baron Munchhausen, pulling himself by his hair out of the mud.) I hope I have managed to avoid the language of the emergent evolution school founded in the 1920s by Teilhard de Chardin, who attributed the appearance of mind, and of the "noosphere," which mind is said to inhabit, to a "law of complexification" governing the evolution of nonliving as well as living matter. The emergent evolutionists have not, in my opinion, made a constructive contribution to this question; on the contrary, they have camouflaged the problem under appealing poetic metaphors. I have tried to look at the problem as a scientist rather than as a poet, as a student of evolution in the widest sense: evolution of the universe, evolution of life, evolution of mind, evolution of culture.

The point of view of the evolutionist forces us to view mind in the context of other aspects of evolution, to draw parallels with other more mundane forms of adaptation, such as the organs of locomotion and of digestion. In the context of evolution, the mind of the adult human, the object of so many centuries of philosophical studies, ceases to be a mysterious phenomenon, a thing unto itself. Rather, mind is seen to be an ✳

adaptive response to selective pressures, just as is nearly everything else in the living world.

We began our search for an answer to our naive question with a brief review of the evolution of the universe, from the big bang, through the genesis of the galaxies and stars, to the formation of our planet Earth. The purpose of this review was to give an impression of the universe prior to life and prior to mind. Our description and understanding of even this earliest, prebiotic part of evolution can be only partly deterministic, in that in many instances amplified statistical fluctuations introduce elements of indeterminacy into the course of events. We then turned to the origin of life from a primal soup, traceable to a definite period in the Earth's history. While the dates of this period of origin are known with reasonable certainty from insights into the physical aspects of terrestrial evolution, almost every other aspect of the origin of life is still deeply obscure. All present forms of life, from the humblest prokaryotes to man, show a tremendous unity in their basic chemical organization. By contrast, a vast gulf separates all creatures, large and small, from inanimate matter, a gulf that seems much wider today than it seemed only a few decades ago. The unity of living matter is manifest in the nucleic acids that are storehouses for genetic information and in the proteins that are executive agents for interpreting genetic information, perceiving signals from both without and within the organism, and making appropriate responses to these signals.

We considered energy metabolism, which exemplifies two general features of evolution: conservatism and opportunism. Thus, if a particular metabolite or chemical reaction step turned out to be capable of performing an essential function, the organisms held onto it, adapting and refining it to suit many diverse situations, rather than developing a new solution from scratch for each novel situation. Hence, contrary to a widely held belief, the anatomical and physiological features of presently extant life forms are not necessarily optimal solutions from the *synchronic* point of view, which takes into account only the present situation. When the features of extant life forms are evaluated from the *diachronic* point of view, which takes into account the succession of historical situations, it appears that evolution used, not what was theoretically optimal, but whatever happened to be available to it and could be appropriated to serve a needed function. The evolutionary process, as envisaged by Darwin, is somewhat analogous to statistical thermodynamics, in that individual steps depend on random events that cannot be predicted with certainty, while the processes and behaviors arising from these steps may well be predictable. For example, given the presence of a molecular substance capable of providing chemical energy in sufficient quantity in the environment, one can safely predict that an organism will evolve to use this substance. The steps in this evolutionary process, however, are not necessarily predictable, and many different paths may lead to the same final result. The first person to see this correspondence between statistical thermodynamics and biological evolution clearly was the logician Charles Peirce, who in 1877, wrote:

> The Darwinian controversy is, in large part, a question of logic. Mr. Darwin proposed to apply the statistical method to biology. The same thing has been done in a widely different branch of science, the theory of gases. Though unable to say what the movements of any particular molecule of gas would be on a certain hypothesis regarding the constitution of this class of bodies, Clausius [who formulated the second law of thermodynamics] and Maxwell were yet able, eight years before the publication of Darwin's immortal work, by the application of the doctrine of probabilities, to predict that in the long run such and such a proportion of the molecules would, under given circumstances, acquire such and such velocities; that there would take place, every second, such and such a relative number of collisions, etc.; and from these propositions were able to deduce certain properties of gases, especially in regard to their heat-relations. In like manner, Darwin, while unable to say what the operation of variation and natural selection in any individual case will be, demonstrates that in the long run they will, or would, adapt animals to their circumstances.

We devoted some attention to the species concept as it applies to sexually propagating organisms and to the process of speciation. Speciation, we learned, does not occur by sudden mutation of a single founder individual, but by bifurcations in the slow drift of evolution of a geographically (or otherwise reproductively) isolated local population. There is also an analogy between evolution and logic: If genes and sets of genes are considered to be the axioms with which evolution operates, the processes of genetic recombination, duplication, inversion, and mutation become formally analogous to deductive reasoning from axioms by the rules of inference. Genomes, and hence species, can then be viewed as statements in a deductive formal language, although there inheres a probabilistic component in the deductive process of evolution: *Which theorems are going to be proved* (i.e., *which* species will be formed) depends very much on random choices. This randomness is a biased one, however, favoring the formulation of genomes of adaptive value.

We considered the broad range of extant genome sizes, as well as conjectures about the organization of the genome and the mechanism by which its information is expressed. Here we saw that a large portion of the information embodied in the genome may be neither expressed nor concerned with the control of gene expression but may be simply dead wood that is carried along without function, just as a large portion of the books carried by great libraries are never checked out.

We then reviewed present notions about the descent of man. The line leading to man is thought to have split off from the apes about five million years ago, with creatures unmistakably identifiable as members of the genus *Homo* dating back at least three million years. Human use and manufacture of tools also began some three million years ago and evolved through many stages. The origin of language, that unique novelty brought to the world by man, is completely obscure, lacking any traces in the paleontological record. But language may be of much more recent origin than tool-making. At the time of the earliest written records, language was already as rich and complex as any modern idiom. There must be a vast developmental gap between the beginnings of language and its extant forms, perhaps as vast as that separating prokaryotes from eukaryotes, or the primal soup from contemporary life. But how that gap was bridged, of that we have no inkling.

The human brain weighs two or three times as much as the brain of our closest living relative in the animal kingdom, the chimpanzee, which lacks the natural gift of language. One is tempted to ask, therefore: Which new parts were added to the primate brain on the step from ape to man, and which of these novel parts is responsible for the gain in linguistic capacity? The answer turns out to be that there are no readily identifiable novel parts, although almost all parts of the brain are bigger in man than in the chimpanzee. But most of that increase in weight may simply be attributable to man's body size being larger than the chimpanzee's, since in all vertebrate species brain weight rises roughly in proportion to body surface area. Admittedly, some parts of the temporal and frontal lobes of the human cerebral cortex are enlarged somewhat disproportionately; but this fact cannot be simply related to the development of language since these enlargements are present in both cerebral hemispheres, while the capacity for language is confined to one hemisphere.

Even if it has not yet been of much help in revealing the nature of language, study of the brain has advanced our understanding of perception and cognition. Analysis of the neural processing of the visual input to the retina has shown that the visual percept that reaches the conscious mind is far removed from the primary sense impression. This conclusion follows both from direct electrophysiological probing of the responses of neural elements of the visual pathway in the brain to diverse features of the visual surround and from psychological tests of visual perception. Both types of studies demonstrate that vision involves a great deal of abstracting and filtering of sensory information at preconscious levels. These features of brain organization endow us with forms of cognition that, to philosophers such as Kant, appeared to be a priori, that is, prior to any experience. As seen from the modern evolutionist view, these forms of cognition are indeed prior to any individual's experience, but they are by no means a priori with respect to the species. Rather, they represent phylogenetic adaptations, evolved for coping with the real world.

In speaking of "perception" and "cognition" we are not referring to concepts extraneous to the physical world, implying the mind of a mysterious "inner man." Rather, we realize that the beginnings of perception are already manifest in microorganisms, as represented by such phenomena as phototaxis in bacteria and phototropism in fungi. Even at this primitive level, the organism receives signals from the outside world, evaluates their significance, and responds appropriately. What do I mean when I say a bacterium or a fungus "evaluates" the significance of signals? I mean no more, and no less, than that the organism possesses structures that permit him to react appropriately, that is, in an evolutionarily adaptive manner. What do I imply by referring to a bacterium or a fungus as "him"? Do I refer to a subject with a consciousness, with a mind? No, I simply refer to the organism as an indivisible object, a functional unit and, as such, an individual.

We turned to Piaget's pioneering studies of the development of cognitive capabilities in childhood. These studies yield a vast array of facts about the behavior of children in a great variety of situations, including free play, directed play, concrete tasks, and verbal responses. The ordering of these facts leads to the notion of identifiable stages of development of the mind. Mind should be viewed as an active rather than as a passive human quality, an activity somewhat like the execution of a computer program. The activity grows by refinement of old programs and their assimilation of new experiences and accommodation to new situations. Mind grows from the moment of birth, when the infant's relation to the world is not yet so organized as to distinguish between self and nonself. Then follows the gradual emergence of this distinction, as well as of such concepts as space, time, causality, object, number, measure, and hierarchical structure.

Piaget's analysis is in no way causal. It is merely descriptive of the unfolding of the mind as it occurs with high regularity in a largely culture-independent manner in every child and is therefore indicative of the human biological heritage. All the same, this hereditarily determined unfolding does not proceed autonomously; it is the result of a dialectic interaction between the developing nervous system and the real world. One empirically demonstrable aspect of this process is provided by the plasticity of the neonatal perceptual apparatus during a specific sensitive period during which it is being set or tuned by environmental influences. We discussed the neurophysiological experiments of Hubel and Wiesel, which showed the role of postnatal visual experience in the formation of functional neural connections in the visual cortex of the kitten, as well as Lorenz's behavioral analog of these experiments, which demonstrated the "imprinting" of a maternal image in neonatal birds.

Thus we constructed a plausible story of how the lifeless, mindless universe came to contain creatures endowed with mind, so endowed by hook or by crook, that is, by phylogeny or by ontogeny. We then proceeded to examine the nature of this mind as reflected in mathematics, physics, biology, and linguistics. What we found was bizarre and ambiguous, often in the most basic respects.

In considering mathematics we concentrated our attention on the marvels of numbers. We looked at the startling simplicity of Euclid's proof that there is no largest prime number; at the fundamental theorem of arithmetic, the proof of which is sufficiently complex to give one an uneasy feeling of being trapped, transcending as it does the grasp of a single glance; and at number theory and some of its unsolved problems (some of which can be stated so simply that they cry out for a decision). We attempted to understand the crisis brought on by the paradoxes involving set theory and the concept of infinity, and we outlined Hilbert's program of proof theory. This program envisaged a procedure of complete formalization of all parts of mathematics, with axioms, rules of inference, and proofs expressed entirely in the form of uninterpreted symbols, that is, symbols whose meaning is irrelevant to the formal system. Hilbert's goal was to show that these formal systems are consistent and complete: consistent in that no contradictory statements can be proved, and complete in that for every legitimate formal statement either it or its negation can be decided.

This program suffered a mortal blow when Gödel showed that undecidable statements can be constructed within any such formal system. It is instructive to view Hilbert's program of formalization and its denouement in a historical perspective. Aristotle introduced the logic of classes, as represented by syllogisms such as:

All men are mortal
Socrates is a man

Therefore, Socrates is mortal

But, as Hilbert and Ackermann pointed out in *Principles of Mathematical Logic*:

> . . . it would be in vain to search for a formal rendering of the logical relation expressed in [these] three sentences. . . . The reason for this is that [Aristotelian syllogisms] depend not only upon the sentences as wholes, but also upon the inner logical structure of the sentences which is expressed grammatically by the relation between subject and predicate and which plays an essential role.

The first explicit proposal for the formalization of logical statements expressed in natural language was made in the 1670s by Newton's contemporary Gottfried Wilhelm von Leibniz, one of the inventors of the differential calculus and a man with a prodigious number of original ideas to his credit. Here are some quotations from Leibniz's writings (translated by Frank Copley):

> All our reasoning is nothing but the joining and substituting of characters, whether these characters be words or symbols or pictures.
>   . . . if we could find characters or signs appropriate for expressing all our thoughts as definitely and as exactly as arithmetic expresses numbers or geometric analysis expresses lines, we could in all subjects *in so far as they are amenable to reasoning* accomplish what is done in Arithmetic and Geometry.
>   For all inquiries which depend on reasoning would be performed by the transposition of characters and by a kind of calculus, which would immediately facilitate the discovery of beautiful results. . . .
>   Moreover, we should be able to convince the world of what we should have found or concluded, since it would be easy to verify the calculation either by doing it over or by trying tests similar to that of casting out nines in arithmetic. And if someone would doubt my results, I should say to him: "let us calculate, Sir," and thus by taking to pen and ink, we should soon settle the question.
>   Following is the rule for constructing the characters: to any given term (that is, the subject or predicate of a statement), let there be assigned a number, but with this one reservation, that a term consisting of a combination of other terms shall have as its number the product of the numbers of those other terms multiplied together. For example, if the term for an "animate being" should be imagined as expressed by the number 2 (or, more generally, a), and the term for "rational" by the number 3 (or, more

generally, *r*), the term for "man" will be expressed by the number 2×3, that is 6, or as the product obtained by multiplying 2 and 3 together (or more generally by the number *ar*).

Nothing is needed, I say, but that philosophic and mathematical procedures, as they call them, be based upon a new method, which I can prescribe and which contains nothing more difficult than other procedures, or more remote from our usual way of understanding, or more foreign to our habits of writing. It will not require much more work than we see already being spent on a good many procedures and on a good many encyclopedias, as they call them. I believe that a number of chosen men can complete the task within five years; within two years they will exhibit the common doctrines of life, that is, metaphysics and morals, in an irrefutable calculus.

Once the characteristic numbers of many ideas have been established, the human race will have a new organon, which will increase the power of the mind much more than the optic glass has aided the eyes, and will be as much superior to microscopes and telescopes as reason is superior to vision.

Today we know that a complete formalization of natural language statements, as here envisaged by Leibniz, is impossible. Even within mathematics, a more restricted universe of discourse than natural language, the theorems of any formal axiomatic system include some that are nondecidable. This is what Gödel's theorem amounts to. Gödel's method of proof is quite analogous to Cantor's procedure for showing that there are more real numbers than rational numbers. In his proof Cantor constructs, for any given seriated pairing of the real with the rational number, a real number not included in the series. Similarly Gödel constructs, for any set of decidable theorems of a formal axiomatic system, a theorem for which it is the case that neither it nor its negation is included in the set. It is, of course, a far cry from Gödel's proof of the *existence* of undecidable statements to the proof that a particular statement is undecidable. In fact, no such proof has yet been delivered for any of the famous undecided statements of number theory, such as Fermat's, Goldbach's, or Riemann's conjectures.

We traced the cognitive roots of physics to our intuitive capacity for measurement. This capacity arises from the concepts of *conservation* (of quantities, such as length or volume, under various operations), *composition* (of a combined entity reflecting the conserved quantities of its parts), and *unit of measurement*. We recapitulated the travails of terrestrial and celestial kinematics, which gradually evolved into the grandiose system of Newtonian mechanics of point masses on which forces act at a distance. We considered the conceptually troublesome role that space, especially empty space, has played in physics. Is space a substance? Can motion relative to it be detected? Are fields of electric, magnetic, and gravitational force "states" of empty space? These vexing and seemingly intractable questions were resolved by the amazing tour de force of the theory of relativity, which demanded an abdication of our intuitive, a priori, or evolutionarily developed, space–time mode of perception. Here "abdication" does not mean discontinuing our intuitive mode of perception in everyday affairs, but merely admitting that we can account for the facts of physics by a scheme that ignores intuition and replaces it with a logically consistent, albeit counterintuitive, four-dimensional world. It is essential to realize, however, that to have standing as a physical theory, the theory of relativity must be connected in a well-defined manner to actual observations of the real world, stated in a language based on our ordinary intuition.

From the point of view of evolutionary epistemology, the principal lesson of both special and general relativity theories is this: Human beings are organisms capable of manipulating internal representations of the world by means of concrete operations and can transcend the bounds of their biologically given perception. They can liberate themselves and construct a view of reality that conflicts with intuition, yet gives a truer, more encompassing view.

Since I have mentioned the word *intuition* rather freely in this essay, I should say a few words about what I mean by it. There is a vast philosophical literature concerning this particular word, which suggests that its meaning is vague enough to cover a multitude of sins. I have been using *intuition* to refer to any *easily accomplished concrete mental operation*. Examples of such mental operations are the reconstruction of three-dimensional objects from two-dimensional perspective projections and the "seeing" of the equivalence of two sets whose members can be paired, and then, from memory, visualizing the cardinal number 7 as a set of seven objects. It is somewhat arbitrary where one sets the boundary between intuition and logical inference. Someone familiar with the four-dimensional geometry of the theory of special relativity may feel secure in dealing with happenings within this framework. We may then say that person has a definite intuition about it, as definite as our own intuition about the ordinary geometry of three dimensions. We would need to have a much better grasp of the biological basis of our three-dimensional intuition before we could decide whether there is a gross difference between it and the four-dimensional intuition acquired by a professional student of the theory of relativity.

We saw that the basic epistemological consequences of the quantum theory are embodied in Heisenberg's uncertainty principle, which sets some kind of limit to the use of concepts developed in classical physics. The problem is to understand as clearly as possible the nature of this limit. How should we reconcile the wave and particle aspects of light and matter? Bohr's complementarity argument seeks to clarify this epistemological conundrum. According to this argument it would be wrong to say "light and matter *really* consist of particles, but unfortunately there are regrettable circumstances that prevent us from following their trajectories; instead we can merely calculate probabilities concerning their whereabouts, by means of an esoteric formalism involving complex variables and symbols that do not commute in multiplication." This is the way most textbooks present the epistemological lesson of the quantum theory, and this presentation is wrong because it strongly implies that some day we might be able to circumvent these regrettable circumstances. Instead, following Bohr, we should take the lesson of quantum theory to be that physical reality is too rich to be caught in the net of the "objective reality" of classical physics. The various aspects of the objects of physics are mutually exclusive. Is there a fundamental difference between this mutual exclusion of various physical aspects of the same object and the mutual exclusion of its visual aspects seen from various vantage points? In the latter case, we have no difficulty in combining the different views seen in a three-dimensional world. Why can't we combine the wave and particle aspects in a similar manner?

The difference lies exactly where it should lie: in the atomicity of the elementary observational act, represented by the quantum of action. In describing an observation we must make a distinction between observer and observed, that is, we must make a Cartesian cut, and this we can do in alternative, mutually exclusive ways, each of which is as real as the other. Quantum theory reconciles these alternative realities. It does not reconcile alternative *views* of one reality; such wording would suggest, wrongly, that there is one reality viewed several ways, as in perspective. No, quantum theory reconciles alternative realities, one or the other of which the observer chooses to let happen. Among the implications of the quantum theory are the loss of the categories of identity of an object and of conservation of objects and a distinct limitation on the category of causality. None of these categorical concepts is possessed by the mind at birth; they constitute part of the unfolding of our inherited cognitive structures during development. It may therefore not be totally unreasonable to believe that the mind can find ways to unburden itself of, or at least deviate from, its biological heritage, a heritage evolved to cope with the directly experienced world of middle dimensions.

Have we, then, answered the naive question we posed at the outset? Did we explain how mind evolved from no mind? Did we find out why so much more was delivered than was ordered, that is, how the mind, having evolved for using stone tools, mounting a minimum of social organization for the hunt, and telling tales about hunting around the hearth, managed to get us to the abstruse reaches of number theory, relativity and quantum theory, elementary particles, and molecular genetics, not to speak of getting us to the moon? Maybe we didn't give any straight answers to these questions, but I think the dilemma "mind from no mind" looks less perplexing than it used to. On the one hand, neurobiological and psychophysical studies of subjective perception have provided insights into how we come to know the world, and cybernetics and even AI have helped a little to illuminate the nature of human thought processes. On the other hand, our ideas about the objective character of the physical world, and hence of the nature of truth have been revised. In other words, mind looks less psychic and matter looks less materialistic, especially in the light of Bohr's complementarity argument, which removed the illusion of total determination and objectivity.

Part, but only part, of the solution to the riddle of how it is possible for the mind to deal so successfully with aspects of the world for dealing with which it was never selected may lie in a combination of *fluctuation* and *illusion*. The fluctuation arises from the vast amplification of simple knowledge through social organization. To fly to the moon does not require monumental intelligence; it requires the cooperation of 500,000 quite ordinary minds. The illusion arises from the preoccupation with our successes and the repression of our failures. The Stone Age people in England constructed Stonehenge 4000 to 5000 years ago, embodying some astronomical information in its architecture. They probably thought very highly of themselves. Little did they know how much they didn't know.

Let us conclude with some general reflections on the peculiar role played by the sciences in this story. The classical natural sciences solidified the feeling that the adult human mind is an absolute: it grasps absolute physical laws concerned with absolute matter embedded in absolute space and time. The Cartesian cut between mind and matter is the rock on which such physical laws stand.

Modern science has gone in the opposite direction. It has forced us to abandon absolute space and time, determinism, and the absolute object. It has shown that these naive notions are applicable only in the middle dimensions of space, time, and energy and must be replaced by more abstract formal schemes. As soon as we move to phenomena at extreme dimensions, our intuitions—that is, our concrete mental operations— become inadequate. This is the point, exactly, where evolutionary thinking is decisively helpful. It suggests, in fact it demands, that our concrete mental operations are indeed adaptations to the mode of life in which we had to compete for survival a long time before the development of science. As such we are saddled with them, just as we are with our organs of locomotion and our eyes and ears. But with science we can transcend our intuitions, just as with electronics we can transcend our eyes and ears.

To the question of how the mental capacity for such transcendence can have arisen in the course of biological evolution I have no satisfactory answer. Indeed, the approach I have sketched in this essay by no means resolves all puzzles, nor does it produce a grand synthesis of the diverse universes of discourse now current in the various sciences. Least of all does it give a basis for a new setting of values in ethics relevant to the life of the individual or to social organization.

The feeling of absurdity evoked by the question "mind from matter?" is perhaps similar to the feeling of absurdity with which we have learned to cope when we permit relativity theory to alter our intuitive concepts of time and space and quantum theory to alter our intuitive concepts of object and causality. If we can learn to accept this ultimate absurdity, there may yet be hope for developing a formal approach that will permit a grand synthesis.

FINIS

REFERENCES

Hilbert, D., and W. Ackermann. 1950. *Principles of Mathematical Logic.* Trans. L. M. Hammond, G. C. Leckie, and F. Steinhardt. Ed. R. E. Luce. New York: Chelsea Publishing.

Leibniz, G. W. von. 1951. *Selections,* ed. P. P. Wiener. New York: Scribners.

Peirce, C. S. 1934. *Collected Papers of C. S. Peirce,* vol. 5. Cambridge: Harvard University Press.

Name Index

Subject Index